UTILITARIANISM

JOHN STUART MILL

UTILITARIANISM
ON LIBERTY
ESSAY ON BENTHAM

together with selected writings of
JEREMY BENTHAM
and
JOHN AUSTIN

Edited with an Introduction
by Mary Warnock
Fellow of St. Hugh's College,
Oxford

A MERIDIAN BOOK

MERIDIAN
Published by the Penguin Group
Penguin Books USA Inc., 375 Hudson Street, New York, New York 10014, U.S.A.
Penguin Books Ltd, 27 Wrights Lane, London W8 5TZ, England
Penguin Books Australia Ltd, Ringwood, Victoria, Australia
Penguin Books Canada Ltd, 2801 John Street, Markham, Ontario, Canada L3R 1B4
Penguin Books (N.Z.) Ltd, 182-190 Wairau Road, Auckland 10, New Zealand

Penguin Books Ltd, Registered Offices: Harmondsworth, Middlesex, England

Published by Meridian, an imprint of New American Library, a division of Penguin
Books USA Inc.

BOOKS ARE AVAILABLE AT QUANTITY DISCOUNTS WHEN USED
TO PROMOTE PRODUCTS OR SERVICES. FOR INFORMATION PLEASE
WRITE TO PREMIUM MARKETING DIVISION, PENGUIN BOOKS USA INC.,
375 HUDSON STREET, NEW YORK, NEW YORK 10014.

REGISTERED TRADEMARK—MARCA REGISTRADA

First Printing/New American Library, March, 1974

13   14   15   16

PRINTED IN THE UNITED STATES OF AMERICA

CONTENTS

INTRODUCTION

by Mary Warnock

Jeremy Bentham was born in London in 1748. His father Jeremiah Bentham was Clerk of the Scriveners' Company, a prosperous man and a Tory. Jeremy was sent to Westminster School, which he hated, in 1755, and to Queen's College, Oxford, which he hated even more, in 1760. He was entered at Lincoln's Inn in 1763, and called to the bar five years later. By this time he had already decided what his life's work should be. In 1768, when he came back to Oxford to record his vote at the University parliamentary election, he happened to go into a circulating library attached to a coffee-house near Queen's, and there he found a copy of Joseph Priestley's new pamphlet *Essay on Government.* In it he found the phrase 'The greatest happiness of the greatest number'. Of this discovery he says : " It was by that pamphlet and this phrase in it that my principles on the subject of morality, public and private, were determined. It was from that pamphlet and that page of it that I drew the phrase, the words and the import of which have been so widely diffused over the civilised world." Upon certain ideas derived from Helvetius and Beccaria and upon this phrase of Priestley's, he decided that he would build a foundation for scientific jurisprudence and for legislation; and in fact he devoted the whole of his life to this task.

In 1776 he published anonymously the *Fragment on Government,* an attack on Blackstone's Commentaries on the Laws of England. In 1785 he left England for Russia, where he went to visit his brother Samuel. He did not return till 1788. He had been urged by his friends to come home and publish something on moral and political philosophy, and in the year after his return he did in fact publish his *Introduction to the Principles of Morals and Legislation,* which is, philo-

sophically, much his most important work, and which sets
out the principles upon which his whole programme was to
rest. He also started work at this time on his project for a
model prison of novel design, the Panopticon, the idea of
which had come to him while he was still in Russia. He
published the first of his pamphlets on this—in his view—
important project in 1791, and another in 1812. His scheme
was sanctioned by Act of Parliament in 1794, and a site
found for the erection of a prison to his specifications in 1799,
but in the end nothing came of the plan. In 1813 Bentham
was paid £23,000 in compensation for the rejection of the
scheme, on which he had indeed spent a great deal of money.
However, the whole affair has some importance for the
development of his thought, in that his disgust with the
behaviour of the government in this matter converted him
to the idea of democracy. He thought that the only possible
reason why a scheme so obviously advantageous should have
been rejected was that Parliament did not really represent
the people, and that therefore they had not the people's interests
at heart.

Meanwhile, in 1802, Bentham's friend and first disciple,
Dumont, published in Paris the *Traités de Legislation Civile
et Penale,* which he had compiled from various papers given
to him by Bentham; and it was on this work that Bentham's
enormous reputation on the Continent was based. Then in
1808 he met James Mill, and a friendship began which
was of central importance in the lives of both men. Bentham,
under the influence of Mill, became much more heavily
engaged in political and social affairs than he had been
before. At the same time he became absorbedly interested
in the education of James Mill's son, John Stuart, who was
early destined by his serious elders to be trained as a disciple
and prophet of their own ideas. The Mill family came to
live near Bentham in London—at 1 Queen's Square, Westminster—where other near neighbours were another Benthamite family, the Austins. Until 1818, in addition, the
whole Mill family spent six months of each year with Bentham
at Ford Abbey, near Chard in Somerset. All this time
Bentham was working steadily at his vast and finally un-

finished *Constitutional Code*. In 1822 he published a "codification proposal addressed by J. Bentham to all nations professing liberal opinions, or idea of a proposed all-comprehensive body of law with an accompaniment of reason ". Besides this, he wrote numerous pamphlets urging reform and exposing abuses, so that his influence on practical affairs and legislation was already considerable by the time of his death. He died in 1832, a week or two after the Great Reform Bill was passed. He gave his body for dissection to the Webb Street School of Anatomy, the first person ever to do so, so far as is known. His skeleton is still in the library of University College, London.

When James Mill met Bentham, John Stuart Mill was two years old. By the time he came to the study of philosophy, the school of radical utilitarians[1] was entirely dominated by Bentham. The younger Mill, the best philosopher of the school, to some extent reacted against it, and introduced new features into utilitarian doctrine, without which it might well have been too rigid and narrow to survive. His education may have been partly responsible for his reaction against strict Benthamism. It is perhaps the most famous of all English educations, and we have Mill's own description of it in the first part of his *Autobiography*. His father taught him Greek at the age of three or four; he started arithmetic and Latin at eight, logic at twelve, political economy at thirteen. Until he was fourteen, he saw no one of his own age, and mixed only with his father's utilitarian friends. He was also required to teach his younger brothers and

[1] The word ' Utilitarian ' appears to have been coined by Bentham. He used it first in a letter dated 1781, and again in a letter, dated, 1801, in which he said "A new religion would be an odd sort of thing without a name", and proposed "Utilitarianism". Mill, however, seems to have been unaware that Bentham used the word, for he claims to have taken it over from John Galt's novel ' Annals of the Parish' (1821) where a character applies it to Benthamite views; and in the essay on Sedgwick's discourse to the University of Cambridge (1835) he feels it necessary to explain it in terms of adherence to the principle of Utility. The word ' Utility' was in fairly common use as a technical term considerably earlier, and is to be found in the writings of Hume.

sisters as much as possible of what his father taught him.
It is scarcely surprising that he once said of himself " I never
was a boy; never played at cricket; it is better to let Nature
have her way." After a visit to France in 1820, Mill began
to read law under the guidance of John Austin, his friend
and neighbour; and though he abandoned the law and
entered India House as a clerk in 1823, he attended Austin's
lectures in 1828. These were the first lectures which Austin
gave after his appointment as professor of Jurisprudence,
in 1826, when London University was founded. An expanded
part of them was published in 1832 (see appendix). Their
influence on Mill's moral philosophy cannot be exaggerated.

In 1826 Mill fell into a mood of deep depression, from
which he did not really emerge until two years later. He
himself, in the *Autobiography*, suggests that his recovery
was largely due to his discovery of Wordsworth; and there
is no doubt that his learning, as he says, from Wordsworth
"what would be the perennial sources of happiness, when
all the greater evils of life shall have been removed " set him
apart from his orthodox Benthamite friends, who had their
eyes so firmly fixed on removing the greater evils that they
never had time to doubt that human welfare consisted in
their removal. Mill's conception of happiness is different
from and richer than theirs. His essay on Bentham (1838)
was published with an accompanying article on the poet
Coleridge, and his favourable judgment of the latter earned him
the disparaging title of ' German metaphysical mystic ' from the
strictly orthodox Benthamite Francis Place. This was certainly unfair; nevertheless, it is clear from the essay on
Bentham, and from his letters, that Mill had come to feel
that the strict utilitarian calculus of pleasures and pains was
too narrow. In a letter to E. Lytton Bulwer in 1836, he
spoke of a programme for a utilitarianism of the whole
of human nature, in which feeling was to be as valuable as
thought, and poetry a necessary condition of philosophy.
In 1830, when this revolution in his thought was almost
complete, Mill met Harriet Taylor, the wife of John Taylor,
a merchant; a beautiful, witty and highly educated woman.
Their famous friendship began at that time, and culminated

at last in their marriage in 1851, after John Taylor's death. There followed seven years of happy married life, though much of it was overshadowed by their ill-health (both had tuberculosis), until the death of Harriet in 1858.

From 1837-40 Mill was owner and director of the *London and Westminster Review*. In the summer of 1840 he completed the first draft of his *Logic,* and from this time onwards his reaction towards Coleridgean romanticism became less marked. He ceased to toy with the idea of ' intuitionism ', and by the time he came to write the *Examination of Sir William Hamilton's philosophy* (1865), his main aim was to reject this very idea in all its forms. In 1865 he was returned to Parliament as member for Westminster. Earlier, in the election of 1851, he had refused an invitation to stand, for the reason, among others, that he still at that time held an important post in the East India Company; but the Company had come to an end in 1858, and he was now relatively free. He remained in Parliament until the General Election of 1868. Among the issues which particularly engaged his interest were the project of extending the franchise to the whole of the working classes and the perennial Irish question. On all these issues Mill spoke with characteristic liberal sentiment, though he had few of the talents conducive to parliamentary success. After his defeat in the General Election, he retired to Avignon, with his step-daughter, Helen Taylor, near to the place where Harriet was buried. They scarcely ever came to England after this time, and Mill died there suddenly, of a local fever, in May 1873.

II

Bentham's life work, as he conceived it, was two-fold. First, he had to provide a secure foundation of theory for any possible legal system; and secondly he had at the same time to criticise existing legal systems in the light of this theoretical foundation. In practice this programme amounted, in large measure, to a testing of existing systems by the criterion

of the 'principle of utility'; for this principle was the
foundation of his general jurisprudence. This was his task;
and it can be seen that he was therefore only very indirectly,
if at all, concerned with moral philosophy. For moral philosophy has traditionally been concerned primarily with the
conduct of the individual—in which Bentham, however, was
interested only in so far as the individual's conduct might
fall under some law, or be subject to some sanction as a
breach of a law. In no case is he particularly interested in
the individual acts of an individual person. His principle
of utility is essentially brought to bear upon whole systems
of laws.

Before considering what his version of the principle was,
it is therefore necessary to look briefly at his theory of
law in general. For this, the best source is the *Fragment
on Government,* his first published work. The *Fragment,*
as we have seen, was an attack on Blackstone's theories,
which had had, in Bentham's opinion, an unmerited and
dangerous public success. What he objected to, among other
things, in the *Commentaries* was their gentlemanly manner,
which would have a wide appeal, he thought, and conduce to the acceptance of certain fundamental muddles and
incoherences. The first and most important of these muddles
lay in the belief in and appeal to *Natural Law.* The second
confused belief which Bentham rejected was the belief in
the *Original Contract,* as the basis for the existence of the
State and of a political obligation binding upon all members
of the State. For both of these beliefs, Bentham substituted
the *principle* of utility. His definition of a law was, in
essence, the same as the more famous definition contained
in Austin's *Province of Jurisprudence Determined*—a definition which has had a permanent and widespread effect
upon English legal theory. According to this definition, a
law is a command of a sovereign, backed up by sanctions, and
maintained by a habit of obedience. Bentham did not insist,
as Austin did, that the sovereign must be absolute, nor
was he precise about the nature, duration or extent of the
habit of obedience. But upon the necessity of a sanction
before there could be any law he was quite definite. This,

then, was the essence of those laws which he proposed to classify, codify and judge by the principle of utility.

His first statement of the principle is to be found in paragraph 54 of the preface to the *Fragment* : " Now then, with respect to actions in general, there is no property in them that is calculated so readily to engage, and so firmly to fix the attention of an observer, as the *tendency* they may have *to,* or *divergency* (if one may so say) *from,* that which may be styled the common *end* of all of them. The end I mean is *Happiness*; and this *tendency* in any act is what we style its *utility;* as this *divergency* is that to which we give the name of *mischievousness.* With respect then to such actions in particular as are among the objects of the Law, to point out to a man the *utility* of them or the mischievousness, is the only way to make him see *clearly* that property of them which every man is in search of; the only, way in fact to give him *satisfaction.* From *utility* then we may denominate a *principle,* that may serve to preside over and govern, as it were, such arrangement as shall be made of the several institutions or combinations of institutions that compose the matter of this science . . . Governed in this manner by a principle that is recognized by all men, the same arrangement that would serve for the jurisprudence of any one country, would serve with little variation for that of any other. Yet more. The mischievousness of a bad Law would be detected, at least the utility of it would be rendered suspicious, by the difficulty of finding a place for it in such an arrangement : while, on the other hand, a *technical* arrangement [the reference is to Blackstone's argument] is a sink that with equal facility will swallow any garbage that is thrown into it." This insistence that by means of the principle of utility he could distinguish good laws from bad was a cardinal feature of Bentham's whole method. Believers in Natural Law appeared to be unable to recognise the possibility of bad laws. For them, a bad law was simply not a law: for law was founded on morality, indeed could not be distinguished from it, and therefore the concept of a bad law was a contradiction. Bentham, on the other hand, insisted upon the difference between law and morality; they need not, though they should, have any connexion with one another. People's actual intentions, and the intentions they ought to have, must be distinguished; and the test of what laws there ought to be, and what laws ought to be obeyed, was utility.

Utility was, moreover, the source of political obligation in the State. In this matter Bentham thought of himself as following the doctrines of Hume, though in fact he appears somewhat to have simplified, if not misunderstood, what Hume actually said. In a footnote to chapter I of the *Fragment* he gives an account of how he came to reject the notion of the Original Contract: " That the foundations of all *virtue* are laid in *utility* is there [Book III of Hume's *Treatise*] demonstrated, after a few exceptions made, with the strongest force of evidence: but I see not, any more than Helvetious saw, what need there was for the exceptions. For my own part, I well remember, no sooner had I read that part of the work that touches on this subject than I felt as if scales had fallen from my eyes. I then for the first time learnt to call the cause of the people the cause of Virtue. Perhaps a short sketch of the wanderings of a raw but well-intentioned mind, in its researches after moral truth, may, on this occasion be not unuseful: for the history of one mind is the history of many. The writings of the honest, but prejudiced, Earl of Clarendon, to whose integrity nothing was wanting, and to whose wisdom little, but the fortune of living somewhat later; and the contagion of a monkish atmosphere; these, and other concurrent causes, had lifted my infant affections on the side of despotism. The Genius of the place I dwelt in, the authority of the state, the voice of the Church in her solemn offices; all these taught me to call Charles a martyr, and his opponents rebels. I saw innovation, where indeed innovation, but a glorious innovation, was, in their efforts to withstand him. I saw falsehood where indeed falsehood was, in their disavowals of innovation. I saw selfishness, and an obedience to the call of passion, in the efforts of the oppressed to rescue themselves from oppression. I saw strong countenance lent in the sacred writings to monarchic government: and none to any other. I saw *passive obedience* deep stamped with the seal of the

Christian Virtues of humility and self-denial. Conversing with lawyers, I found them full of the virtues of their Original Contract, as a recipe of sovereign efficacy for reconciling the accidental necessity of resistance with the general duty of submission. This drug of theirs they administered to me to calm my scruples. But my unpractised stomach revolted against their opiate. I bid them open to me that page of history in which the solemnization of this important contract was recorded. They shrunk from this challenge; nor could they, when thus pressed, do otherwise than our Author [Blackstone] has done, confess the whole to be a fiction. This, methought, looked ill. It seemed to me the acknowledgment of a bad cause, the bringing a fiction to support it. ' To prove fiction, indeed,' said I ' there is need of fiction; but it is the characteristic of truth to need no proof but truth. Have you then really any such privilege as that of coining facts? You are spending argument to no purpose. Indulge yourselves in the licence of supposing that to be true which is not, and as well may you suppose that proposition itself to be true which you wish to prove, as that other whereby you hope to prove it.' Thus continued I unsatisfying, and unsatisfied, till I learnt to see that *utility* was the test and measure of all virtue; of loyalty as much as any; and that the obligation to minister to general happiness, was an obligation paramount to and inclusive of every other. Having thus got the instruction I stood in need of, I sat down to make my profit of it. I bid adieu to the original contract: and I left it to those to amuse themselves with this rattle, who could think they needed it."

Rejecting natural law, then, Bentham defined laws as *commands* backed up by *sanctions*, some of which would and some of which would not conform to the dictates of morality, the test here being the test of utility. Rejecting the original contract, he saw both the origin of the laws and the obligation to obey them as derivable from the principle of utility. He seems to see, though perhaps confusedly, a distinction between general and particular obligation. For in the passage quoted above he speaks of 'the obligation to minister to general happiness' as the overriding obligation, the most general duty of all. But elsewhere, in chapter 5 of the *Fragment,* he defines duty more narrowly, in the following way : " That is my *duty* to do, which I am liable to be *punished,* according to law, if I do not do : this is the original, ordinary, and proper sense of the word *duty."* In this passage he is interested in denying what Blackstone asserts, that ' supreme governors ' can themselves have duties. It is possible that he has here merely forgotten that, earlier, he spoke of the overriding duty of maximising happiness, which would, if it existed, certainly fall upon the supreme governors and law-makers above everyone else; but it may also be that he is here making the distinction between asking what I am at present constrained to do by the existing laws—what my present duty is, and, on the other hand, asking whether the present laws are such as are conducive to happiness, that is, whether they are good laws and should, in general, be obeyed.

Now to obey laws in general is conducive to happiness. So utility, according to Humean doctrine, provides the answer to the most general question of all, namely, why have laws and government rather than anarchy? But Bentham's main interest lay in showing that utility would also provide the answer to a question less general than this, but more important, namely whether a whole given system of law is a good system. In one sense, I have a duty to obey only so far as utility allows, that is, as far as the law is good; in another sense, I have a duty of obedience as soon as a law with sanctions exists at all. The point, then, of Bentham's codification proposals would be to ensure that only those laws which I have a duty to obey in the first sense should impose on me a duty of obedience in the second sense, that is, should be included as laws in the system.

It is clear that in order to proceed with the plan of codification, Bentham had to show how the principle of utility could actually be applied; and it is to this task that he is addressing himself in the *Introduction to the Principles of Morals and Legislation.* He re-states the principle, in slightly different terms from his earlier definition, in chapter I of the *Principles*; the method of its application is expounded in Chapter IV. The rest of the *Principles* is devoted to expanding what is contained in essence in these two chapters. In chapter I, the principle is said to be an ' act of mind ', or a ' sentiment ', which when it is applied to an act or an object ' approves of its utility, as that quality of it by which the measure of approbation or disapprobation bestowed upon it ought to be governed '. Utility itself is defined as that property in an object whereby it ' tends to produce benefit, advantage, pleasure, good or happiness '. (All these, he says, in the present case come to the same thing.) An action is conformable to utility when the tendency it has to augment the happiness of the community is greater than any it has to diminish it. Of such an action it is possible to say that it is right, or that it ought to be done. " When thus interpreted the words *ought,* and *right* and *wrong,* and others of that stamp, have a meaning : when otherwise, they have none."

It is noticeable that Bentham does not here use the word ' duty '; and on the whole he confines this word to its use in the second of the senses noticed above, namely that sense which is derived from the existence of an actual law, with a sanction attached. However, he is prepared to allow that there are sanctions other than legal punishments, and therefore duties not strictly derived from an actual law. For in the *Fragment,* he lists three kinds of sanction, legal, divine and moral—moral sanction being the mortification arising from the ill-will of the community at large. These three kinds of sanction give rise to three kinds of duty. " When in any of these three senses a man asserts a point of conduct to be a duty, what he asserts is the existence, actual or probable, of an *external* event : viz. of a punishment issuing from one or other of these sources in consequence of a contravention of the duty . . . If he persists in asserting it to be a duty, but without meaning it should be understood that it is on any one of these three accounts that he looks upon it as such; all he then asserts is his own internal *sentiment* : all he means then is, that he feels himself *pleased* or *displeased* at the thoughts of the point of conduct in question, but without being able to tell *why.* In this case he should e'en say so; and not seek to give undue influence to his own single suffrage, by delivering it in terms that purport to declare the voice either of God, or of the law, or of the people."

Now this passage is very severe about sentiment. Bentham seems to be saying that sentiment is no kind of standard by which to distinguish what is a duty from what is not. On the other hand, as we have seen, in the *Principles* he defines his own principle of Utility in terms of a *sentiment* of approbation. However, there are two points to be borne in mind before accusing him of radical inconsistency. First, in the *Fragment* he is confining himself to discussing the word ' duty ' (though in the wide sense, which may include moral as well as strictly legal duties); while in the *Principles* this term seems to be deliberately avoided. Secondly, as we have noticed already, the context of the passage in the *Fragment* is highly polemical; for he is there primarily concerned to use his definition of duty in terms of punishment, for the purpose of rebutting a particular point of Blackstone's. But more important than either of these points is the fact that when, in the *Principles,* he speaks of ' sentiment ', it is *not,* as it is in the *Fragment,* just a feeling of pleasure or pain that he has in mind; it is rather a sentiment—that is, a particular feeling which can arise *only* if the object of it can be shown to be conducive to happiness; and whether or not an object is conducive to happiness is a matter of fact, which can, Bentham thinks, be demonstrated. So a ' sentiment ' in the *Principles* is not a mere chance or whimsical feeling of pleasure, but a feeling based on certain features of the situation; a feeling of *justified* pleasure. (In fact, the concept of this sentiment which constitutes the principle of utility is, whether knowingly or not, derived directly from Hume, by whom the peculiar *moral* feeling of approbation is held to arise only where the characters judged to be virtuous actually possess certain ascertainable features.) It is, therefore, crucial to the whole theory that Bentham should be able to show that whether or not an object is conformable to the principle of utility can be conclusively established, that it is not a matter of guess-work but at least of rational probability.

This is what he sets out to do in the fourth chapter of the *Principles,* entitled 'Value of a lot of pleasure and pain, how to be measured'. This celebrated 'calculus' of pleasures and pains is said by him to be that 'on which the whole fabric of morals and legislation may be seen to rest'. Bentham was perfectly aware that this part of his theory would meet with sharp criticism, and he was ready with answers to many objections. But no objection would ever have made him give it up. For the calculus was not invented for its own sake, as a theoretical contribution to moral philosophy; it was meant to be *used.* Bentham's confidence that, with this tool in hand, he could infallibly, and for all countries alike, discriminate good laws from bad, was the formative principle of the whole of his long life's work, both as a theorist and as a reformer. Later Utilitarians, who felt that this tool could no longer be relied on, lost none of their reforming zeal; nevertheless they lost perhaps the bland assurance that the causes they took up could be *proved* to be right.

To believe wholeheartedly in the 'felicific calculus', to act on the assurance that 'quantities' of happiness can thus be exactly calculated, is in effect to deny the relevance of differences between one sort of person and another (though some of these differences are classified in chapter VI of the *Principles*). Now the legislator is not usually required to take such differences into account—indeed, in many ways, he is obliged not to. But one of Mill's main problems was to reconcile his romantic belief in the sanctity of the individual with the legislator's indifference to idiosyncrasy in which he had been brought up; and this was a problem for him only because he, unlike Bentham, was really interested in moral theory, not merely in legal codification and practical reform. His work is best understood, in fact, as an attempt to apply a jurisprudential theory to the sphere of private morality.

This attempt finds its clearest expression in *Utilitarianism.* But it is necessary first to consider Mill's essay *On Liberty*; for this, besides being one of his most famous writings and quite his most moving, well illustrates a stage in his move away from Benthamism in the strictest sense. The deficiencies which, perhaps with some exaggeration, he imputes to his master in the essay on Bentham are remedied by the theory embodied in *On Liberty*. 'Man, that most complex being, is a very simple one in his eyes': but according to the new doctrine, the first requirement for a good system of laws is that the individual whom Bentham in Mill's view so much over-simplified should be allowed freedom for self-development in the way he wishes to go. "I regard", he says, "utility as the ultimate appeal on all ethical questions; but it must be utility in the largest sense, grounded on the permanent interests of a man as a progressive being." Again, "The only freedom which deserves the name, is that of pursuing our own good in our own way, so long as we do not attempt to deprive others of theirs, or impede their efforts to obtain it." This freedom is what a system of law and government which is truly conformable to the principle of utility must work to ensure. 'The greatest happiness of the greatest number', upon which Bentham claimed to found all jurisprudence and all morals, is still to be the principle of government; but "we have now recognised", Mill writes, "the necessity to the mental well-being of mankind (on which all their other well-being depends) of freedom of opinion, and freedom of the expression of opinion . . ."; and he goes on to recapitulate his four powerful arguments for this recognition. But he says "The greatest difficulty to be encountered does not lie in the appreciation of means towards an acknowledged end, but in the indifference of persons in general to the end itself. If it were felt that the free development of individuality is one of the leading essentials of well-being; that it is not only a co-ordinate element with all that is designated by the terms civilisation, instruction, education, culture, but is itself a necessary part and condition of all those things; there would be no danger that liberty should be undervalued, and the adjustment of the boundaries between it and social control would present no extraordinary difficulty." Freedom to make up one's own mind, to make one's own decisions, and to hold whatever opinions seem to one to be true, do not come into Bentham's list of pleasures, nor does deprivation of his freedom appear in his list of pains. To write of freedom and individuality as necessary conditions of well-being is, in fact, to move decisively away from the mechanics of the felicific calculus.

Nevertheless, the essay *On Liberty* is still close to Bentham in that its subject-matter is legal systems and government; a criterion is offered by which to distinguish good government from bad. The criterion is new, but the purpose is familiar. For moral theory proper we must turn to *Utilitarianism*. This short work, published in 1863, is not only the most complete statement of Mill's moral philosophy, but has also become one of the most discussed of all texts in the subject. Critics of utilitarianism in general, while admitting that it is a highly idiosyncratic work, often pick on it as their particular target, while Mill's own peculiar arguments have also come in for an exceptional amount of attention. This is understandable for *Utilitarianism* is short, absorbing and in some ways ambiguous, all ideal qualifications for celebrity in a philosophical text. The two most frequent criticisms are, briefly, that utilitarianism in any version, Mill's included, is untenable, since it holds that acts are good in so far as their consequences are good, whereas we cannot in fact ever find out for certain what the consequences of actions are; yet we are often certain that some acts are right and others wrong, and therefore our judgment must have some other foundation. Secondly, it is often held that Mill's version particularly is confused, for he claims to derive all morality from the *fact* that other people's happiness is an end, and the supreme end, while the most that he is really entitled to do is to suggest that we *ought* to adopt this sort of end; but if he were then asked *why* we ought to, he could offer no answer. For to answer in terms of the principle of utility would be plainly circular employing the principle to justify itself; while to answer that it was *right*, or *good*, to adopt the ‘ greatest happiness ’ as an end would be to give up the principle as itself the sole and sufficient foundation of morality.

By taking these objections in order, we may come at a reasonably clear view of Mill's moral philosophy.

First, then, it is held that utilitarianism is in general untenable. On this point it is essential to be clear whether it is to *types or classes* of action that we are to assign moral value by looking to their consequences, or to *individual acts*. For to determine the consequence of an individual act is a matter of predicting the future in a given particular case; sometimes we can do this and sometimes, certainly, we cannot. But if we are concerned with *types* of act, then our position is better. For the past here supplies us with evidence that *in general*, if A occurs, B will follow. Now although we cannot be certain, and generally make no claim to be certain, that there will be no exceptions whatever to such a statement, still its form is meant to be general and to cover the majority of cases. It is a 'law-like' statement, which can be uttered without any reference to a particular time or place. The analogy between such general statements of consequences and full-blown scientific laws is not without importance. Bentham had claimed to make morality *scientific*; and Mill, in his *System of Logic* (1843) had investigated the method of establishing scientific generalisations, and in particular, causal laws. It is very likely that he was aware of the possible bearing of his logical upon his ethical inquiries; for in Bentham's version of Utilitarianism there is no real place for the particular. We have seen already that he was concerned with systems of laws which apply to everyone equally; so he is concerned also with the legislator's characteristic interest in the *tendency* of acts to good or ill. This language of 'tendency', which Bentham constantly employs, makes no sense if applied to a single act. We may speak of the tendency of theft, in general, to cause pain or harm of various kinds, but not of the tendency of a particular act of thieving to do so. Besides, the point of legislation is to encourage or discourage acts of a certain class, and very rarely (if ever) to require that *one particular action* be done or not done. In short, there is no doubt that when Bentham speaks of 'an act' he means 'a kind of act' for example, murder. More explicitly still, John Austin, from whom we may say that Mill learned more of moral philosophy than he could have learned from Bentham, discussed this very problem in his lectures *The Province of Jurisprudence Determined* (see Appendix). In the second lecture, he says : " Trying to collect the tendency (of a human action) we must not consider the action as if it were single or insulated, but must look at the class of actions to which it belongs. The probable specific consequences of doing that single act are not the objects of the inquiry. The question to be solved is this : if acts of the class were generally done or generally forborne or omitted, what would be the probable effect on the general happiness or good?" To go further back, Hume had made a distinction between *natural* and *artificial* virtues, the latter being those whose exercise was not necessarily on every single occasion productive of pleasure in those who contemplated it, but which had all the same a tendency to produce pleasure if they were thought of as generally exercised. Such generalising, the raising for instance of the question whether, if everyone acted in this or that way, the consequences would be beneficial, Hume claimed gave rise to general rules, and these rules laid down ' all the great lines of our duty '.

It is therefore undoubtedly in the tradition of utilitarianism to consider, above all, the consequences of general classes of acts, and to inquire about these whether they tend to produce more pleasure than pain. If Mill paid less attention than Hume to particular cases, it is because Bentham had come between, for whom individual acts of virtue or vice were hardly of interest at all

Mill, however, is not unaware that sometimes the principle of utility may have to be applied directly to a particular case in order that the agent may determine what he should do. In most cases ' secondary principles ' will be enough—such principles, that is, as ' It is wrong to deceive ' —and it is such general principles as these which would be justified, if challenged, by an appeal to utility. But Mill claims only that these secondary principles will suffice to guide us in the majority of cases. There may be some situ-

ations in which they prove inadequate, or at any rate need
to be revised. In the fragment on *Aphorisms* (1837) Mill
says : " Every really existing Thing is a compound of such
innumerable properties, and has such an infinity of relations
with all other things in the universe that almost every law to
which it appears to be subject, is liable to be set aside or
frustrated . . .; and as no one can possibly foresee or grasp
all these contingencies, much less express them in such an
imperfect language as that of words, no one needs flatter
himself that he can lay down propositions sufficiently specific
to be available for practice, which he may afterwards apply
mechanically without any exercise of thought. It is given to
no human being to stereotype a set of truths, and walk
safely by their guidance with his mind's eye closed." And
two years earlier, in the article on " Professor Sedgwick's
Discourse on the Studies of the University of Cambridge ",
Mill himself answered one version of the many accusations
against utilitarianism in these words : " Who ever said that
it was necessary to foresee all the consequences of each individual action, ' as they go down into the countless ages
of coming time '? Some of the consequences of an action
are accidental; others are its natural result, according to
the known laws of the universe. The former for the most part
cannot be foreseen; but the whole course of human life
is founded upon the fact that the latter can." Mill rightly
goes on to remark that it is not only for the sake of morality,
but in every other practical connection, that we assume that
single instances *can* be subsumed, more or less accurately,
under general laws, and that in this way consequences *can*
in general be predicted according to these laws. " The com-
monest person lives according to maxims of prudence wholly
founded on foresight of consequences." The utilitarians,
then, are not claiming the impossible when they claim that
the rightness of an act depends upon its consequences. An
individual act may be treated as a case of a general type
of act, and the general type of act may be learned, inductively,
generally to have consequences of a pleasurable or painful
kind, though such rules of thumb will be subject to qualifications and exceptions, as such rules usually are. We may

claim to *know* that a certain particular act is wrong, because we may know without doubt that it is an act in breach of a general rule of morality; and the rule of morality has been adopted as such because the general breach of it causes harm. This is Mill's position. We may criticise it as being unadventurous, or unduly conservative, as leaving too little rocm for moral innovation or reform; but we cannot reasonably dismiss it as simply impossible.

The second main set of criticisms levelled against Mill's *Utilitarianism* is that he is muddled about the foundation of the theory. He tries to show that pleasure or happiness is desirable, and that it is the only thing which is desirable, as an end; he also tries to show that it is not only our own happiness which we desire, but the happiness of other people as well; and finally he asserts, though he does not seriously try to prove, that some kinds of happiness are more desirable than others. On all these counts he has been held guilty of confusion. Numbers of people have been very severe with his arguments, especially those contained in the fourth chapter of *Utilitarianism,* which is entitled ' Of what sort of proof the principle of Utility is susceptible '. It is upon this chapter that G.E. Moore concentrates his fire when, in his *Principia Ethica,* he is arguing against the ' naturalistic fallacy'. This fallacy was supposed by Moore to consist in attempting to define the term ' good ', which was, he thought, in fact indefinable, and more particularly in attempting to define it in terms of natural phenomena, such as pleasure. Since Moore, and indeed at all times, it has been very widely held that anyone who attempts to derive ethical concepts such as ' ought' or ' right ' or ' good ' from non-ethical concepts such as ' pleasure ' or ' happiness ' must be committing a fallacy, and that therefore their philosophy, being founded on error, does not merit very serious attention. But Mill at any rate was not interested in defining ' good ' nor in deriving its meaning from anything else, but in saying *what things are good*; and he states at the beginning of this chapter that questions of ultimate ends are not susceptible of proof. He is not, then, trying to *prove* that one and only one thing is supremely valuable, but rather, assuming that people do adopt something as an ultimate end, he is trying to find out empirically what it is that they do so value. The answer to this is that they value happiness, or pleasure. When Mill uses his much-criticised argument from the analogy between 'visible' and 'desirable', he is attempting to establish what things are good. He holds that, if people did not already regard some things as ends, and therefore desire them, it would be impossible to prove to them that these things were ends. He asks 'How is it possible to prove that health is good?' The answer is that it is not possible, but neither is it necessary. For everyone knows that it is good, and shows this by desiring it. When he says that 'the sole evidence it is possible to produce that anything is desirable is that people actually desire it', he is making the same point. He is not trying to *prove* that happiness is good, but to produce evidence that people already know, without waiting for any proof, that it is good. You can find out what people recognise as ultimate ends by finding out what they desire. What they desire, Mill goes on to say, is happiness.

So far Mill's arguments seem perfectly sound, though not adventurous; but it is this very passage which has outraged moral philosophers more than any other. Of it Moore wrote : 'The fallacy in this step is so obvious that it is quite wonderful how Mill failed to see it'. If Mill had indeed defined 'good' as 'desirable', and then had gone on to define 'desirable' as 'desired', he might well have been open to serious objection. But in fact it was no part of his interest to *define* 'good', or 'desirable', at all. However, though his procedure so far seems unexceptionable, his efforts to show that pleasure or happiness is the *only* thing desirable in itself are less successful. He says that whether or not this is true is a psychological matter, which should therefore be settled on empirical grounds. But it is difficult not to conclude that in the end he is asserting that it is a logical necessity that we desire only pleasure. For he concludes with the words : 'To desire anything, except in proportion as the idea of it is pleasant, is a physical and metaphysical impossibility'; and this is hard to interpret except as meaning it is *contradictory* to deny that what we desire is pleasure. It is possible for Mill to argue in this way because of the extreme ambiguity which attaches to such phrases as 'desire it for its own sake' and 'desire it for the sake of pleasure'. These two phrases may be used to say very much the same thing and so whatever is suggested as an ultimate end will turn out to be desired for the sake of pleasure. There is a further indeterminacy in the concept of pleasure itself. Is absolutely *any* satisfaction, including the satisfaction of satisfying a desire, to be included under the term 'pleasure'? If it is, then of course there is no difficulty in showing that all we desire is pleasure. Mill does not appear to grapple with these difficulties very successfully, or even to be adequately aware of them.

Even if it is allowed that happiness is the ultimate end of life, that this is what people value above everything else, and (more dubiously) that they desire nothing *except* happiness or pleasure, there still remains the question *whose* happiness the individual is supposed to take as his ultimate end. Mill says: 'The happiness which forms the utilitarian standard of what is right in conduct is not the agent's own happiness but that of all concerned'; and he rightly contends that this standard is high, and is such as to foster the beautiful and exalted developments of human nature. But it is one thing to adopt the general happiness as a test for whether a kind of action is virtuous, and quite another to say that the general happiness actually *is* the object of all our desires. The latter could not possibly be maintained. But if not, then what is the connexion between the proposition that all that we desire is happiness or pleasure, and the proposition that the happiness of others is the standard of moral goodness? There appears to be none. An altruistic concern for the happiness of others might well be taken to be the essential requirement of a moral system, but it in no way follows from this that all that we desire is happiness. Nor could the latter be taken to entail the former. It will be seen that this problem is not satisfactorily resolved by Mill in *Utilitarianism*. Once again, the problem did not arise for Bentham, simply because he was not concerned with the sphere of private morality. If we consider the legislator, he may be judged a good legislator if he works for the general happiness, and if his system of laws promotes it; and in working in this way for the general good he will thereby be working for his own, since the laws govern his life as well as other people's. His *private* advantage or pleasure, as distinct from the good of people at large, does not enter into the question of legislation. But as soon as the subject is changed from legislation to morals, from regulating people's conduct in general by means of sanctions, to deciding for a particular man faced with a particular problem how he ought to behave, then the possible conflict between private interest and the well-being of others is liable at once to become the most pressing question of all. And though it may well be that Mill's altruistic principle of utility is a good principle to use, there is nothing to suggest that every one uses it nor that it is the only possible principle.

But still, even though the connexion between the principle as Mill employs it and his arguments to show that we all desire pleasure is not made out, there remains great merit in his exposition of the principle in the private sphere; and if he sometimes seems to suggest that it is only if a ' secondary principle' is conformable to the principle of utility that it will count as a *moral* principle at all, then this is all to the good, for there is much to recommend such a view. Perhaps it is not going too far in interpretation, moreover, to suggest that Mill may really mean, not that we all *do* desire the greatest happiness of the greatest number, but that, since we are rational human beings, we are *capable of learning* to desire it. The principle of utility would on this view be a rational principle, the *only* rational principle of morality there could be. Because we can learn to recognise this, we can learn also to frame explicit rules, and to build up social customs, which produce in us and others the habit of conformity, so that gradually we learn to value virtue for its own sake. We develop, that is, a ' moral sense '. There is a good deal in Mill's writings to confirm such an interpretation. For example, in the essay on Sedgwick's Discourse, in arguing against an *innate* moral sense he says : " Young children have affections, but not moral feelings;

and children whose will is never resisted, never acquire them. There is no selfishness equal to that of children, as everyone who is acquainted with children well knows. It is not the hard, cold selfishness of a grown person, for the most affectionate children have it, where their affection is not supplying a counter-impulse; but the most selfish of grown persons does not come up to a child in the reckless seizing of any pleasure to himself, regardless of the consequences to others. The pains of others, though naturally painful to us, are not so until we have realized them by an act of imagination, implying voluntary attention; and that no very young child ever pays, while under the impulse of a present desire. If a child restrains the indulgence of any wish, it is either from affection or sympathy which are quite other feelings than those of morality; or else (whatever Mr. Sedgwick may think) because he has been taught to do so." There is something peculiar to the nature of man which makes such moral teaching possible : " The idea of the pain of another is naturally painful; the idea of the pleasure of another is naturally pleasurable. From this fact in our natural constitution, all our affections both of love and aversion towards human beings, in so far as they are different from those we entertain towards mere inanimate objects which are pleasant or disagreeable to us, are held by the best teachers of the theory of utility to originate."

This perhaps optimistic belief that men have a better, rational and imaginative part which is capable among other things of an interest in others, explains how it is that Mill is prepared to discriminate between different kinds of pleasure, in a way in which Bentham was not. Mill's critics point out the incompatibility between strict Benthamism and the assertion in Chapter II of *Utilitarianism* that there are different *qualities* of pleasure. "No intelligent human being would consent to be a fool, no instructed person would be an ignoramus, no person of feeling and conscience would be selfish and base, even though they should be persuaded that the fool, the dunce, or the rascal is better satisfied with his lot than they are with theirs." Mill's attempt to explain different qualities of pleasure by explaining how you judge one to be ' higher '

than the other (namely, by appeal to competent judges)
need not be taken very seriously. But his introduction of the
distinction in the first place is yet one more instance of
his departure from the purest Benthamism. Just as in the
essay *On Liberty* he had insisted that the government must,
to conform to the principle of Utility, allow for individual
freedom and self-improvement, but could hardly *prove* that
this was the most important benefit, so in private morality
he can state that the pleasures of intelligence should not be
overlooked, but can hardly, according to the principle, *prove*
that they are to be preferred to others. That he tried to do
so is evidence simply of his temperamental sympathy with
the Wordsworthian estimate of the value to be set on personal experience. These are the ' perennial sources of happiness ' to which Wordsworth had opened his eyes.

Since the time of Mill, Utilitarianism has proved to be
a plant of most sturdy growth. In Mill's life-time ideas and
principles of Utilitarian tendency had already been firmly
implanted in English public life; they were not the only, but
they were a major, influence in that general though gradual
overhauling of the machinery of politics and government
which, in the last century, achieved so much in the direction
of rational reform. In this field the utilitarian spirit led
men to ask, of more and more of their institutions, not whether
they were familiar, venerable, picturesque, or even defensible,
but whether they *worked well*—whether they were framed,
as social institutions should be, in such a way as to secure
for society some tangible benefit. With this practical success
Bentham would have been delighted, and perhaps content;
Mill too was at all times concerned with such practical matters
but perhaps valued more highly than Bentham would have
done the addition of theoretical success, that is the acceptance
of his principles by other thinkers.

On this point a student of the recent history of ethics
might well be misled by fairly recent literature. In the
earlier years of this century academic moral philosophy was
largely dominated by ' intuitionists ', in whose view it was
a fundamental mistake to look for *any* justification of moral
principles; there simply were, so to speak, formal facts, to

be accepted as such and neither questioned nor explained. In their writings, accordingly, it is not uncommon to find Utilitarianism dismissed in a phrase or two at the very beginning, as being quite fundamentally misconceived—as attempting to produce the ultimate, underlying justification for principles which neither need nor admit of any justification whatever. It is, however, more than doubtful whether the views of this school were ever found very widely persuasive, partly because their own positive content was so very arid—it might almost be said that the intuitionists declined, on principle, to argue at all. More recent writers, in any case—of whom we may mention S. E. Toulmin and P. H. Nowell-Smith in Britain and C. L. Stevenson in America—have wished to reopen the question of the *grounds* of our moral convictions, and in so doing have said much that Mill would have been happy to agree with. Very recently, the ' naturalistic fallacy ' itself, the philosophical bludgeon with which Moore and many others had sought to destroy Utilitarianism for ever, has been critically re-appraised, and some well-argued doubts expressed of its very existence. For is it not a *fact* that some types of behaviour tend to do good, and others to do harm? And how in the end, if not on the basis of this fact, can we make sense of discriminating some actions as *right* in morals, and others as *wrong*? To raise these questions is, not perhaps to carry on where Bentham and Mill left off, but very nearly, in effect, to go back to the point from which they started.

AN INTRODUCTION TO THE PRINCIPLES OF MORALS AND LEGISLATION

by Jeremy Bentham

CHAPTER I

OF THE PRINCIPLE OF UTILITY

1. Nature has placed mankind under the governance of two sovereign masters, *pain* and *pleasure*. It is for them alone to point out what we ought to do, as well as to determine what we shall do. On the one hand the standard of right and wrong, on the other the chain of causes and effects, are fastened to their throne. They govern us in all we do, in all we say, in all we think : every effort we can make to throw off our subjection, will serve but to demonstrate and confirm it. In words a man may pretend to abjure their empire : but in reality he will remain subject to it all the while. The *principle of utility*[1] recognises this subjection, and assumes it for the

---

[1] Note by the Author, July 1822.

To this denomination has of late been added, or substituted, the *greatest happiness* or *greatest felicity* principle : this for shortness, instead of saying at length *that principle* which states the greatest happiness of all those whose interest is in question, as being the right and proper, and only right and proper and universally desirable, end of human action : of human action in every situation, and in particular in that of a functionary or set of functionaries exercising the powers of Government. The word *utility* does not so clearly point to the ideas of *pleasure* and *pain* as the words *happiness* and *felicity* do : nor does it lead us to the consideration of the *number,* of the interests affected; to the *number,* as being the circumstance, which contributes, in the largest proportion, to the formation of the standard here in question; the *standard of right and wrong,* by which alone the propriety of human conduct, in every situation, can with

foundation of that system, the object of which is to rear the fabric of felicity by the hands of reason and of law. Systems which attempt to question it, deal in sounds instead of senses, in caprice instead of reason, in darkness instead of light.

But enough of metaphor and declamation: it is not by such means that moral science is to be improved.

2. The principle of utility is the foundation of the present work: it will be proper therefore at the outset to give an explicit and determinate account of what is meant by it. By the principle[2] of utility is meant that principle which approves or disapproves of every action whatsoever, according to the tendency which it appears to have to augment or diminish the happiness of the party whose interest is in question: or, what is the same thing in other words, to promote or to oppose that happiness. I say of every action whatsoever; and therefore not only of every action of a private individual, but of every measure of government.

3. By utility is meant that property in any object, whereby it tends to produce benefit, advantage, pleasure, good, or happiness, (all this in the present case comes to the same thing) or (what comes again to the same thing) to prevent the happening of mischief, pain, evil, or unhappiness to the party whose interest is considered: if that party be the com-

---

propriety be tried. This want of a sufficiently manifest connexion between the ideas of *happiness* and *pleasure* on the one hand, and the idea of *utility* on the other, I have every now and then found operating, and with but too much efficiency, as a bar to the acceptance, that might otherwise have been given, to this principle.

[2] The word principle is derived from the Latin principium: which seems to be compounded of the two words *primus,* first, or chief, and *cipium,* a termination which seems to be derived from *capio,* to take, as in *mancipium, municipium;* to which are analogous, *auceps, forceps,* and others. It is a term of very vague and very extensive signification: it is applied to any thing which is conceived to serve as a foundation or beginning to any series of operations: in some cases, of physical operations; but of mental operations in the present case.

The principle here in question may be taken for an act of the mind; a sentiment; a sentiment of approbation; a sentiment which, when applied to an action, approves of its utility, as that quality of it by which the measure of approbation or disapprobation bestowed upon it ought to be governed.

munity in general, then the happiness of the community : if a particular individual, then the happiness of that individual.

4. The interest of the community is one of the most general expressions that can occur in the phraseology of morals : no wonder that the meaning of it is often lost. When it has a meaning, it is this. The community is a fictitious *body,* composed of the individual persons who are considered as constituting as it were its *members.* The interest of the community then is, what?—the sum of the interests of the several members who compose it.

5. It is in vain to talk of the interest of the community, without understanding what is the interest of the individual.[3] A thing is said to promote the interest, or to be *for* the interest, of an individual, when it tends to add to the sum total of his pleasures : or, what comes to the same thing, to diminish the sum total of his pains.

6. An action then may be said to be conformable to the principle of utility, or, for shortness sake, to utility, (meaning with respect to the community at large) when the tendency it has to augment the happiness of the community is greater than any it has to diminish it.

7. A measure of government (which is but a particular kind of action, performed by a particular person or persons) may be said to be conformable to or dictated by the principle of utility, when in like manner the tendency which it has to augment the happiness of the community is greater than any which it has to diminish it.

8. When an action, or in particular a measure of government, is supposed by a man to be conformable to the principle of utility, it may be convenient, for the purposes of discourse, to imagine a kind of law or dictate, called a law or dictate of utility; and to speak of the action in question, as being conformable to such law or dictate.

9. A man may be said to be a partisan of the principle of utility, when the approbation or disapprobation he annexes to any action, or to any measure, is determined by and pro-portioned to the tendency which he conceives it to have

[3] Interest is one of those words, which not having any superior *genus,* cannot in the ordinary way be defined.

to augment or to diminish the happiness of the community : or in other words, to its conformity or uncomformity to the laws or dictates of utility.

10. Of an action that is conformable to the principle of utility one may always say either that it is one that ought to be done, or at least that it is not one that ought not to be done. One may say also, that it is right it should be done; at least that it is not wrong it should be done : that it is a right action; at least that it is not a wrong action. When thus interpreted, the words *ought,* and *right* and *wrong,* and others of that stamp, have a meaning : when otherwise, they have none.

11. Has the rectitude of this principle been ever formally contested? It should seem that it had, by those who have not known what they have been meaning. Is it susceptible of any direct proof? it should seem not : for that which is used to prove every thing else, cannot itself be proved : a chain of proofs must have their commencement somewhere. To give such proof is as impossible as it is needless.

12. Not that there is or ever has been that human creature breathing, however stupid or perverse, who has not on many, perhaps on most occasions of his life, deferred to it. By the natural constitution of the human frame, on most occasions of their lives men in general embrace this principle, without thinking of it : if not for the ordering of their own actions, yet for the trying of their own actions, as well as of those of other men. There have been, at the same time, not many, perhaps, even of the most intelligent, who have been disposed to embrace it purely and without reserve. There are even few who have not taken some occasion or other to quarrel with it, either on account of their not understanding always how to apply it, or on account of some prejudice or other which they were afraid to examine into, or could not bear to part with. For such is the stuff that man is made of : in principle and in practice, in a right track and in a wrong one, the rarest of all human qualities is consistency.

13. When a man attempts to combat the principle of utility, it is with reasons drawn, without his being aware of it, from that very principle itself.[4] His arguments, if they

[4] ' The principle of utility, (I have heard it said) is a dangerous

prove any thing, prove not that the principle is *wrong,* but that, according to the applications he supposes to be made of it, it is *misapplied.* Is it possible for a man to move the earth? Yes; but he must first find out another earth to stand upon.

14. To disprove the propriety of it by arguments is im-

---

principle: it is dangerous on certain occasions to consult it.' This is as much as to say, what? that it is not consonant to utility, to consult utility: in short, that it is *not* consulting it, to consult it.

Addition by the Author, July 1822.

Not long after the publication of the Fragment on Government, anno 1776, in which, in the character of an all-comprehensive and all-commanding principle, the principle of *utility* was brought to view, one person by whom observation to the above effect was made was *Alexander Wedderburn,* at that time Attorney or Solicitor General, afterwards successively Chief Justice of the Common Pleas, and Chancellor of England, under the successive titles of Lord Loughborough and Earl of Rosslyn. It was made—not indeed in my hearing, but in the hearing of a person by whom it was almost immediately communicated to me. So far from being self-contradictory, it was a shrewd and perfectly true one. By that distinguished functionary, the state of the Government was thoroughly understood: by the obscure individual, at that time not so much as supposed to be so: his disquisitions had not been as yet applied, with any thing like a comprehensive view, to the field of Constitutional Law, nor therefore to those features of the English Government, by which the greatest happiness of the ruling *one* with or without that of a favoured few, are now so plainly seen to be the only ends to which the course of it has at any time been directed. The *principle of utility* was an appellative, at that time employed—employed by me, as it had been by others, to designate that which in a more perspicuous and instructive manner, may, as above, be designated by the name of the *greatest happiness principle.* 'This principle (said Wedderburn) is a dangerous one.' Saying so, he said that which, to a certain extent, is strictly true: a principle, which lays down, as the only *right·* and justifiable end of Government, the greatest happiness of the greatest number— how can it be denied to be a dangerous one? dangerous it unquestionably is, to every government which has for its *actual* end or object, the greatest happiness of a certain *one,* with or without the addition of some comparatively small number of others, whom it is a matter of pleasure or accommodation to him to admit, each of them, to a share in the concern, on the footing of so many junior partners. *Dangerous* it therefore really was, to the interest—

possible; but, from the causes that have been mentioned, or from some confused or partial view of it, a man may happen to be disposed not to relish it. Where this is the case, if he thinks the settling of his opinions on such a subject worth the trouble, let him take the following steps and at length, perhaps, he may come to reconcile himself to it.

1. Let him settle with himself, whether he would wish to discard this principle altogether; if so, let him consider what it is that all his reasonings (in matters of politics especially) can amount to?

2. If he would, let him settle with himself, whether he would judge and act without any principle, or whether there is any other he would judge and act by?

3. If there be, let him examine and satisfy himself whether the principle he thinks he has found is really any separate intelligible principle; or whether it be not a mere principle in words, a kind of phrase, which at bottom expresses neither more nor less than the mere averment of his own unfounded sentiments; that is, what in another person he might be apt to call caprice?

4. If he is inclined to think that his own approbation or disapprobation, annexed to the idea of an act, without any regard to its consequences, is a sufficient foundation for him to judge and act upon, let him ask himself whether his sentiment is to be a standard of right and wrong, with respect to every other man, or whether every man's sentiment has the same privilege of being a standard to itself?

5. In the first case, let him ask himself whether his

---

the sinister interest—of all those functionaries, himself included, whose interest it was, to maximise delay, vexation, and expense, in judicial and other modes of procedure, for the sake of the profit, extractible out of the expense. In a Government which had for its end in view the greatest happiness of the greatest number, Alexander Wedderburn might have been Attorney General and then Chancellor: but he would not have been Attorney General with £15,000 a year, nor Chancellor, with a peerage with a veto upon all justice, with £25,000 a year, and with 500 sinecures at his disposal, under the name of Ecclesiastical Benefices, besides *et cæteras*.

principle is not despotical, and hostile to all the rest of human race?

6. In the second case, whether it is not anarchical, and whether at this rate there are not as many different standards of right and wrong as there are men? and whether even to the sane man, the same thing, which is right to-day, may not (without the least change in its nature) be wrong to-morrow? and whether the same thing is not right and wrong in the same place at the same time? and in either case, whether all argument is not at an end? and whether, when two men have said, 'I like this,' and 'I don't like it,' they can (upon such a principle) have any thing more to say?

7. If he should have said to himself, No: for that the sentiment which he proposes as a standard must be grounded on reflection, let him say on what particulars the reflection is to turn? if on particulars having relation to the utility of the act, then let him say whether this is not deserting his own principle, and borrowing assistance from that very one in opposition to which he sets it up: or if not on those particulars, on what other particulars?

8. If he should be for compounding the matter, and adopting his own principle in part, and the principle of utility in part, let him say how far he will adopt it?

9. When he has settled with himself where he will stop, then let him ask himself how he justifies to himself the adopting it so far? and why he will not adopt it any farther?

10. Admitting any other principle than the principle of utility to be a right principle, a principle that it is right for a man to pursue; admitting (what is not true) that the word *right* can have a meaning without reference to utility, let him say whether there is any such thing as a *motive* that a man can have to pursue the dictates of it: if there is, let him say what that motive is, and how it is to be distinguished from those which enforce the dictates of utility: if not, then lastly let him say what it is this other principle can be good for?

CHAPTER II

OF PRINCIPLES ADVERSE TO THAT
OF UTILITY

1. If the principle of utility be a right principle to be governed by, and that in all cases, it follows from what has been just observed, that whatever principle differs from it in any case must necessarily be a wrong one. To prove any other principle, therefore, to be a wrong one, there needs no more than just to show it to be what it is, a principle of which the dictates are in some point or other different from those of the principle of utility: to state it is to confute it.

2. A principle may be different from that of utility in two ways: 1. By being constantly opposed to it: this is the case with a principle which may be termed the principle of *asceticism*.[1] 2. By being sometimes opposed to it, and sometimes not, as it may happen: this is the case with another,

[1] Ascetic is a term that has been sometimes applied to Monks. It comes from a Greek word which signifies *exercise*. The practices by which Monks sought to distinguish themselves from other men were called their Exercises. These exercises consisted in so many contrivances they had for tormenting themselves. By this they thought to ingratiate themselves with the Deity For the Deity, said they, is a Being of infinite benevolence: now a Being of the most ordinary benevolence is pleased to see others make themslves as happy as they can: therefore to make ourselves as unhappy as we can is the way to please the Deity. If any body asked them, what motive they could find for doing all this? Oh! said they, you are not to imagine that we are punishing ourselves for nothing: we know very well what we are about. You are to know, that for every grain of pain it costs us now, we are to have a hundred grains of pleasure by and by. The case is, that God loves to see us torment ourselves at present: indeed he has as good as told us so. But this is done only to try us, in order just to see how we should behave: which it is plain he could not know, without making the experiment. Now, then, from the satisfaction it gives him to see us make ourselves as unhappy as we can make ourselves in this present life, we have a sure proof of the satisfaction it will give him to see us as happy as he can make us in a life to come.

which may be termed the principle of *sympathy* and *antipathy*.

3. By the principle of asceticism I mean that principle, which, like the principle of utility, approves or disapproves of any action, according to the tendency which it appears to have to augment or diminish the happiness of the party whose interest is in question; but in an inverse manner: approving of actions in as far as they tend to diminish his happiness; disapproving of them in as far as they tend to augment it.

4. It is evident that any one who reprobates any the least particle of pleasure, as such, from whatever source derived, is *pro tanto* a partisan of the principle of asceticism. It is only upon that principle, and not from the principle of utility, that the most abominable pleasure which the vilest of male-factors ever reaped from his crime would be reprobated, if it stood alone. The case is, that it never does stand alone; but is necessarily followed by such a quantity of pain (or, what comes to the same thing, such a chance for a certain quantity of pain) that the pleasure in comparison of it, is as nothing: and this is the true and sole, but perfectly sufficient, reason for making it a ground for punishment

5. There are two classes of men of very different com-plexions, by whom the principle of asceticism appears to have been embraced; the one a set of moralists, the other a set of religionists. Different accordingly have been the motives which appear to have recommended it to the notice of these different parties. Hope, that is the prospect of pleasure, seems to have animated the former: hope, the aliment of philosophic pride: the hope of honour and reputation at the hands of men. Fear, that is the prospect of pain, the latter: fear the offspring of superstitious fancy: the fear of future punishment at the hands of a splenetic and revengeful Deity. I say in this case fear: for of the invisible future, fear is more powerful than hope. These circumstances characterise the two different parties among the partisans of the principle of asceticism; the parties and their motives different, the principle the same.

6. The religious party, however, appear to have carried it farther than the philosophical: they have acted more consistently and less wisely. The philosophical party have

scarcely gone farther than to reprobate pleasure: the religious
party have frequently gone so far as to make it a matter of
merit and of duty to court pain. The philosophical party have
hardly gone farther than the making pain a matter of
indifference. It is no evil, they have said: they have not
said, it is a good. They have not so much as reprobated all
pleasure in the lump. They have discarded only what they
have called the gross; that is, such as are organical, or of
which the origin is easily traced up to such as are organical:
they have even cherished and magnified the refined. Yet
this, however, not under the name of pleasure: to cleanse
itself from the sordes of its impure original, it was necessary
it should change its name: the honourable, the glorious, the
reputable, the becoming, the *honestum,* the *decorum,* it was
to be called: in short, any thing but pleasure.

7. From these two sources have flowed the doctrines from
which the sentiments of the bulk of mankind have all along
received a tincture of this principle; some from the philosophical, some from the religious, some from both. Men of
education more frequently from the philosophical, as more
suited to the elevation of their sentiments: the vulgar more
frequently from the superstitious, as more suited to the
narrowness of their intellect, undilated by knowledge: and
to the abjectness of their condition, continually open to the
attacks of fear. The tinctures, however, derived from the
two sources, would naturally intermingle, insomuch that a
man would not always know by which of them he was most
influenced: and they would often serve to corroborate and
enliven one another. It was this conformity that made a kind
of alliance between parties of a complexion otherwise so
dissimilar: and disposed them to unite upon various occasions
against the common enemy, the partisan of the principle of
utility, whom they joined in branding with the odious name
of Epicurean.

8. The principle of asceticism, however, with whatever
warmth it may have been embraced by its partisans as a rule of
private conduct, seems not to have been carried to any considerable length, when applied to the business of government.
In a few instances it has been carried a little way by the

philosophical party : witness the Spartan regimen. Though
then, perhaps, it may be considered as having been a measure
of security : and an application, though a precipitate and
perverse application, of the principle of utility. Scarcely in
any instances, to any considerable length, by the religious :
for the various monastic orders, and the societies of the
Quakers, Dumplers, Moravians, and other religionists, have
been free societies, whose regimen no man has been astricted to
without the intervention of his own consent. Whatever merit
a man may have thought there would be in making himself
miserable, no such notion seems ever to have occurred to any
of them, that it may be a merit, much less a duty, to make
others miserable : although it should seem, that if a certain
quantity of misery were a thing so desirable, it would not
matter much whether it were brought by each man upon
himself, or by one man upon another. It is true, that from the
same source from whence, among the religionists, the attachment to the principle of asceticism took its rise, flowed
other doctrines and practices, from which misery in abundance was produced in one man by the instrumentality
of another : witness the holy wars, and the persecutions for
religion. But the passion for producing misery in these cases
proceeded upon some special ground : the exercise of it was
confined to persons of particular descriptions : they were
tormented, not as men, but as heretics and infidels. To have
inflicted the same miseries on their fellow-believers and fellow-
sectaries, would have been as blameable in the eyes even of
these religionists, as in those of a partisan of the principle of
utility. For a man to give himself a certain number of stripes
was indeed meritorious : but to give the same number of
stripes to another man, not consenting, would have been a
sin. We read of saints, who for the good of their souls, and
the mortification of their bodies, have voluntarily yielded
themselves a prey to vermin : but though many persons of
this class have wielded the reins of empire, we read of none
who have set themselves to work, and made laws on purpose,
with a view of stocking the body politic with the breed of
highwaymen, housebreakers, or incendiaries. If at any time they
have suffered the nation to be preyed upon by swarms of idle

pensioners, or useless placemen, it has rather been from negligence and imbecility, than from any settled plan for oppressing and plundering of the people. If at any time they have sapped the sources of national wealth, by cramping commerce, and driving the inhabitants into emigration, it has been with other views, and in pursuit of other ends. If they have declaimed against the pursuit of pleasure, and the use of wealth, they have commonly stopped at declamation : they have not, like Lycurgus, made express ordinances for the purpose of banishing the precious metals. If they have established idleness by a law, it has been not because idleness, the mother of vice and misery, is itself a virtue, but because idleness (say they) is the road to holiness. If under the notion of fasting, they have joined in the plan of confining their subjects to a diet, thought by some to be of the most nourishing and prolific nature, it has been not for the sake of making them tributaries to the nations by whom that diet was to be supplied, but for the sake of manifesting their own power, and exercising the obedience of the people. If they have established, or suffered to be established, punishments for the breach of celibacy, they have done no more than comply with the petitions of those deluded rigorists, who, dupes to the ambitious and deep-laid policy of their rulers, first laid themselves under that idle obligation by a vow.

9. The principle of asceticism seems originally to have been the reverie of certain hasty speculators, who having perceived, or fancied, that certain pleasures, when reaped in certain circumstances, have, at the long run, been attended with pains more than equivalent to them, took occasion to quarrel with every thing that offered itself under the name of pleasure. Having then got thus far, and having forgot the point which they set out from, they pushed on, and went so much further as to think it meritorious to fall in love with pain. Even this, we see, is at bottom but the principle of utility misapplied.

10. The principle of utility is capable of being consistently pursued; and it is but tautology to say, that the more consistently it is pursued, the better it must ever be for human-kind. The principle of asceticism never was, nor ever can be, consistently pursued by any living creature. Let but

one tenth part of the inhabitants of this earth pursue it consistently, and in a day's time they will have turned it into a hell.

11. Among principles adverse[2] to that of utility, that

[2] The following Note was first printed in January 1789.

It ought rather to have been styled, more extensively, the principle of *caprice*. Where it applies to the choice of actions to be marked out for injunction or prohibition, for reward or punishment, (to stand, in a word, as subjects for *obligations* to be imposed,) it may indeed with propriety be termed, as in the text, the principle of *sympathy* and *antipathy*. But this appellative does not so well apply to it, when occupied in the choice of the *events* which are to serve as sources of *title* with respect to *rights*: where the actions prohibited and allowed, the obligations and rights, being already fixed, the only question is, under what circumstances a man is to be invested with the one or subjected to the other? from what incidents occasion is to be taken to invest a man, or to refuse to invest him, with the one, or to subject him to the other? In the latter case it may more appositely be characterised by the name of the *phantastic principle*. Sympathy and antipathy are affections of the *sensible* faculty. But the choice of *titles* with respect to *rights,* especially with respect to proprietary rights, upon grounds unconnected with utility, has been in many instances the work, not of the affections but of the imagination.

When, in justification of an article of English Common Law, calling uncles to succeed in certain cases in preference to fathers, Lord Coke produced a sort of ponderosity he had discovered in rights, disqualifying them from ascending in a straight line, it was not that he *loved* uncles particularly, or *hated* fathers, but because the analogy, such as it was, was what his imagination presented him with, instead of a reason, and because, to a judgment unobservant of the standard of utility, or unacquainted with the art of consulting it, where affection is out of the way, imagination is the only guide.

When I know not what ingenious grammarian invented the proposition *Delegatus non potest delegare,* to serve as a rule of law, it was not surely that he had any antipathy to delegates of the second order, or that it was any pleasure to him to think of the ruin which, for want of a manager at home, may befall the affairs of a traveller, whom an unforeseen accident has deprived of the object of his choice: it was, that the incongruity, of giving the same law to objects so contrasted as *active* and *passive* are, was not to be surmounted, and that *-atus* chimes, as well as it contrasts, with *-are.*

When that inexorable maxim, (of which the dominion is no

which at this day seems to have most influence in matters of
government, is what may be called the principle of sympathy
and antipathy. By the principle of sympathy and antipathy, I
mean that principle which approves or disapproves of certain
actions, not on account of their tending to augment the

---

more to be defined, than the date of its birth, or the name of its
father, is to be found,) was imported from England for the government of Bengal, and the whole fabric of judicature was crushed
by the thunders of *ex post facto* justice, it was not surely that the
prospect of a blameless magistracy perishing in prison afforded any
enjoyment to the unoffended authors of their misery; but that the
music of the maxim, absorbing the whole imagination, had drowned
the cries of humanity along with the dictates of common sense.[a]

---

[a] Additional Note by the Author, July 1822.

Add, and that the bad system, of Mahomedan and other native law
was to be put down at all events, to make way for the inapplicable
and still more mischievous system of English Judge-made law, and,
by the hand of his accomplice Hastings, was to be put into the
pocket of Impey—Importer of this instrument of subversion, £8,000
a-year contrary to law, in addition to the £8,000 a-year lavished
upon him, with the customary profusion, by the hand of law.—
See the Account of this transaction in *Mill's British India.*

To this Governor a statue is erecting by a vote of East India
Directors and Proprietors: on it should be inscribed—*Let it but
put money into our pockets, no tyranny too flagitious to be worshipped
by us.*

To this statue of the Arch-malefactor should be added, for a companion, that of the long-robed accomplice: the one lodging the
bribe in the hand of the other. The hundred millions of plundered
and oppressed Hindoos and Mahomedans pay for the one; a Westminster Hall subscription might pay for the other.

What they have done for Ireland with her seven millions of souls,
the authorised dealers and perverters of justice have done for Hindostan with her hundred millions. In this there is nothing wonderful.
The wonder is—that, under such institutions, men, though in ever
such small number, should be found, whom the view of the injustices
which, by *English Judge-made law,* they are compelled to commit,
and the miseries they are thus compelled to produce, deprive of
health and rest. Witness the Letter of an English Hindostan Judge,
Sept. 1, 1819, which lies before me. I will not make so cruel a
requital for his honesty, as to put his name in print: indeed the
House of Commons' Documents already published leave little need
of it.

happiness, nor yet on account of their tending to diminish the happiness of the party whose interest is in question, but merely because a man finds himself disposed to approve or disapprove of them : holding up that approbation or disapprobation as a sufficient reason for itself, and disclaiming the

---

Fiat Justitia, ruat cælum, says another maxim, as full of extravagance as it is of harmony : Go heaven to wreck—so justice be but done : — and what is the ruin of kingdoms, in comparison of the wreck of heaven?

So again, when the Prussian chancellor, inspired with the wisdom of I know not what Roman sage, proclaimed in good Latin, for the edification of German ears, *Servitus servitutis non datur,* [Cod. Fred. tom. ii. par. 2. liv. 2. tit. x. § 6. p. 308.] it was not that he had conceived any aversion to the life-holder who, during the continuance of his term, should wish to gratify a neighbour with a right of way or water, or to the neighbour who should wish to accept of the indulgence; but that, to a jurisprudential ear, *-tus -tutis* sound little less melodious than *-atus -are.* Whether the melody of the maxim was the real reason of the rule, is not left open to dispute : for it is ushered in by the conjunction *quia,* reason's appointed harbinger : *quia servitus servitutis non datur.*

Neither would equal melody have been produced, nor indeed could similar melody have been called for, in either of these instances, by the opposite provision : it is only when they are opposed to general rules, and not when by their conformity they are absorbed in them, that more specific ones can obtain a separate existence. *Delegatus potest delegare,* and *Servitus servitutis datur,* provisions already included under the general adoption of contracts, would have been as unnecessary to the apprehension and the memory, as, in comparison of their energetic negatives, they are insipid to the ear.

Were the inquiry diligently made, it would be found that the goddess of harmony has exercised more influence, however latent, over the dispensations of Themis, than her most diligent historiographers, or even her most passionate panegyrists, seem to have been aware of. Every one knows, how, by the ministry of Orpheus, it was she who first collected the sons of men beneath the shadow of the sceptre : yet, in the midst of continual experience, men seem yet to learn, with what successful diligence she has laboured to guide it in its course. Every one knows, that measured numbers were the language of the infancy of law : none seem to have observed, with what imperious sway they have governed her maturer age. In English jurisprudence in particular, the connexion betwixt law and music, however less perceived than in Spartan legislation, is

necessity of looking out for any extrinsic ground. Thus far in the general department of morals : and in the particular department of politics, measuring out the quantum (as well as determining the ground) of punishment, by the degree of the disapprobation.

---

not perhaps less real nor less close. The music of the Office, though not of the same kind, is not less musical in its kind, than the music of the Theatre; that which hardens the heart, than that which softens it : —sostenutos as long, cadences as sonorous; and those governed by rules, though not yet promulgated, not less determinate. Search indictments, pleadings, proceedings in chancery, conveyances : whatever trespasses you may find against truth or common sense, you will find none against the laws of harmony. The English Liturgy, just as this quality has been extolled in that sacred office, possesses not a greater measure of it, than is commonly to be found in an English Act of Parliament. Dignity, simplicity, brevity, precision, intelligibility, possibility of being retained or so much as apprehended, every thing yields to Harmony. Volumes might be filled, shelves loaded, with the sacrifices that are made to this insatiate power. Expletives, her ministers in Grecian poetry are not less busy, though in different shape and bulk, in English legislation : in the former, they are monosyllables[b] : in the latter, they are whole lines.[c]

To return to the *principle of sympathy and antipathy* : a term preferred at first, on account of its impartiality, to the *principle of caprice*. The choice of an appellative, in the above respects too narrow, was owing to my not having, at that time, extended my views over the civil branch of law, any otherwise than as I had found it inseparably involved in the penal. But when we come to the former branch, we shall see the *phantastic* principle making at least as great a figure there, as the principle of *sympathy and antipathy* in the latter.

In the days of Lord Coke, the light of utility can scarcely be said to have as yet shone upon the face of Common Law. If a faint ray of it, under the name of the *argumentum ab inconvenienti,* is to be found in a list of about twenty topics exhibited by that great lawyer as the co-ordinate leaders of that all-perfect system, the admission, so circumstanced, is as sure a proof of neglect, as, to the status of Brutus and Cassius, exclusion was a cause of notice. It stands, neither in the front, nor in the rear, nor in any post of honour; but

[b] Μεν, τοι, γε, νυν, &c.

[c] And be it further enacted by the authority aforesaid, that—Provided always, and it is hereby further enacted and declared that—&c. &c.

12. It is manifest, that this is rather a principle in name than in reality : it is not a positive principle of itself, so much as a term employed to signify the negation of all principle. What one expects to find in a principle is something that points out some external consideration, as a means of warranting and guiding the internal sentiments of approbation and disapprobation : this expectation is but ill fulfilled by a proposition, which does neither more nor less than hold up each of those sentiments as a ground and standard for itself.

13. In looking over the catalogue of human actions (says a partisan of this principle) in order to determine which of them are to be marked with the seal of disapprobation, you need but to take counsel of your own feelings : whatever you find in yourself a propensity to condemn, is wrong for that very reason. For the same reason it is also meet for punishment : in what proportion it is adverse to utility, or whether it be adverse to utility at all, is a matter that makes no difference. In that same *proportion* also is it meet for punishment : if you hate much, punish much : if you hate little, punish little : punish as you hate. If you hate not at all, punish not at all : the fine feelings of the soul are not to

---

huddled in towards the middle, without the smallest mark of preference. [Coke, Littleton, II. a.] Nor is this Latin *inconvenience* by any means the same thing with the English one. It stands distinguished from *mischief*: and because by the vulgar it is taken for something less bad, it is given by the learned as something worse. *The law prefers a mischief to an inconvenience,* says an admired maxim, and the more admired because as nothing is expressed by it, the more is supposed to be understood.

Not that there is any avowed, much less a constant opposition, between the prescriptions of utility and the operations of the common law : such constancy we have seen to be too much even for ascetic fervor. [Supra, par x.] From time to time instinct would unavoidably betray them into the paths of reason : instinct which, however it may be cramped, can never be killed by education. The cobwebs spun out of the materials brought together by 'the competition of opposite analogies,' can never have ceased being warped by the silent attraction of the rational principle : though it should have been, as the needle is by the magnet, without the privity of conscience.

be overborne and tyrannised by the harsh and rugged dictates of political utility.

14. The various systems that have been formed concerning the standard of right and wrong, may all be reduced to the principle of sympathy and antipathy. One account may serve for all of them. They consist all of them in so many contrivances for avoiding the obligation of appealing to any external standard, and for prevailing upon the reader to accept of the author's sentiment or opinion as a reason for itself. The phrase is different, but the principle the same.[8]

[8] It is curious enough to observe the variety of inventions men have hit upon, and the variety of phrases they have brought forward, in order to conceal from the world, and, if possible, from themselves, this very general and therefore very pardonable self-sufficiency.

1. One man says, he has a thing made on purpose to tell him what is right and what is wrong; and that it is called a *moral sense*: and then he goes to work at his ease, and says, such a thing is right, and such a thing is wrong—why? 'because my moral sense tells me it is.'

2. Another man comes and alters the phrase: leaving out *moral*, and putting in *common*, in the room of it. He then tells you, that his common sense teaches him what is right and wrong, as surely as the other's moral sense did: meaning by common sense, a sense of some kind or other, which, he says, is possessed by all mankind: the sense of those, whose sense is not the same as the author's, being struck out of the account as not worth taking. This contrivance does better than the other; for a moral sense, being a new thing, a man may feel about him a good while without being able to find it out: but common sense is as old as the creation; and there is no man but would be ashamed to be thought not to have as much of it as his neighbours. It has another great advantage: by appearing to share power, it lessens envy: for when a man gets up upon this ground, in order to anathematise those who differ from him, it is not by a *sic volo sic jubeo*, but by a *velitis jubeatis*.

3. Another man comes, and says, that as to a moral sense indeed, he cannot find that he has any such thing: that however he has an *understanding*, which will do quite as well. This understanding, he says, is the standard of right and wrong: it tells him so and so. All good and wise men understand as he does: if other men's understandings differ in any point from his, so much the worse

15. It is manifest, that the dictates of this principle will frequently coincide with those of utility, though perhaps without intending any such thing. Probably more frequently than not : and hence it is that the business of penal justice is

---

for them : it is a sure sign they are either defective or corrupt.

4. Another man says, that there is an eternal and immutable Rule of Right : that the rule of right dictates so and so : and then he begins giving you his sentiments upon any thing that comes uppermost : and these sentiments (you are to take for granted) are so many branches of the eternal rule of right.

5. Another man, or perhaps the same man (it's no matter) says, that there are certain practices conformable, and others repugnant, to the Fitness of Things; and then he tells you, at his leisure, what practices are conformable and what repugnant : just as he happens to like a practice or dislike it.

6. A great multitude of people are continually talking of the Law of Nature; and then they go on giving you their sentiments about what is right and what is wrong : and these sentiments, you are to understand, are so many chapters and sections of the Law of Nature.

7. Instead of the phrase, Law of Nature, you have sometimes, Law of Reason, Right Reason, Natural Justice, Natural Equity, Good Order. Any of them will do equally well. This latter is most used in politics. The three last are much more tolerable than the others, because they do not very explicitly claim to be any thing more than phrases : they insist but feebly upon the being looked upon as so many positive standards of themselves, and seem content to be taken, upon occasion, for phrases expressive of the conformity of the thing in question to the proper standard, whatever that may be. On most occasions, however, it will be better to say *utility* : *utility* is clearer, as referring more explicitly to pain and pleasure.

8. We have one philosopher, who says, there is no harm in any thing in the world but in telling a lie : and that if, for example, you were to murder your own father, this would only be a particular way of saying, he was not your father. Of course, when this philosopher sees any thing that he does not like, he says, it is a particular way of telling a lie. It is saying, that the act ought to be done, or may be done, when, *in truth,* it ought not to be done.

9. The fairest and openest of them all is that sort of man who speaks out, and says, I am of the number of the Elect : now God himself takes care to inform the Elect what is right : and that with so good effect, and let them strive ever so, they cannot help not

carried on upon that tolerable sort of footing upon which
we see it carried on in common at this day. For what more
natural or more general ground of hatred to a practice can
there be, than the mischievousness of such practice? What

---

only knowing it but practising it. If therefore a man wants to know
what is right and what is wrong, he has nothing to do but to
come to me.

It is upon the principle of antipathy that such and such acts
are often reprobated on the score of their being *unnatural*: the
practice of exposing children, established among the Greeks and
Romans, was an unnatural practice. Unnatural, when it means any
thing, means unfrequent: and there it means something; although
nothing to the present purpose. But here it means no such thing:
for the frequency of such acts is perhaps the great complaint. It
therefore means nothing; nothing, I mean which there is in the
act itself. All it can serve to express is, the disposition of the
person who is talking of it: the disposition he is in to be angry at
the thoughts of it. Does it merit his anger? Very likely it may: but
whether it does or no is a question, which, to be answered rightly,
can only be answered upon the principle of utility.

Unnatural, is as good a word as moral sense, or common sense;
and would be as good a foundation for a system. Such an act is
unnatural; that is, repugnant to nature: for I do not like to
practise it: and, consequently, do not practise it. It is therefore
repugnant to what ought to be the nature of everybody else.

The mischief common to all these ways of thinking and arguing
(which, in truth, as we have seen, are but one and the same method,
couched in different forms of words) is their serving as a cloke,
and pretence, and aliment, to despotism: if not a despotism in
practice, a despotism however in disposition: which is but too
apt, when pretence and power offer, to show itself in practice.
The consequence is, that with intentions very commonly of the
purest kind, a man becomes a torment either to himself or his
fellow-creatures. If he be of the melancholy cast, he sits in silent
grief, bewailing their blindness and depravity: if of the irascible,
he declaims with fury and virulence against all who differ from
him; blowing up the coals of fanaticism, and branding with the
charge of corruption and insincerity, every man who does not think,
or profess to think, as he does.

If such a man happens to possess the advantages of style, his book
may do a considerable deal of mischief before the nothingness of it is
understood.

These principles, if such they can be called, it is more frequent to

all men are exposed to suffer by, all men will be disposed to hate. It is far yet, however, from being a constant ground : for when a man suffers, it is not always that he knows what it is he suffers by. A man may suffer grievously, for instance,

---

see applied to morals than to politics : but their influence extends itself to both. In politics, as well as morals, a man will be at least equally glad of a pretence for deciding any question in the manner that best pleases him, without the trouble of inquiry. If a man is an infallible judge of what is right and wrong in the actions of private individuals, why not in the measures to be observed by public men in the direction of those actions? accordingly (not to mention other chimeras) I have more than once known the pretended law of nature set up in legislative debates, in opposition to arguments derived from the principle of utility.

'But is it never, then, from any other considerations than those of utility, that we derive our notions of right and wrong?' I do not know : I do not care. Whether a moral sentiment can be originally conceived from any other source than a view of utility, is one question : whether upon examination and reflection it can, in point of fact, be actually persisted in and justified on any other ground, by a person reflecting within himself, is another : whether in point of right it can properly be justified on any other ground, by a person addressing himself to the community, is a third. The two first are questions of speculation : it matters not, comparatively speaking, how they are decided. The last is a question of practice : the decision of it is of as much importance as that of any can be.

'I feel in myself,' (say you) 'a disposition to approve of such or such an action in a moral view : but this is not owing to any notions I have of its being a useful one to the community. I do not pretend to know whether it be an useful one or not : it may be, for aught I know, a mischievous one.' 'But is it then,' (say I) 'a mischievous one? examine; and if you can make yourself sensible that it is so, then if duty means any thing, that is, moral duty, it is your *duty* at least to abstain from it : and more than that, if it is what lies in your power, and can be done without too great a sacrifice, to endeavour to prevent it. It is not your cherishing the notion of it in your bosom, and giving it the name of virtue, that will excuse you.'

'I feel in myself,' (say you again) 'a disposition to detest such or such an action in a moral view; but this is not owing to any notions I have of its being a mischievous one to the community. I do not pretend to know whether it be a mischievous one or not : it may be not a mischievous one : it may be, for aught I know,

by a new tax, without being able to trace up the cause of his sufferings to the injustice of some neighbour, who has eluded the payment of an old one.

16. The principle of sympathy and antipathy is most apt to err on the side of severity. It is for applying punishment in many cases which deserve none : in many cases which deserve some, it is for applying more than they deserve. There is no incident imaginable, be it ever so trivial, and so remote from mischief, from which this principle may not extract a ground of punishment. Any difference in taste : any difference in opinion : upon one subject as well as upon another. No disagreement so trifling which perseverance and altercation will not render serious. Each becomes in the other's eyes an enemy, and if laws permit, a criminal.[4] This is one

---

an useful one.'—' May it indeed,' (say I) ' an useful one? but let me tell you then, that unless duty, and right and wrong, be just what you please to make them, if it really be not a mischievous one, and any body has a mind to do it, it is no duty of yours, but, on the contrary, it would be very wrong in you, to take upon you to prevent him : detest it within yourself as much as you please; that it may be a very good reason (unless it be also a useful one) for your not doing it yourself : but if you go about, by word or deed, to do any thing to hinder him, or make him suffer for it, it is you, and not he, that have done wrong : it is not your setting yourself to blame his conduct, or branding it with the name of vice, that will make him culpable, or you blameless. Therefore, if you can make yourself content that he shall be of one mind, and you of another, about this matter, and so continue, it is well : but if nothing will serve you, but that you and he must needs be of the same mind, I'll tell you what you have to do : it is for you to get the better of your antipathy, not for him to truckle to it.'

[4] King James the First of England had conceived a violent antipathy against Arians : two of whom he burnt.[a] This gratification he procured himself without much difficulty : the notions of the times were favourable to it. He wrote a furious book against Vorstius, for being what was called an Arminian : for Vorstius was at a distance. He also wrote a furious book, called ' A Counterblast to Tobacco,' against the use of that drug, which Sir Walter Raleigh had then lately introduced. Had the notions of the times co-operated with him, he would have burnt the Anabaptist and the smoke of

---

[a] Hume's Hist. vol. 6.

of the circumstances by which the human race is distinguished (not much indeed to its advantage) from the brute creation.

17. It is not, however, by any means unexampled for this principle to err on the side of lenity. A near and perceptible mischief moves antipathy. A remote and imperceptible mischief, though not less real, has no effect. Instances in proof of this will occur in numbers in the course of the work.[5] It would be breaking in upon the order of it to give them here.

18. It may be wondered, perhaps, that in all this while no mention has been made of the *theological* principle; meaning that principle which professes to recur for the standard of right and wrong to the will of God. But the case is, this is not in fact a distinct principle. It is never any thing more or less than one or other of the three before-mentioned principles presenting itself under another shape.

---

tobacco in the same fire. However, he had the satisfaction of putting Raleigh to death afterwards, though for another crime.

Disputes concerning the comparative excellence of French and Italian music have occasioned very serious bickerings at Paris. One of the parties would not have been sorry (says Mr. D'Alembert[b]) to have brought government into the quarrel. Pretences were sought after and urged. Long before that, a dispute of like nature, and of at least equal warmth, had been kindled at London upon the comparative merits of two composers at London; where riots between the approvers and disapprovers of a new play are, at this day, not unfrequent. The ground of quarrel between the Big-endians and the Little-endians in the fable, was not more frivolous than many an one which has laid empires desolate. In Russia, it is said, there was a time when some thousands of persons lost their lives in a quarrel, in which the government had taken part, about the number of fingers to be used in making the sign of the cross. This was in days of yore: the ministers of Catherine II are better *instructed*[c] than to take any other part in such disputes, than that of preventing the parties concerned from doing one another a mischief.

[5] See ch. XVI [Division], par. 42, 44.

---

[b] Melanges Essai sur la Liberté de la Musique.

[c] Instruct. art. 474, 475, 476.

The *will* of God here meant cannot be his revealed will, as contained in the sacred writings : for that is a system which nobody ever thinks of recurring to at this time of day, for the details of political administration : and even before it can be applied to the details of private conduct, it is universally allowed, by the most eminent divines of all persuasions, to stand in need of pretty ample interpretations; else to what use are the works of those divines? And for the guidance of these interpretations, it is also allowed, that some other standard must be assumed. The will then which is meant on this occasion, is that which may be called the *presumptive* will : that is to say, that which is presumed to be his will on account of the conformity of its dictates to those of some other principle. What then may be this other principle? it must be one or other of the three mentioned above : for there cannot, as we have seen, be any more. It is plain, therefore, that setting revelation out of the question, no light can ever be thrown upon the standard of right and wrong, by any thing that can be said upon the question, what is God's will. We may be perfectly sure, indeed, that whatever is right is conformable to the will of God : but so far is that from answering the purpose of showing us what is right, that it is necessary to know first whether a thing is right in order to know from thence whether it be conformable to the will of God.[6]

[6] The principle of theology refers every thing to God's pleasure. But what is God's pleasure? God does not, he confessedly does not now, either speak or write to us. How then are we to know what is his pleasure? By observing what is our own pleasure, and pronouncing it to be his. Accordingly what is called the pleasure of God, is and must necessarily be (revelation apart) neither more nor less than the good pleasure of the person, whoever he be, who is pronouncing what he believes, or pretends, to be God's pleasure. How know you it to be God's pleasure that such or such an act should be abstained from? whence come you even to suppose as much? 'Because the engaging in it would, I imagine, be prejudicial upon the whole to the happiness of mankind;' says the partisan of the principle of utility : 'Because the commission of it is attended with a gross and sensual, or at least with a trifling and transient satisfaction;' says the partisan of the principle of asceticism : 'Because I detest the thought of it; and I cannot, neither ought I

19. There are two things which are very apt to be confounded, but which it imports us carefully to distinguish :—the motive or cause, which, by operating on the mind of an individual, is productive of any act : and the ground or reason which warrants a legislator, or other by-stander, in regarding that act with an eye of approbation. When the act happens, in the particular instance in question, to be productive of effects which we approve of, much more if we happen to observe that the same motive may frequently be productive, in other instances, of the like effects, we are apt to transfer our approbation to the motive itself, and to assume, as the just ground for the approbation we bestow on the act, the circumstance of its originating from that motive. It is in this way that the sentiment of antipathy has often been considered as a just ground of action. Antipathy, for instance, in such or such a case, is the cause of an action which is attended with good effects : but this does not make it a right ground of action in that case, any more than in any other. Still farther. Not only the effects are good, but the agent sees beforehand that they will be so. This may make the action indeed a perfectly right action : but it does not make antipathy a right ground of action. For the same sentiment of antipathy, if implicitly deferred to, may be, and very frequently is, productive of the very worst effects. Antipathy, therefore, can never be a right ground of action. No more, therefore, can resentment, which, as will be seen more particularly hereafter, is but a modification of antipathy. The only right ground of action, that can possibly subsist, is, after all, the consideration of utility, which if it is a right principle of action, and of approbation, in any one case, is so in every other. Other principles in abundance, that is, other motives, may be the reasons why such and such an act *has* been done : that is, the reasons or causes of its

---

to be called upon to tell why;' says he who proceeds upon the principle of antipathy. In the words of one or other of these must that person necessarily answer (revelation apart) who professes to take for his standard the will of God.

being done : but it is this alone that can be the reason why it might or ought to have been done. Antipathy or resentment requires always to be regulated, to prevent its doing mischief : to be regulated by what? always by the principle of utility. The principle of utility neither requires nor admits of any other regulator than itself.

CHAPTER III

OF THE FOUR SANCTIONS OR SOURCES OF PAIN AND PLEASURE

1. It has been shown that the happiness of the individuals, of whom a community is composed, that is their pleasures and their security, is the end and the sole end which the legislator ought to have in view: the sole standard, in conformity to which each individual ought, as far as depends upon the legislator, to be *made* to fashion his behaviour. But whether it be this or any thing else that is to be *done,* there is nothing by which a man can ultimately be *made* to do it, but either pain or pleasure. Having taken a general view of these two grand objects (*viz.,* pleasure, and what comes to the same thing, immunity from pain) in the character of *final* causes; it will be necessary to take a view of pleasure and pain itself, in the character of *efficient* causes or means.

2. There are four distinguishable sources from which pleasure and pain are in use to flow: considered separately, they may be termed the *physical,* the *political,* the *moral,* and the *religious*: and inasmuch as the pleasures and pains belonging to each of them are capable of giving a binding force to any law or rule of conduct, they may all of them be termed *sanctions.*[1]

[1] Sanctio, in Latin, was used to signify the *act of binding,* and, by a common grammatical transition, *any thing which serves to bind a man*: to wit, to the observance of such or such a mode of conduct. According to a Latin grammarian,[a] the import of the word is derived by rather a far-fetched process (such as those commonly are, and in a great measure indeed must be, by which intellectual ideas are derived from sensible ones) from the word *sanguis,* blood: because, among the Romans, with a view to inculcate into the people a persuasion that such or such a mode of conduct would be rendered obligatory upon a man by the force of which I call the religious sanction (that is, that he would be made to suffer by the extra-

---

[a] Servius. See Ainsworth's Dict. ad verbum *Sanctio.*

3. If it be in the present life, and from the ordinary course of nature, not purposely modified by the interposition of the will of any human being, nor by any extraordinary interposition of any superior invisible being, that the pleasure or the pain takes place or is expected, it may be said to issue from or to belong to the *physical sanction.*

4. If at the hands of a *particular* person or set of persons in the community, who under names correspondent to that of *judge,* are chosen for the particular purpose of dispensing it, according to the will of the sovereign or supreme ruling power in the state, it may be said to issue from the *political sanction.*

5. If at the hands of such *chance* persons in the community, as the party in question may happen in the course of his life to have concerns with, according to each man's spontaneous disposition, and not according to any settled or concerted rule, it may be said to issue from the *moral* or *popular sanction.*[2]

6. If from the immediate hand of a superior invisible being, either in the present life, or in a future, it may be said to issue from the *religious sanction.*

7. Pleasures or pains which may be expected to issue from the *physical, political,* or *moral* sanctions, must all of them be

---

ordinary interposition of some superior being, if he failed to observe the mode of conduct in question) certain ceremonies were contrived by the priests: in the course of which ceremonies the blood of victims was made use of.

A Sanction then is a source of obligatory powers or *motives*: that is, of *pains* and *pleasures*; which, according as they are connected with such or such modes of conduct, operate, and are indeed the only things which can operate, as *motives.* See Chap. x. [Motives].

[2] Better termed *popular,* as more directly indicative of its constituent cause; as likewise of its relation to the more common phrase *public opinion,* in French *opinion publique,* the name there given to that tutelary power, of which of late so much is said, and by which so much is done. The latter appellation is however unhappy and inexpressive; since if *opinion* is material, it is only in virtue of the influence it exercises over action, through the medium of the affections and the will.

expected to be experienced, if ever, in the *present* life : those which may be expected to issue from the *religious* sanction, may be expected to be experienced either in the *present* life or in a *future*.

8. Those which can be experienced in the present life, can of course be no others than such as human nature in the course of the present life is susceptible of : and from each of these sources may flow all the pleasures or pains of which, in the course of the present life, human nature is susceptible. With regard to these then (with which alone we have in this place any concern) those of them which belong to any one of those sanctions, differ not ultimately in kind from those which belong to any one of the other three : the only difference there is among them lies in the circumstances that accompany their production. A suffering which befalls a man in the natural and spontaneous course of things, shall be styled, for instance, a *calamity*; in which case, if it be supposed to befall him through any imprudence of his, it may be styled a punishment issuing from the physical sanction. Now this same suffering, if inflicted by the law, will be what is commonly called a *punishment*; if incurred for want of any friendly assistance, which the misconduct, or supposed misconduct, of the sufferer has occasioned to be withholden, a punishment issuing from the *moral* sanction; if through the immediate interposition of a particular providence, a punishment issuing from the religious sanction.

9. A man's goods, or his person, are consumed by fire. If this happened to him by what is called an accident, it was a calamity : if by reason of his own imprudence (for instance, from his neglecting to put his candle out) it may be styled a punishment of the physical sanction : if it happened to him by the sentence of the political magistrate, a punishment belonging to the political sanction; that is, what is commonly called a punishment : if for want of any assistance which his *neighbour* withheld from him out of some dislike to his *moral* character, a punishment of the *moral* sanction : if by an immediate act of *God's* displeasure, manifested on account of some *sin* committed by him, or through any distraction of

mind, occasioned by the dread of such displeasure, a punishment of the *religious* sanction.[3]

10. As to such of the pleasures and pains belonging to the religious sanction, as regard a future life, of what kind these may be we cannot know. These lie not open to our observation. During the present life they are matter only of expectation : and, whether that expectation be derived from natural or revealed religion, the particular kind of pleasure or pain, if it be different from all those which lie open to our observation, is what we can have no idea of. The best ideas we can obtain of such pains and pleasures are altogether unliquidated in point of quality. In what other respects our ideas of them *may* be liquidated will be considered in another place.[4]

11. Of these four sanctions the physical is altogether, we may observe, the ground-work of the political and the moral : so is it also of the religious, in as far as the latter bears relation to the present life. It is included in each of those other three. This may operate in any case, (that is, any of the pains or pleasures belonging to it may operate) independently of *them* : none of *them* can operate but by means of this. In a word, the powers of nature may operate of themselves; but neither the magistrate, nor men at large, *can* operate, nor is God in the case in question *supposed* to operate, but through the powers of nature.

12. For these four objects, which in their nature have so much in common, it seemed of use to find a common name. It seemed of use, in the first place, for the convenience of giving a name to certain pleasures and pains, for which a name equally characteristic could hardly otherwise have been found : in the second place, for the sake of holding up the efficacy of certain moral forces, the influence of which is apt not to be sufficiently attended to. Does the political sanction exert an influence over the conduct of mankind? The

[3] A suffering conceived to befall a man by the immediate act of God, as above, is often, for shortness' sake, called a *judgment* : instead of saying, a suffering inflicted on him in consequence of a special judgment formed, and resolution thereupon taken, by the Deity.

[4] See ch. XIII [Cases unmeet] par. 2. note.

moral, the religious sanctions do so too. In every inch of his career are the operations of the political magistrate liable to be aided or impeded by these two foreign powers: who, one or other of them, or both, are sure to be either his rivals or his allies. Does it happen to him to leave them out of his calculations? he will be sure almost to find himself mistaken in the result. Of all this we shall find abundant proofs in the sequel of this work. It behoves him, therefore, to have them continually before his eyes; and that under such a name as exhibits the relation they bear to his own purposes and designs.

CHAPTER IV

VALUE OF A LOT OF PLEASURE OR PAIN, HOW TO BE MEASURED

1. Pleasures then, and the avoidance of pains, are the *ends* which the legislator has in view : it behoves him therefore to understand their *value*. Pleasures and pains are the *instruments* he has to work with : it behoves him therefore to understand their force, which is again, in other words, their value.

2. To a person considered *by himself,* the value of a pleasure or pain considered *by itself,* will be greater or less, according to the four following circumstances[1] :

    1. Its *intensity.*
    2. Its *duration.*
    3. Its *certainty* or *uncertainty.*
    4. Its *propinquity* or *remoteness.*

3. These are the circumstances which are to be considered in estimating a pleasure or a pain considered each of them by itself. But when the value of any pleasure or pain is considered for the purpose of estimating the tendency of any *act* by which it is produced, there are two other circumstances to be taken into account; these are,

5. Its *fecundity,* or the chance it has of being followed by sensations of the *same* kind : that is, pleasures, if it be a pleasure : pains, if it be a pain.

---

[1] These circumstances have since been denominated *elements* or *dimensions* of *value* in a pleasure or a pain.

Not long after the publication of the first edition, the following memoriter verses were framed, in the view of lodging more effectually, in the memory, these points, on which the whole fabric of morals and legislation may be seen to rest.

    Intense, long, certain, speedy, fruitful, pure—
    Such marks in *pleasures* and in *pains* endure.
    Such pleasures seek if *private* be thy end:
    If it be *public,* wide let them *extend.*
    Such *pains* avoid, whichever be thy view:
    If pains *must* come, let them *extend* to few.

6. Its *purity*, or the chance it has of *not* being followed by sensations of the *opposite* kind : that is, pains, if it be a pleasure : pleasures, if it be a pain.

These two last, however, are in strictness scarcely to be deemed properties of the pleasure or the pain itself; they are not, therefore, in strictness to be taken into the account of the value of that pleasure or that pain. They are in strictness to be deemed properties only of the act, or other event, by which such pleasure or pain has been produced; and accordingly are only to be taken into the account of the tendency of such act or such event.

4. To a *number* of persons, with reference to each of whom the value of a pleasure or a pain is considered, it will be greater or less, according to seven circumstances : to wit, the six preceding ones; *viz.*

1. Its *intensity*.
2. Its *duration*.
3. Its *certainty* or *uncertainty*.
4. Its *propinquity* or *remoteness*.
5. Its *fecundity*.
6. Its *purity*.

And one other; to wit :

7. Its *extent*; that is, the number of persons to whom it *extends*; or (in other words) who are affected by it.

5. To take an exact account then of the general tendency of any act, by which the interests of a community are affected, proceed as follows. Begin with any one person of those whose interests seem most immediately to be affected by it : and take an account,

1. Of the value of each distinguishable *pleasure* which appears to be produced by it in the *first* instance.

2. Of the value of each *pain* which appears to be produced by it in the *first* instance.

3. Of the value of each pleasure which appears to be produced by it *after* the first. This constitutes the *fecundity* of the first *pleasure* and the *impurity* of the first *pain*.

4. Of the value of each *pain* which appears to be produced by it after the first. This constitutes the *fecundity* of the first *pain*, and the *impurity* of the first pleasure.

5. Sum up all the values of all the *pleasures* on the one side, and those of all the pains on the other. The balance, if it be on the side of pleasure, will give the *good* tendency of the act upon the whole, with respect to the interests of that *individual* person; if on the side of pain, the *bad* tendency of it upon the whole.

6. Take an account of the *number* of persons whose interests appear to be concerned; and repeat the above process with respect to each. *Sum up* the numbers expressive of the degrees of *good* tendency, which the act has, with respect to each individual, in regard to whom the tendency of it is *good* upon the whole : do this again with respect to each individual, in regard to whom the tendency of it is *bad* upon the whole. Take the *balance;* which, if on the side of *pleasure,* will give the general *good tendency* of the act, with respect to the total number or community of individuals concerned; if on the side of pain, the general *evil tendency,* with respect to the same community.

6. It is not to be expected that this process should be strictly pursued previously to every moral judgment, or to every legislative or judicial operation. It may, however, be always kept in view : and as near as the process actually pursued on these occasions approaches to it, so near will such process approach to the character of an exact one.

7. The same process is alike applicable to pleasure and pain, in whatever shape they appear : and by whatever denomination they are distinguished : to pleasure, whether it be called *good* (which is properly the cause or instrument of pleasure) or *profit* (which is distant pleasure, or the cause or instrument of distant pleasure,) or *convenience,* or *advantage, benefit, emolument, happiness,* and so forth : to pain, whether it be called *evil,* (which corresponds to *good*) or *mischief,* or *inconvenience,* or *disadvantage,* or *loss,* or *unhappiness,* and so forth.

8. Nor is this a novel and unwarranted, any more than it is a useless theory. In all this there is nothing but what the practice of mankind, wheresoever they have a clear view of their own interest, is perfectly conformable to. An article of property, an estate in land, for instance, is valuable, on

what account? On account of the pleasures of all kinds which it enables a man to produce, and what comes to the same thing the pains of all kinds which it enables him to avert. But the value of such an article of property is universally understood to rise or fall according to the length or shortness of the time which a man has in it : the certainty or uncertainty of its coming into possession : and the nearness or remoteness of the time at which, if at all, it is to come into possession. As to the *intensity* of the pleasures which a man may derive from it, this is never thought of, because it depends upon the use which each particular person may come to make of it; which cannot be estimated till the particular pleasures he may come to derive from it, or the particular pains he may come to exclude by means of it, are brought to view. For the same reason, neither does he think of the *fecundity* or *purity* of those pleasures.

Thus much for pleasure and pain, happiness and unhappiness, in *general*. We come now to consider the several particular kinds of pain and pleasure.

CHAPTER V

PLEASURES AND PAINS, THEIR KINDS

1. Having represented what belongs to all sorts of pleasures and pains alike, we come now to exhibit, each by itself, the several sorts of pains and pleasures. Pains and pleasures may be called by one general word, interesting perceptions. Interesting perceptions are either simple or complex. The simple ones are those which cannot any one of them be resolved into more: complex are those which are resolvable into divers simple ones. A complex interesting perception may accordingly be composed either, 1. Of pleasures alone: 2. Of pains alone: or, 3. Of a pleasure or pleasures, and a pain or pains together. What determines a lot of pleasure, for example, to be regarded as one complex pleasure, rather than as divers simple ones, is the nature of the exciting cause. Whatever pleasures are excited all at once by the action of the same cause, are apt to be looked upon as constituting all together but one pleasure.

2. The several simple pleasures of which human nature is susceptible, seem to be as follows: 1. The pleasures of sense. 2. The pleasures of wealth. 3. The pleasures of skill. 4. The pleasures of amity. 5. The pleasures of a good name. 6. The pleasures of power. 7. The pleasures of piety. 8. The pleasures of benevolence. 9. The pleasures of malevolence. 10. The pleasures of memory. 11. The pleasures of imagination. 12. The pleasures of expectation. 13. The pleasures dependent on association. 14. The pleasures of relief.

3. The several simple pains seem to be as follows: 1. The pains of privation. 2. The pains of the senses. 3. The pains of awkwardness. 4. The pains of enmity. 5. The pains of an ill name. 6. The pains of piety. 7. The pains of benevolence.

8. The pains of malevolence. 9. The pains of the memory.
10. The pains of the imagination. 11. The pains of expectation. 12. The pains dependent on association.[1]

4. 1. The pleasures of sense seem to be as follows: 1.
The pleasures of the taste or palate; including whatever
pleasures are experienced in satisfying the appetites of hunger
and thirst. 2 The pleasure of intoxication. 3. The pleasures
of the organ of smelling. 4. The pleasures of the touch. 5.
The simple pleasures of the ear; independent of association.
6. The simple pleasures of the eye; independent of association. 7. The pleasure of the sexual sense. 8. The pleasure
of health: or, the internal pleasurable feeling or flow of
spirits (as it is called) which accompanies a state of full
health and vigour; especially at times of moderate bodily
exertion. 9. The pleasures of novelty: or, the pleasures
derived from the gratification of the appetite of curiosity,
by the application of new objects to any of the senses.[2]

5. 2. By the pleasures of wealth may be meant those
pleasures which a man is apt to derive from the consciousness
of possessing any article or articles which stand in the list of
instruments of enjoyment or security, and more particularly
at the time of his first acquiring them; at which time the
pleasure may be styled a pleasure of gain or a pleasure of
acquisition: at other times a pleasure of possession.

3. The pleasures of skill, as exercised upon particular

[1] The catalogue here given, is what seemed to be a complete list
of the several simple pleasures and pains of which human nature
is susceptible: insomuch, that if, upon any occasion whatsoever,
a man feels pleasure or pain, it is either referable at once to some
one or other of these kinds, or resolvable into such as are. It might
perhaps have been a satisfaction to the reader, to have seen an
analytical view of the subject, taken upon an exhaustive plan, for
the purpose of demonstrating the catalogue to be what it purports
to be, a complete one. The catalogue is in fact the result of such
an analysis; which, however, I thought it better to discard at
present, as being of too metaphysical a cast, and not strictly within
the limits of this design. See Chap. XIII [Cases unmeet], par. 2.
Note.

[2] There are also pleasures of novelty, excited by the appearance
of new ideas: these are pleasures of the imagination. See infra
13.

objects, are those which accompany the application of such particular instruments of enjoyment to their uses, as cannot be so applied without a greater or less share of difficulty or exertion.[3]

6. 4. The pleasures of amity, or self-recommendation, are the pleasures that may accompany the persuasion of a man's being in the acquisition or the possession of the good-will of such or such assignable person or persons in particular : or, as the phrase is, of being upon good terms with him or them : and as a fruit of it, of his being in a way to have the benefit of their spontaneous and gratuitous services.

7. 5. The pleasures of a good name are the pleasures that accompany the persuasion of a man's being in the acquisition or the possession of the good-will of the world about him; that is, of such members of society as he is likely to have concerns with; and as a means of it, either their love or their esteem, or both : and as a fruit of it, of his being in the way to have the benefit of their spontaneous and gratuitous services. These may likewise be called the pleasures of good repute, the pleasures of honour, or the pleasures of the moral sanction.[4]

8. 6. The pleasures of power are the pleasures that accompany the persuasion of a man's being in a condition to dispose people, by means of their hopes and fears, to give him the benefit of their services : that is, by the hope of some service, or by the fear of some disservice, that he may be in the way to render them.

9. 7. The pleasures of piety are the pleasures that accompany the belief of a man's being in the acquisition or in possession of the good-will or favour of the Supreme Being : and as a fruit of it, of his being in a way of enjoying pleasures to be received by God's special appointment, either in this life,

---

[3] For instance, the pleasure of being able to gratify the sense of hearing, by singing, or performing upon any musical instrument. The pleasure thus obtained, is a thing superadded to, and perfectly distinguishable from, that which a man enjoys from hearing another person perform in the same manner.

[4] See Chap. III [Sanctions].

or in a life to come. These may also be called the pleasures of religion, the pleasures of a religious disposition, or the pleasures of the religious sanction.[5]

10. 8. The pleasures of benevolence are the pleasures resulting from the view of any pleasures supposed to be possessed by the beings who may be the objects of benevolence; to wit, the sensitive beings we are acquainted with; under which are commonly included, 1. The Supreme Being. 2. Human beings. 3. Other animals. These may also be called the pleasures of good-will, the pleasures of sympathy, or the pleasures of the benevolent or social affections.

11. 9. The pleasures of malevolence are the pleasures resulting from the view of any pain supposed to be suffered by the beings who may become the objects of malevolence : to wit, 1. Human beings. 2. Other animals. These may also be styled the pleasures of ill-will, the pleasures of the irascible appetite, the pleasures of antipathy, or the pleasures of the malevolent or dissocial affections.

12. 10. The pleasures of the memory are the pleasures which after having enjoyed such and such pleasures, or even in some case after having suffered such and such pains, a man will now and then experience, at recollecting them exactly in the order and in the circumstances in which they were actually enjoyed or suffered. These derivative pleasures may of course be distinguished into as many species as there are of original perceptions, from whence they may be copied. They may also be styled pleasures of simple recollection.

13. 11. The pleasures of the imagination are the pleasures which may be derived from the contemplation of any such pleasures as may happen to be suggested by the memory, but in a different order, and accompanied by different groups of circumstances. These may accordingly be referred to any one of the three cardinal points of time, present, past, or future. It is evident they may admit of as many distinctions as those of the former class.

14. 12. The pleasures of expectation are the pleasures that result from the contemplation of any sort of pleasure, referred

[5] See Chap. III [Sanctions].

to time *future*, and accompanied with the sentiment of *belief*. These also may admit of the same distinctions.[6]

15. 13. The pleasures of association are the pleasures which certain objects or incidents may happen to afford, not of themselves, but merely in virtue of some association they have contracted in the mind with certain objects or incidents which are in themselves pleasurable. Such is the case, for instance, with the pleasure of skill, when afforded by such a set of incidents as compose a game of chess. This derives its pleasurable quality from its association partly with the pleasure of skill, as exercised in the production of incidents pleasurable of themselves : partly from its association with the pleasures of power. Such is the case also with the pleasure of good luck, when afforded by such incidents as compose the game of hazard, or any other game of chance, when played at for nothing. This derives its pleasurable quality from its association with one of the pleasures of wealth; to wit, with the pleasure of acquiring it.

16. 14. Farther on we shall see pains grounded upon pleasures; in like manner may we now see pleasures grounded upon pains. To the catalogue of pleasures may accordingly be added the pleasures of *relief* : or, the pleasures which a man experiences when, after he has been enduring pain of any kind for a certain time, it comes to cease, or to abate. These may of course be distinguished into as many species as there are of pains : and may give rise to so many pleasures of memory, of imagination, and of expectation.

17. 1. Pains of privation are the pains that may result from the thought of not possessing in the time present any of the several kinds of pleasures. Pains of privation may accordingly be resolved into as many kinds as there are of pleasures to which they may correspond, and from the absence whereof they may be derived.

18. There are three sorts of pains which are only so many modifications of the several pains of privation. When the enjoyment of any particular pleasure happens to be particularly desired, but without any expectation approaching to

[6] In contradistinction to these, all other pleasures may be termed pleasures of *enjoyment*.

assurance, the pain of privation which thereupon results takes a particular name, and is called the pain of *desire,* or of unsatisfied desire.

19. Where the enjoyment happens to have been looked for with a degree of expectation approaching to assurance, and that expectation is made suddenly to cease, it is called a pain of disappointment.

20. A pain of privation takes the name of a pain of regret in two cases : 1. Where it is grounded on the memory of a pleasure, which having been once enjoyed, appears not likely to be enjoyed again : 2. Where it is grounded on the idea of a pleasure, which was never actually enjoyed, nor perhaps so much as expected, but which might have been enjoyed (it is supposed), had such or such a contingency happened, which, in fact, did not happen.

21. 2. The several pains of the senses seem to be as follows : 1. The pains of hunger and thirst : or the disagreeable sensations produced by the want of suitable substances which need at times to be applied to the alimentary canal. 2. The pains of the taste : or the disagreeable sensations produced by the application of various substances to the palate, and other superior parts of the same canal. 3. The pains of the organ of smell : or the disagreeable sensations produced by the effluvia of various substances when applied to that organ. 4. The pains of the touch : or the disagreeable sensations produced by the application of various substances to the skin. 5. The simple pains of the hearing, or the disagreeable sensations excited in the organ of that sense by various kinds of sounds : independently (as before), of association. 6. The simple pains of the sight : or the disagreeable sensations if any such there be, that may be excited in the organ of that sense by visible images, independent of the principle of association. 7[7]. The pains resulting from excessive heat or cold, unless these be referable to the touch. 8. The pains of disease : or the acute and uneasy sensations result-

[7] The pleasure of the sexual sense seems to have no positive pain to correspond to it : it has only a pain of privation, or pain of the mental class, the pain of unsatisfied desire. If any positive pain of body result from the want of such indulgence, it belongs to the head of pains of disease.

ing from the several diseases and indispositions to which human nature is liable. 9. The pain of exertion, whether bodily or mental : or the uneasy sensation which is apt to accompany any intense effort, whether of mind or body.

22. 3[8]. The pains of awkwardness are the pains which sometimes result from the unsuccessful endeavour to apply any particular instruments of enjoyment or security to their uses, or from the difficulty a man experiences in applying them.[9]

23. 4. The pains of enmity are the pains that may accompany the persuasion of a man's being obnoxious to the ill-will of such or such an assignable person or persons in particular : or, as the phrase is, of being upon ill terms with him or them : and, in consequence, of being obnoxious to certain pains of some sort or other, of which he may be the cause.

24. 5. The pains of an ill-name, are the pains that accompany the persuasion of a man's being obnoxious, or in a way to be obnoxious to the ill-will of the world about him. These may likewise be called the pains of ill-repute, the pains of dishonour, or the pains of the moral sanction.[10]

[8] The pleasures of novelty have no positive pains corresponding to them. The pain which a man experiences when he is in the condition of not knowing what to do with himself, that pain, which in French is expressed by a single word *ennui*, is a pain of privation : a pain resulting from the absence, not only of all the pleasures of novelty, but of all kinds of pleasure whatsoever.

The pleasures of wealth have also no positive pains corresponding to them : the only pains opposed to them are pains of privation. If any positive pains result from the want of wealth, they are referable to some other class of positive pains; principally to those of the senses. From the want of food, for instance, result the pains of hunger; from the want of clothing, the pains of cold; and so forth.

[9] It may be a question, perhaps, whether this be a positive pain of itself, or whether it be nothing more than a pain of privation, resulting from the consciousness of a want of skill. It is, however, but a question of words, nor does it matter which way it be determined.

[10] In as far as a man's fellow-creatures are supposed to be determined by any event not to regard him with any degree of esteem or *good* will, or to regard him with a less degree of esteem or *good*

25. 6.[11] The pains of piety are the pains that accompany the belief of a man's being obnoxious to the displeasure of the Supreme Being: and in consequence to certain pains to be inflicted by his especial appointment, either in this life or in a life to come. These may also be called the pains of religion; the pains of a religious disposition; or the pains of the religious sanction. When the belief is looked upon as well-grounded, these pains are commonly called religious terrors; when looked upon as ill-grounded, superstitious terrors.[12]

26. 7. The pains of benevolence are the pains resulting from the view of any pains supposed to be endured by other beings. These may also be called the pains of good-will, of sympathy, or the pains of the benevolent or social affections.

27. 8. The pains of malevolence are the pains resulting from the view of any pleasures supposed to be enjoyed by any beings who happen to be the objects of a man's displeasure. These may also be styled the pains of ill-will, of antipathy, or the pains of the malevolent or dissocial affections.

28. 9. The pains of the memory may be grounded on every

---

will than they would otherwise; not to do him any sorts of *good* offices, or not to do him so many *good* offices as they would otherwise; the pain resulting from such consideration may be reckoned a pain of privation: as far as they are supposed to regard him with such a degree of aversion or disesteem as to be disposed to do him positive *ill* offices, it may be reckoned a positive pain. The pain of privation, and the positive pain, in this case run one into another indistinguishably.

[11] There seem to be no positive pains to correspond to the pleasures of power. The pains that a man may feel from the want or the loss of power, in as far as power is distinguished from all other sources of pleasure, seem to be nothing more than pains of privation.

[12] The positive pains of piety, and the pains of privation, opposed to the pleasures of piety, run one into another in the same manner as the positive pains of enmity, or of an ill name, do with respect to the pains of privation, opposed to the pleasures of amity, and those of a good name. If what is apprehended at the hands of God is barely the not receiving pleasure, the pain is of the privative class: if, moreover, actual pain be apprehended, it is of the class of positive pains.

one of the above kinds, as well of pains of privation as of positive pains. These correspond exactly to the pleasures of the memory.

29. 10. The pains of the imagination may also be grounded on any one of the above kinds, as well of pains of privation as of positive pains; in other respects they correspond exactly to the pleasures of the imagination.

30. 11. The pains of expectation may be grounded on each one of the above kinds, as well of pains of privation as of positive pains. These may be also termed pains of apprehension.[13]

31. 12. The pains of association correspond exactly to the pleasures of association.

32. Of the above list there are certain pleasures and pains which suppose the existence of some pleasure or pain of some other person, to which the pleasure or pain of the person in question has regard : such pleasures and pains may be termed *extra-regarding*. Others do not suppose any such thing : these may be termed *self-regarding*.[14] The only pleasures and pains of the extra-regarding class are those of benevolence and those of malevolence : all the rest are self-regarding.[15]

33. Of all these several sorts of pleasures and pains, there is scarce any one which is not liable, on more accounts than one, to come under the consideration of the law. Is an offence committed? It is the tendency which it has to destroy, in such or such persons, some of these pleasures, or to produce some of these pains, that constitutes the mischief of it, and the ground for punishing it. It is the prospect of some of these pleasures, or of security from some of these pains, that constitutes the motive or temptation, it is the attainment of them that constitutes the profit of the offence. Is the offender to be

[13] In contradistinction to these, all other pains may be termed pains of *sufferance*.

[14] See Chap. x [Motives].

[15] By this means the pleasures and pains of amity may be the more clearly distinguished from those of benevolence : and on the other hand, those of enmity from those of malevolence. The pleasures and pains of amity and enmity are of the self-regarding cast : those of benevolence and malevolence of the extra-regarding.

punished? It can be only by the production of one or more of these pains, that the punishment can be inflicted.[16]

[16] It would be a matter not only of curiosity, but of some use, to exhibit a catalogue of the several complex pleasures and pains, analysing them at the same time into the several simple ones, of which they are respectively composed. But such a disquisition would take up too much room to be admitted here. A short specimen, however, for the purpose of illustration, can hardly be dispensed with.

The pleasures taken in at the eye and ear are generally very complex. The pleasures of a country scene, for instance, consist commonly, amongst others, of the following pleasures:

I. PLEASURES OF THE SENSES

1. The simple pleasures of sight, excited by the perception of agreeable colours and figures, green fields, waving foliage, glistening water, and the like.
2. The simple pleasure of the ears, excited by the perceptions of the chirping of birds, the murmuring of waters, the rustling of the wind among the trees.
3. The pleasures of the smell, excited by the perceptions of the fragrance of flowers, of new-mown hay, or other vegetable substances, in the first stages of fermentation.
4. The agreeable inward sensation, produced by a brisk circulation of the blood, and the ventilation of it in the lungs by a pure air, such as that in the country frequently is in comparison of that which is breathed in towns.

II. PLEASURES OF THE IMAGINATION PRODUCED BY ASSOCIATION

1. The idea of the plenty, resulting from the possession of the objects that are in view, and of the happiness arising from it.
2. The idea of the innocence and happiness of the birds, sheep, cattle, dogs, and other gentle or domestic animals.
3. The idea of the constant flow of health, supposed to be enjoyed by all these creatures: a notion which is apt to result from the occasional flow of health enjoyed by the supposed spectator.
4. The idea of gratitude, excited by the contemplation of the all-powerful and beneficent Being, who is looked up to as the author of these blessings.

These four last are all of them, in some measure at least, pleasures of sympathy.

The depriving a man of this group of pleasures is one of the evils apt to result from imprisonment: whether produced by illegal violence, or in the way of punishment, by appointment of the laws.

BENTHAM[1]

by John Stuart Mill

There are two men, recently deceased, to whom their country is indebted not only for the greater part of the important ideas which have been thrown into circulation among its thinking men in their time, but for a revolution in its general modes of thought and investigation. These men, dissimilar in almost all else, agreed in being closet-students —secluded in a peculiar degree, by circumstances and character, from the business and intercourse of the world: and both were, through a large portion of their lives, regarded by those who took the lead in opinion (when they happened to hear of them) with feelings akin to contempt. But they were destined to renew a lesson given to mankind by every age, and always disregarded—to show that speculative philosophy, which to the superficial appears a thing so remote from the business of life and the outward interests of men, is in reality the thing on earth which most influences them, and in the long run overbears every other influence save those which it must itself obey. The writers of whom we speak have never been read by the multitude; except for the more slight of their works, their readers have been few: but they have been the teachers of the teachers; there is hardly to be found in England an individual of any importance in the world of mind, who (whatever opinions he may have afterwards adopted) did not first learn to think from one of these two; and though their influences have but begun to diffuse themselves through these intermediate channels over society at large, there is already scarcely a publication of any consequence addressed to the educated classes, which, if these persons had not existed, would not have been different from what it is. These men are, Jeremy Bentham and Samuel Taylor Cole-

[1] *London and Westminster Review,* August 1838.

ridge—the two great seminal minds of England in their age.

No comparison is intended here between the minds or influences of these remarkable men : this were impossible unless there were first formed a complete judgment of each, considered apart. It is our intention to attempt, on the present occasion, an estimate of one of them; the only one, a complete edition of whose works is yet in progress, and who, in the classification which may be made of all writers into Progressive and Conservative, belongs to the same division with ourselves. For although they were far too great men to be correctly designated by either appellation exclusively, yet in the main, Bentham was a Progressive philosopher, Coleridge a Conservative one. The influence of the former has made itself felt chiefly on minds of the Progressive class; of the latter on those of the Conservative : and the two systems of concentric circles which the shock given by them is spreading over the ocean of mind, have only just begun to meet and intersect. The writings of both contain severe lessons to their own side, on many of the errors and faults they are addicted to : but to Bentham it was given to discern more particularly those truths with which existing doctrines and institutions were at variance; to Coleridge, the neglected truths which lay *in* them.

A man of great knowledge of the world, and of the highest reputation for practical talent and sagacity among the official men of his time (himself no follower of Bentham, nor of any partial or exclusive school whatever) once said to us, as the result of his observation, that to Bentham more than to any other source might be traced the questioning spirit, the disposition to demand the *why* of everything, which had gained so much ground and was producing such important consequences in these times. The more this assertion is examined, the more true it will be found. Bentham has been in this age and country the great questioner of things established. It is by the influence of the modes of thought with which his writings inoculated a considerable number of thinking men, that the yoke of authority has been broken, and innumerable opinions, formerly received on tradition as incontestable, are put upon their defence, and required to give an account of themselves. Who, before Bentham, (whatever controversies might exist on points of detail) dared to speak disrespectfully, in express terms, of the British Constitution, or the English Law? He did so; and his arguments and his example together encouraged others. We do not mean that his writings caused the Reform Bill, or that the Appropriation Clause owns him as its parent : the changes which have been made, and the greater changes which will be made, in our institutions, are not the work of philosophers, but of the interests and instincts of large portions of society recently grown into strength. But Bentham gave voice to those interests and instincts : until he spoke out, those who found our institutions unsuited to them did not dare to say so, did not dare consciously to think so; they had never heard the excellence of those institutions questioned by cultivated men, by men of acknowledged intellect; and it is not in the nature of uninstructed minds to resist the united authority of the instructed. Bentham broke the spell. It was not Bentham by his own writings; it was Bentham through the minds and pens which those writings fed—through the men in more direct contact with the world, into whom his spirit passed. If the superstition about ancestorial wisdom has fallen into decay; if the public are grown familiar with the idea that their laws and institutions are in great part not the product of intellect and virtue, but of modern corruption grafted upon ancient barbarism; if the hardiest innovation is no longer scouted because it is an innovation—establishments no longer considered sacred because they are establishments—it will be found that those who have accustomed the public mind to these ideas have learnt them from Bentham's school, and that the assault on ancient institutions has been, and is, carried on for the most part with his weapons. It matters not although these thinkers, or indeed thinkers of any descriptions, have been but scantily found among the persons prominently and ostensibly at the head of the Reform movement. All movements, except directly revolutionary ones, are headed, not by those who originate them, but by those who know best how to compromise between the old opinions and the new. The father of English innovation, both in doctrines and in institutions, is Bentham : he is the great *subversive,* or, in the language of continental philosophers, the great *critical* thinker of his age and country.

We consider this, however, to be not his highest title to fame. Were this all, he were only to be ranked among the lowest order of the potentates of mind—the negative, or destructive philosophers; those who can perceive what is false, but not what is true; who awaken the human mind to the inconsistencies and absurdities of time-sanctioned opinions and institutions, but substitute nothing in the place of what they take away. We have no desire to undervalue the services of such persons : mankind has been deeply indebted to them; nor will there ever be a lack of work for them, in a world in which so many false things are believed, in which so many which have been true, are believed long after they have ceased to be true. The qualities, however, which fit men for perceiving anomalies, without perceiving the truths which would rectify them, are not among the rarest of endowments. Courage, verbal acuteness, command over the forms of argumentation, and a popular style, will make, out of the shallowest man, with a sufficient lack of reverence, a considerable negative philosopher. Such men have never been wanting in periods of culture; and the period in which Bentham formed his early impressions was emphatically their reign, in proportion to its barrenness in the more noble products of the human mind. An age of formalism in the Church and corruption in the State, when the most valuable part of the meaning of traditional doctrines had faded from the minds even of those who retained from habit a mechanical belief in them, was the time to raise up all kinds of sceptical philosophy. Accordingly, France had Voltaire, and his school of negative thinkers, and England (or rather Scotland) had the profoundest negative thinker on record, David Hume : a man, the peculiarities of whose mind qualified him to detect failure of proof, and want of logical consistency, at a depth which French sceptics, with their comparatively feeble powers of analysis and abstraction, *stopped* far short of, and which German subtlety alone could thoroughly appreciate or hope to rival.

If Bentham had merely continued the work of Hume, he

would scarcely have been heard of in philosophy; for he was
far inferior to Humè in Hume's qualities, and was in no
respect fitted to excel as a metaphysician. We must not look
for subtlety, or the power of recondite analysis, among his
intellectual characteristics. In the former quality, few great
thinkers have ever been so deficient; and to find the latter,
in any considerable measure, in a mind acknowledging any
kindred with his, we must have recourse to the late Mr.
Mill—a man who united the great qualities of the metaphysicians of the eighteenth century, with others of a different
complexion, admirably qualifying him to complete and correct
their work. Bentham had not these peculiar gifts; but he
possessed others, not inferior, which were not possessed by
any of his precursors; which have made him a source of light
to a generation which has far outgrown their influence, and,
as we called him, the chief subversive thinker of an age which
has long lost all that they could subvert.

To speak of him first as a merely negative philosopher—
as one who refutes illogical arguments, exposes sophistry,
detects contradiction and absurdity; even in that capacity
there was a wide field left vacant for him by Hume, and which
he has occupied to an unprecedented extent; the field of
practical abuses. This was Bentham's peculiar province : to
this he was called by the whole bent of his disposition : to
carry the warfare against absurdity into things practical. His
was an essentially practical mind. It was by practical abuses
that his mind was first turned to speculation—by the abuses
of the profession which was chosen for him, that of the
law. He has himself stated what particular abuse first gave
that shock to his mind, the recoil of which has made the
whole mountain of abuse totter; it was the custom of making
the client pay for three attendances in the office of a Master
in Chancery, when only one was given. The law, he found,
on examination, was full of such things. But were these
discoveries of his? No; they were known to every lawyer
who practised, to every judge who sat on the bench, and neither
before nor for long after did they cause any apparent uneasiness to the consciences of these learned persons, nor
hinder them from asserting, whenever occasion offered, in

books, in parliament, or on the bench, that the law was the
perfection of reason. During so many generations, in each
of which thousands of educated young men were successively
placed in Bentham's position and with Bentham's opportunities, he alone was found with sufficient moral sensibility
and self-reliance to say to himself that these things, however
profitable they might be, were frauds and that between them
and himself there should be a gulf fixed. To this rare union
of self-reliance and moral sensibility we are indebted for
all that Bentham has done. Sent to Oxford by his father at
the unusually early age of fifteen—required, on admission,
to declare his belief in the Thirty-nine Articles—he felt it
necessary to examine them; and the examination suggested
scruples, which he sought to get removed, but instead of the
satisfaction he expected, was told that it was not for boys
like him to step up their judgment against the great men
of the Church. After a struggle, he signed; but the impression that he had done an immoral act, never left him;
he considered himself to have committed a falsehood, and
throughout life he never relaxed in his indignant denun-
ciations of all laws which command such falsehoods, all
institutions which attach rewards to them.

By thus carrying the war of criticism and refutation, the
conflict with falsehood and absurdity, into the field of practical
evils, Bentham, even if he had done nothing else, would
have earned an important place in the history of intellect.
He carried on the warfare without intermission. To this, not
only many of his most piquant chapters, but some of the most
finished of his entire works, are entirely devoted : the ' Defence of Usury;' the ' Book of Fallacies;' and the onslaught
upon Blackstone, published anonymously under the title of
' A Fragment on Government,' which, though a first production, and of a writer afterwards so much ridiculed for
his style, excited the highest admiration no less for its composition than for its thoughts, and was attributed by turns
to Lord Mansfield, to Lord Camden, and (by Dr. Johnson)
to Dunning, one of the greatest masters of style among the
lawyers of his day. These writings are altogether original;
though of the negative school, they resemble nothing previously

produced by negative philosophers; and would have sufficed
to create for Bentham, among the subversive thinkers of
modern Europe, a place peculiarly his own. But it is not these
writings that constitute the real distinction between him and
them. There was a deeper difference. It was that they were
purely negative thinkers, he was positive; they only assailed
error, he made it a point of conscience not to do so until
he thought he could plant instead the corresponding truth.
Their character was exclusively analytic, his was synthetic.
They took for their starting-point the received opinion on any
subject, dug round it with their logical implements, pronounced its foundations defective, and condemned it : he
began *de novo,* laid his own foundations deeply and firmly,
built up his own structure, and bade mankind compare the
two; it was when he had solved the problem himself, or
thought he had done so, that he declared all other solutions to
be erroneous. Hence, what they produced will not last;
it must perish, much of it has already perished, with the
errors which it exploded : what he did has its own value, by
which it must outlast all errors to which it is opposed.
Though we may reject, as we often must, his practical conclusions, yet his premises, the collections of facts and observations from which his conclusions were drawn, remain
for ever, a part of the materials of philosophy.

A place, therefore, must be assigned to Bentham among
the masters of wisdom, the great teachers and permanent
intellectual ornaments of the human race. He is among those
who have enriched mankind with imperishable gifts; and
although these do not transcend all other gifts, nor entitle
him to those honours ' above all Greek, above all Roman
fame,' which by a natural reaction against the neglect and
contempt of the ignorant, many of his admirers were once disposed to accumulate upon him, yet to refuse an admiring
recognition of what he was, on account of what he was not,
is a much worse error, and one which, pardonable in the
vulgar, is no longer permitted to any cultivated and instructed
mind.

If we were asked to say, in the fewest possible words,
what we conceive to be Bentham's place among these great

intellectual benefactors of humanity; what he was, and what
he was not; what kind of service he did and did not render
to truth; we should say—he was not a great philosopher, but
he was a great reformer in philosophy. He brought into
philosophy something which it greatly needed, and for want
of which it was at a stand. It was not his doctrines which
did this, it was his mode of arriving at them. He introduced
into morals and politics those habits of thought and modes
of investigation, which are essential to the idea of science;
and the absence of which made those departments of inquiry,
as physics had been before Bacon, a field of interminable
discussion, leading to no result. It was not his opinions,
in short, but his method that constituted the novelty and
the value of what he did; a value beyond all price, even
though we should reject the whole, as we unquestionably must
a large part, of the opinions themselves.

Bentham's method may be shortly described as the method
of detail; of treating wholes by separating them into their
parts, abstractions by resolving them into Things,—classes
and generalities by distinguishing them into the individuals
of which they are made up; and breaking every question into
pieces before attempting to solve it. The precise amount of
originality of this process, considered as a logical conception
—its degree of connexion with the methods of physical
science, or with the previous labours of Bacon, Hobbes or
Locke—is not an essential consideration in this place. Whatever originality there was in the method—in the subjects he
applied it to, and in the rigidity with which he adhered to
it, there was the greatest. Hence his interminable classifications. Hence his elaborate demonstrations of the most acknowledged truths. That murder, incendiarism, robbery, are mischievous actions, he will not take for granted without proof;
let the thing appear ever so self-evident, he will know the
why and the how of it with the last degree of precision;
he will distinguish all the different mischiefs of a crime,
whether of the *first,* the *second,* or the *third* order, namely,
1. the evil to the sufferer, and to his personal connexions;
2. the *danger* from example, and the *alarm* or painful feeling
of insecurity; and 3. the discouragement to industry and

useful pursuits arising from the *alarm,* and the trouble and
resources which must be expended in warding off the *danger.*
After this enumeration, he will prove from the laws of human
feeling, that even the first of these evils, the sufferings
of the immediate victim, will on the average greatly outweigh
the pleasure reaped by the offender; much more when all the
other evils are taken into account. Unless this could be
proved, he would account the infliction of punishment un-
warrantable; and for taking the trouble to prove it formally,
his defence is, ' there are truths which it is necessary to
prove, not for their own sakes, because they are acknowledged,
but that an opening may be made for the reception of other
truths which depend upon them. It is in this manner we
provide for the reception of first principles, which, once received, prepare the way for admission of all other truths.'[2]
To which may be added, that in this manner also we discipline the mind for practising the same sort of dissection
upon questions more complicated and of more doubtful
issue.

It is a sound maxim, and one which all close thinkers
have felt, but which no one before Bentham ever so consistently
applied, that error lurks in generalities : that the human
mind is not capable of embracing a complex whole, until it
has surveyed and catalogued the parts of which that whole is
made up; that abstractions are not realities *per se,* but an
abridged mode of expressing facts, and that the only practical mode of dealing with them is to trace them back to the
facts (whether of experience or of consciousness) of which
they are the expression. Proceeding on this principle, Bentham
makes short work with the ordinary modes of moral and
political reasoning. These, it appeared to him, when hunted
to their source, for the most part terminated in *phrases.* In
politics, liberty, social order, constitution, law of nature, social
compact, etc, were the catch-words : ethics had its analogous
ones. Such were the arguments on which the gravest questions of morality and policy were made to turn; not reasons,
but allusions to reasons; sacramental expressions, by which
a summary appeal was made to some general sentiment of

[2] Part I. pp. 161-2, of the collected edition.

mankind, or to some maxim in familiar use, which might be true or not, but the limitations of which no one had ever critically examined. And this satisfied other people; but not Bentham. He required something more than opinion as a reason for opinion. Whenever he found a *phrase* used as an argument for or against anything, he insisted upon knowing what it meant; whether it appealed to any standard, or gave intimation of any matter of fact relevant to the question; and if he could not find that it did either, he treated it as an attempt on the part of the disputant to impose his own individual sentiment on other people, without giving them a reason for it; a 'contrivance for avoiding the obligation of appealing to any external standard, and for prevailing upon the reader to accept of the author's sentiment and opinion as a reason, and that a sufficient one, for itself.' Bentham shall speak for himself on this subject: the passage is from his first systematic work, 'Introduction to the Principles of Morals and Legislation,' and we could scarcely quote anything more strongly exemplifying both the strength and weakness of his mode of philosophising.

'It is curious enough to observe the variety of inventions men have hit upon, and the variety of phrases they have brought forward, in order to conceal from the world, and, if possible, from themselves, this very general and therefore very pardonable self-sufficiency.

1. One man says, he has a thing made on purpose to tell him what is right and what is wrong; and that it is called a 'moral sense:' and then he goes to work at his ease, and says, such a thing is right, and such a thing is wrong —why? 'Because my moral sense tells me it is.'

2. Another man comes and alters the phrase : leaving out *moral,* and putting in *common* in the room of it. He then tells you that his common sense tells him what is right and wrong, as surely as the other's moral sense did : meaning by common sense a sense of some kind or other, which, he says, is possessed by all mankind : the sense of those whose sense is not the same as the author's being struck out as not worth taking. This contrivance does better than the other; for a moral sense being a

new thing, a man may feel about him a good while
without being able to find it out : but common sense is
as old as the creation; and there is no man but would be
ashamed to be thought not to have as much of it as his
neighbours. It has another great advantage : by appearing to share power, it lessens envy; for when a man
gets up upon this ground, in order to anathematise those
who differ from him, it is not by a *sic volo sic jubeo,* but
by a *velitis jubeatis.*

3. Another man comes, and says, that as to a moral
sense indeed, he cannot find that he has any such thing :
that, however, he has an *understanding,* which will do
quite as well. This understanding, he says, is the
standard of right and wrong : it tells him so and so.
All good and wise men understand as he does : if
other men's understandings differ in any part from his
so much the worse for them : it is a sure sign they are
either defective or corrupt.

4. Another man says, that there is an eternal and
immutable Rule of Right : that that rule of right dictates
so and so : and then he begins giving you his sentiments
upon anything that comes uppermost : and these sentiments (you are to take for granted) are so many branches
of the eternal rule of right.

5. Another man, or perhaps the same man (it is no
matter), says that there are certain practices conformable,
and others repugnant, to the Fitness of Things; and
then he tells you, at his leisure, what practices are
conformable, and what repugnant : just as he happens
to like a practice or dislike it.

6. A great multitude of people are continually talking
of the Law of Nature; and then they go on giving
you their sentiments about what is right and what is
wrong : and these sentiments, you are to understand, are
so many chapters and sections of the Law of Nature.

7. Instead of the phrase, Law of Nature, you have
sometimes Law of Reason, Right Reason, Natural Justice,
Natural Equity, Good Order. Any of them will do equally
well. This latter is most used in politics. The three

last are much more tolerable than the others, because they do not very explicitly claim to be anything more than phrases : they insist but feebly upon the being looked upon as so many positive standards of themselves, and seem content to be taken, upon occasion, for phrases expressive of the conformity of the thing in question to the proper standard, whatever that may be. On most occasions, however, it will be better to say *utility* : *utility* is clearer, as referring more explicitly to pain and pleasure.

8. We have one philosopher, who says, there is no harm in anything in the world but in telling a lie; and that if, for example, you were to murder your own father, this would only be a particular way of saying, he was not your father. Of course when this philosopher sees anything that he does not like, he says it is a particular way of telling a lie. It is saying, that the act ought to be done, or may be done, when, *in* truth, it ought not to be done.

9. The fairest and openest of them all is that sort of man who speaks out, and says, I am of the number of the Elect : now God himself takes care to inform the Elect what is right : and that with so good effect, and let them strive ever so, they cannot help not only knowing it but practising it. If therefore a man wants to know what is right and what is wrong, he has nothing to do but to come to me.'

Few will contend that this is a perfectly fair representation of the *animus* of those who employ the various phrases so amusingly animadverted on; but that the phrases contain no argument, save what is grounded on the very feelings they are adduced to justify, is a truth which Bentham had the eminent merit of first pointing out.

It is the introduction into the philosophy of human conduct, of this method of detail—of this practice of never reasoning about wholes until they have been resolved into their parts, nor about abstractions until they have been translated into realities—that constitutes the originality of Bentham in philosophy, and makes him the great reformer of the moral and political branch of it. To what he terms the 'exhaustive method of classification,' which is but one branch of this more general method, he himself ascribes everything original in the systematic and elaborate work from which we have quoted. The generalities of his philosophy itself have little or no novelty : to ascribe any to the doctrine that general utility is the foundation of morality, would imply great ignorance of the history of philosophy, of general literature, and of Bentham's own writings. He derived the idea, as he says himself, from Helvetius; and it was the doctrine no less, of the religious philosophers of that age, prior to Reid and Beattie. We never saw an abler defence of the doctrine of utility than in a book written in refutation of Shaftesbury, and now little read—Brown's[3] 'Essays on the Characteristics;' and in Johnson's celebrated review of Soame Jenyns, the same doctrine is set forth as that both of the author and the reviewer. In all ages of philosophy one of its schools has been utilitarian—not only from the time of Epicurus, but long before. It was by mere accident that this opinion became connected in Bentham with his peculiar method. The utilitarian philosophers antecedent to him had no more claims to the method than their antagonists. To refer, for instance, to the Epicurean philosophy, according to the most complete view we have of the moral part of it, by the most accomplished scholar of antiquity, Cicero; we ask any one who has read his philosophical writings, the 'De Finibus' for instance, whether the arguments of the Epicureans do not, just as much as those of the Stoics or Platonists, consist of mere rhetorical appeals to common notions, to εἰκότα and σημεῖα instead of τεκμηρία, notions picked up as it were casually, and when true at all, never so narrowly looked into as to ascertain in what sense and under what limitations they are true. The application of a real inductive philosophy to the problems of ethics, is as unknown to the Epicurean moralists as to any of the other schools; they never take a question to pieces, and join

[3] Author of another book which made no little sensation when it first appeared,—' An Estimate of the Manners of the Times.'

issue on a definite point. Bentham certainly did not learn his sifting and anatomising method from them.

This method Bentham has finally installed in philosophy; has made it henceforth imperative on philosophers of all schools. By it he has formed the intellects of many thinkers, who either never adopted, or have abandoned, many of his peculiar opinions. He has taught the method to men of the most opposite schools to his; he has made them perceive that if they do not test their doctrines by the method of detail, their adversaries will. He has thus, it is not too much to say, for the first time introduced precision of thought into moral and political philosophy. Instead of taking up their opinions by intuition, or by ratiocination from premises adopted on a mere rough view, and couched in language so vague that it is impossible to say exactly whether they are true or false, philosophers are now forced to understand one another, to break down the generality of their propositions, and join a precise issue in every dispute. This is nothing less than a revolution in philosophy. Its effect is gradually becoming evident in the writings of English thinkers of every variety of opinion, and will be felt more and more in proportion as Bentham's writings are diffused, and as the number of minds to whose formation they contribute is multiplied.

It will naturally be presumed that of the fruits of this great philosophical improvement some portion at least will have been reaped by its author. Armed with such a potent instrument, and wielding it with such singleness of aim; cultivating the field of practical philosophy with such unwearied and such consistent use of a method right in itself, and not adopted by his predecessors; it cannot be but that Bentham by his own inquiries must have accomplished something considerable. And so, it will be found, he has; something not only considerable, but extraordinary; though but little compared with what he has left undone, and far short of what his sanguine and almost boyish fancy made him flatter himself that he had accomplished. His peculiar method, admirably calculated to make clear thinkers, and sure ones to the extent of their materials, has not equal efficacy for making those materials complete. It is a security for accuracy, but not for comprehensiveness; or rather, it is a security for one sort of comprehensiveness, but not for another.

Bentham's method of laying out his subject is admirable as a preservative against one kind of narrow and partial views. He begins by placing before himself the whole of the field of inquiry to which the particular question belongs, and divides down until he arrives at the thing he is in search of; and thus by successively rejecting all which is not the thing, he gradually works out a definition of what it is. This, which he calls the exhaustive method, is as old as philosophy itself. Plato owes everything to it, and does everything by it; and the use made of it by that great man in his Dialogues, Bacon, in one of those pregnant logical hints scattered through his writings, and so much neglected by most of his pretended followers, pronounces to be the nearest approach to a true inductive method in the ancient philosophy. Bentham was probably not aware that Plato had anticipated him in the process to which he too declared that he owed everything. By the practice of it, his speculations are rendered eminently systematic and consistent; no question, with him, is ever an insulated one; he sees every subject in connexion with all the other subjects with which in his view it is related, and from which it requires to be distinguished; and as all that he knows, in the least degree allied to the subject, has been marshalled in an orderly manner before him, he does not, like people who use a looser method, forget and overlook a thing on one occasion to remember it on another. Hence there is probably no philosopher of so wide a range, in whom there are so few inconsistencies. If any of the truths which he did not see, had come to be seen by him, he would have remembered it everywhere and at all times, and would have adjusted his whole system to it. And this is another admirable quality which he has impressed upon the best of the minds trained in his habits of thought : when those minds open to admit new truths, they digest them as fast as they receive them.

But this system, excellent for keeping before the mind of the thinker all that he knows, does not make him know enough; it does not make a knowledge of some of the properties of a thing suffice for the whole of it, nor render a rooted habit of surveying a complex object (though ever so carefully) in only one of its aspects, tantamount to the power of contemplating it in all. To give this last power, other qualities are required: whether Bentham possessed those other qualities we now have to see.

Bentham's mind, as we have already said, was eminently synthetical. He begins all his inquiries by supposing nothing to be known on the subject, and reconstructs all philosophy *ab initio,* without reference to the opinions of his predecessors. But to build either a philosophy or anything else, there must be materials. For the philosophy of matter, the materials are the properties of matter; for moral and political philosophy, the properties of man, and of man's position in the world. The knowledge which any inquirer possesses of these properties constitutes a limit beyond which, as a moralist or a political philosopher, whatever be his powers of mind, he cannot reach. Nobody's synthesis can be more complete than his analysis. If in his survey of human nature and life he has left any element out, then, wheresoever that element exerts any influence, his conclusions will fail, more or less, in their application. If he has left out many elements, and those very important, his labours may be highly valuable; he may have largely contributed to that body of partial truths which, when completed and corrected by one another, constitute practical truth; but the applicability of his system to practice in its own proper shape will be of an exceedingly limited range.

Human nature and human life are wide subjects, and whoever would embark in an enterprise requiring a thorough knowledge of them, has need both of large stores of his own, and of all aids and appliances from elsewhere. His qualifications for success will be proportional to two things: the degree in which his own nature and circumstances furnish him with a correct and complete picture of man's nature and circumstances; and his capacity of deriving light from other minds.

Bentham failed in deriving light from other minds. His writings contain few traces of the accurate knowledge of any

schools of thinking but his own; and many proofs of his
entire conviction that they could teach him nothing worth
knowing. For some of the most illustrious of previous thinkers,
his contempt was unmeasured. In almost the only passage of
the 'Deontology' which, from its style, and from its having
before appeared in print, may be known to be Bentham's,
Socrates, and Plato are spoken of in terms distressing to his
greatest admirers; and the incapacity to appreciate such men,
is a fact perfectly in unison with the general habits of
Bentham's mind. He had a phrase, expressive of the view
he took of all moral speculations to which his method had
not been applied, or (which he considered as the same thing)
not founded on a recognition of utility as the moral standard;
this phrase was 'vague generalities.' Whatever presented
itself to him in such a shape, he dismissed as unworthy of
notice, or dwelt upon only to denounce as absurd. He did
not heed, or rather the nature of his mind prevented it from
occurring to him, that these generalities contained the whole
unanalysed experience of the human race.

Unless it can be asserted that mankind did not know anything until logicians taught it to them—that until the last
hand has been put to a moral truth by giving it a meta-
physically precise expression, all the previous rough-hewing
which it has undergone by the common intellect at the
suggestion of common wants and common experience is to go
for nothing; it must be allowed, that even the originality
which can, and the courage which dares, think for itself, is not
a more necessary part of the philosophical character than a
thoughtful regard for previous thinkers, and for the collective
mind of the human race. What has been the opinion of mankind, has been the opinion of persons of all tempers and dispositions, of all partialities and prepossessions, of all varieties
in position, in education, in opportunities of observation and
inquiry. No one inquirer is all this; every inquirer is either
young or old, rich or poor, sickly or healthy, married or
unmarried, meditative or active, a poet or a logician, an
ancient or a modern, a man or a woman; and if a thinking
person, has, in addition, the accidental peculiarities of his
individual modes of thought. Every circumstance which gave a

character to the life of a human being, carries with it its peculiar biases; its peculiar facilities for perceiving some things, and for missing or forgetting others. But, from points of view different from his, different things are perceptible; and none are more likely to have seen what he does not see, than those who do not see what he sees. The general opinion of mankind is the average of the conclusions of all minds, stripped indeed of their choicest and most recondite thoughts, but freed from their twists and partialities : a net result, in which everybody's particular point of view is represented, nobody's predominant. The collective mind does not penetrate below the surface, but it sees all the surface; which profound thinkers, even by reason of their profundity, often fail to do : their intenser view of a thing in some of its aspects diverting their attention from others.

The hardiest assertor, therefore, of the freedom of private judgment—the keenest detector of the errors of his predecessors, and of the inaccuracies of current modes of thought —is the very person who most needs to fortify the weak side of his own intellect, by study of the opinions of mankind in all ages and nations, and of the speculations of philosophers of the modes of thought most opposite to his own. It is there that he will find the experiences denied to himself —the remainder of the truth of which he sees but half—the truths, of which the errors he detects are commonly but the exaggerations. If, like Bentham, he brings with him an improved instrument of investigation, the greater is the probability that he will find ready prepared a rich abundance of rough ore, which was merely waiting for that instrument. A man of clear ideas errs grievously if he imagines that whatever is seen confusedly does not exist : it belongs to him, when he meets with such a thing, to dispel the mist, and fix the outlines of the vague form which is looming through it.

Bentham's contempt, then, of all other schools of thinkers; his determination to create a philosophy wholly out of the materials furnished by his own mind, and by minds like his own; was his first disqualification as a philosopher. His second, was the incompleteness of his own mind as a repre-

sentative of universal human nature. In many of the most
natural and strongest feelings of human nature he had no
sympathy; from many of its graver experiences he was altogether cut off; and the faculty by which one mind understands
a mind different from itself, and throws itself into the
feelings of that other mind, was denied him by his deficiency
of Imagination.

With Imagination in the popular sense, command of
imagery and metaphorical expression, Bentham was, to a
certain degree, endowed. For want, indeed, of poetical culture,
the images with which his fancy supplied him were seldom
beautiful, but they were quaint and humorous, or bold, forcible,
and intense : passages might be quoted from him both of
playful irony, and of declamatory eloquence, seldom sur-
passed in the writings of philosophers. The Imagination
which he had not, was that to which the name is generally
appropriated by the best writers of the present day; that
which enables us, by a voluntary effort, to conceive the
absent as if it were present, the imaginary as if it were
real, and to clothe it in the feelings which, if it were
indeed real, it would bring along with it. This is the power
by which one human being enters into the mind and circumstances of another. This power constitutes the poet, in so far as
he does anything but melodiously utter his own actual feelings.
It constitutes the dramatist entirely. It is one of the constituents of the historian; by it we understand other times;
by it Guizot interprets to us the middle ages; Nisard, in
his beautiful Studies on the later Latin poets, places us in
the Rome of the Caesars; Michelet disengages the distinctive
characters of the different races and generations of mankind
from the facts of their history. Without it nobody knows
even his own nature, further than circumstances have actually
tried it and called it out; nor the nature of his fellow-
creatures, beyond such generalisations as he may have been
enabled to make from his observation of their outward conduct.

By these limits, accordingly, Bentham's knowledge of human
nature is bounded. It is wholly empirical; and the empiricism
of one who has had little experience. He had neither internal

experience nor external; the quiet, even tenor of his life, and his healthiness of mind, conspired to exclude him from both. He never knew prosperity and adversity, passion nor satiety : he never had even the experiences which sickness gives; he lived from childhood to the age of eighty-five in boyish health. He knew no dejection, no heaviness of heart. He never felt life a sore and a weary burthen. He was a boy to the last. Self-consciousness, that daemon of the men of genius of our time, from Wordsworth to Byron, from Goethe to Chateaubriand, and to which this age owes so much both of its cheerful and its mournful wisdom, never was awakened in him. How much of human nature slumbered in him he knew not, neither can we know. He had never been made alive to the unseen influences which were acting on himself, nor consequently on his fellow-creatures. Other ages and other nations were a blank to him for purposes of instruction. He measured them but by one standard; their knowledge of facts, and their capability to take correct views of utility, and merge all other objects in it. His own lot was cast in a generation of the leanest and barrenest men whom England had yet produced, and he was an old man when a better race came in with the present century. He saw accordingly in man little but what the vulgarest eye can see; recognised no diversities of character but such as he who runs may read. Knowing so little of human feelings, he knew still less of the influences by which those feelings are formed : all the more subtle workings both of the mind upon itself, and of external things upon the mind, escaped him; and no one, probably, who, in a highly instructed age, ever attempted to give a rule to all human conduct, set out with a more limited conception either of the agencies by which human conduct *is,* or of those by which it *should* be, influenced.

This, then is our idea of Bentham. He was a man both of remarkable endowments for philosophy, and of remarkable deficiencies for it : fitted, beyond almost any man, for drawing from his premises, conclusions not only correct, but sufficiently precise and specific to be practical : but whose general conception of human nature and life, furnished him with an unusually slender stock of premises. It is obvious

what would be likely to be achieved by such a man; what a
thinker, thus gifted and thus disqualified, could do in philosophy. He could, with close and accurate logic, hunt half-
truths to their consequences and practical applications, on
a scale both of greatness and of minuteness not previously
exemplified; and this is the character which posterity will
probably assign to Bentham.

We express our sincere and well-considered conviction
when we say, that there is hardly anything positive in
Bentham's philosophy which is not true : that when his
practical conclusions are erroneous, which in our opinion they
are very often, it is not because the considerations which he
urges are not rational and valid in themselves, but because
some more important principle, which he did not perceive,
supersedes those considerations, and turns the scale. The
bad part of his writings is his resolute denial of all that he
does not see, of all truths but those which he recognises. By
that alone has he exercised any bad influence upon his age;
by that he has, not created a school of deniers, for this
is an ignorant prejudice, but put himself at the head of the
school which exists always, though it does not always find
a great man to give it the sanction of philosophy : thrown
the mantle of intellect over the natural tendency of men in
all ages to deny or disparage all feelings and mental states
of which they have no consciousness in themselves.

The truths which are not Bentham's, which his philosophy
takes no account of, are many and important; but his non-
recognition of them does not put them out of existence;
they are still with us, and it is a comparatively easy task
that is reserved for us, to harmonise those truths with his.
To reject his half of the truth because he overlooked the
other half, would be to fall into his error without having
his excuse. For our own part, we have a large tolerance
for one-eyed men, provided their one eye is a penetrating
one : if they saw more, they probably would not see so
keenly, nor so eagerly pursue one course of inquiry. Almost
all rich veins of original and striking speculation have been
opened by systematic half-thinkers : though whether these
new thoughts drive out others as good, or are peacefully

superadded to them, depends on whether these half-thinkers are or are not followed in the same track by complete thinkers. The field of man's nature and life cannot be too much worked, or in too many directions; until every clod is turned up the work is imperfect; no whole truth is possible but by combining the points of view of all the fractional truths, nor, therefore, until it has been fully seen what each fractional truth can do by itself.

What Bentham's fractional truths could do, there is no such good means of showing as by a review of his philosophy : and such a review, though inevitably a most brief and general one, it is now necessary to attempt.

The first question in regard to any man of speculation is, what is his theory of human life? In the minds of many philosophers, whatever theory they have of this sort is latent, and it would be a revelation to themselves to have it pointed out to them in their writings as others can see it, unconsciously moulding everything to its own likeness. But Bentham always knew his own premises, and made his reader know them : it was not his custom to leave the theoretic grounds of his practical conclusions to conjecture. Few great thinkers have afforded the means of assigning with so much certainty the exact conception which they had formed of man and of man's life.

Man is conceived by Bentham as a being susceptible of pleasures and pains, and governed in all his conduct partly by the different modifications of self-interest, and the passions commonly classed as selfish, partly by sympathies, or occasionally antipathies, towards other beings. And here Bentham's conception of human nature stops. He does not exclude religion; the prospect of divine rewards and punishments he includes under the head of ' self-regarding interest,' and the devotional feeling under that of sympathy with God. But the whole of the impelling or restraining principles, whether of this or of another world, which he recognises, are either self-love, or love or hatred towards other sentient beings. That there might be no doubt of what he thought on the subject, he has not left us to the general evidence of his writings, but has drawn out a ' Table of the Springs of Action,' an express enumeration and classification of human motives, with their various names, laudatory, vituperative, and neutral : and this table, to be found in Part I of his collected works, we recommend to the study of those who would understand his philosophy.

Man is never recognised by him as a being capable of pursuing spiritual perfection as an end; of desiring, for its own sake, the conformity of his own character to his standard of excellence, without hope of good or fear of evil from other source than his own inward consciousness. Even in the more limited form of Conscience, this great fact in human nature escapes him. Nothing is more curious than the absence of recognition in any of his writings of the existence of conscience, as a thing distinct from philanthropy, from affection for God or man, and from self-interest in this world or in the next. There is a studied abstinence from any of the phrases which, in the mouths of others, import the acknowledgment of such a fact.[4] If we find the words 'Conscience,' 'Principle,' 'Moral Rectitude,' 'Moral Duty,' in his Table of the Springs of Action, it is among the synonyms of the 'love of reputation;' with an intimation as to the two former phrases, that they are also sometimes synonymous with the *religious* motive, or the motive of *sympathy*. The feeling of moral approbation or disapprobation properly so called, either towards ourselves or our fellow-creatures, he seems unaware of the existence of; and neither the word *self-respect,* nor the idea to which that word is appropriated, occurs even once, so far as our recollection serves us, in his whole writings.

Nor is it only the moral part of man's nature, in the strict sense of the term—the desire of perfection, or the feeling of an approving or of an accusing conscience—that he overlooks; he but faintly recognises, as a fact in human

---

[4] In a passage in the last volume of his book on Evidence, and possibly in one or two other places, the 'love of justice' is spoken of as a feeling inherent in almost all mankind. It is impossible, without explanations now unattainable, to ascertain what sense is to be put upon casual expressions so inconsistent with the general tenor of his philosophy.

nature, the pursuit of any other ideal end for its own sake. The sense of *honour*, and personal dignity—that feeling of personal exaltation and degradation which acts independently of other people's opinion, or even in defiance of it; the love of *beauty*, the passion of the artist; the love of *order*, of congruity, of consistency in all things, and conformity to their end; the love of *power*, not in the limited form of power over other human beings, but abstract power, the power of making our volitions effectual; the love of *action*, the thirst for movement and activity, a principle scarcely of less influence in human life than its opposite, the love of ease :—None of these powerful constituents of human nature are thought worthy of a place among the ' Springs of Action;' and though there is possibly no one of them of the existence of which an acknowledgment might not be found in some corner of Bentham's writings, no conclusions are ever founded on the acknowledgment. Man, that most complex being, is a very simple one in his eyes. Even under the head of *sympathy*, his recognition does not extend to the more complex forms of the feeling—the love of *loving*, the need of a sympathising support, or of objects of admiration and reverence. If he thought at all of any of the deeper feelings of human nature, it was but as idiosyncrasies of taste, with which the moralist no more than the legislator had any concern, further than to prohibit such as were mischievous among the actions to which they might chance to lead. To say either that man should, or that he should not, take pleasure in one thing, displeasure in another, appeared to him as much an act of despotism in the moralist as in the political ruler.

It would be most unjust to Bentham to surmise (as narrow-minded and passionate adversaries are apt in such cases to do) that this picture of human nature was copied from himself; that all those constituents of humanity which he rejected from his table of motives, were wanting in his own breast. The unusual strength of his early feelings of virtue, was, as we have seen, the original cause of all his speculations; and a noble sense of morality, and especially of justice, guides and pervades them all. But having been early accustomed to keep before his mind's eye the happiness

of mankind (or rather of the whole sentient world), as the
only thing desirable in itself, or which rendered anything
else desirable, he confounded all disinterested feelings which
he found in himself, with the desire of general happiness :
just as some religious writers, who loved virtue for its own
sake as much perhaps as men could do, habitually confounded their love of virtue with their fear of hell. It
would have required greater subtlety than Bentham possessed,
to distinguish from each other, feelings which, from long
habit, always acted in the same direction; and his want of
imagination prevented him from reading the distinction, where
it is legible enough, in the hearts of others.

Accordingly, he has not been followed in this grand oversight
by any of the able men who, from the extent of their
intellectual obligations to him, have been regarded as his
disciples. They may have followed him in his doctrine
of utility, and in his rejection of a moral sense as the test
of right and wrong : but while repudiating it as such, they
have, with Hartley, acknowledged it as a fact in human
nature; they have endeavoured to account for it, to assign
its laws : nor are they justly chargeable either with under-
valuing this part of our nature, or with any disposition to
throw it into the background of their speculations. If any
part of the influence of this cardinal error has extended
itself to them, it is circuitously, and through the effect on
their minds of other parts of Bentham's doctrines.

Sympathy, the only disinterested motive which Bentham
recognised, he felt the inadequacy of, except in certain
limited cases, as a security for virtuous action. Personal
affection, he well knew, is as liable to operate to the injury
of third parties, and requires as much to be kept under
government, as any other feeling whatever : and general
philanthropy, considered as a motive influencing mankind in
general, he estimated at its true value when divorced from
the feeling of duty—as the very weakest and most unsteady
of all feelings. There remained, as a motive by which
mankind are influenced, and by which they may be guided to
their good, only personal interest. Accordingly, Bentham's
idea of the world is that of a collection of persons pursuing

each his separate interest or pleasure, and the prevention
of whom from jostling one another more than is unavoidable,
may be attempted by hopes and fears derived from three
sources—the law, religion, and public opinion. To these
three powers, considered as binding human conduct, he gave
the name of *sanctions* : the *political* sanction, operating by the
rewards and penalties of the law; the *religious* sanction,
by those expected from the Ruler of the Universe; and the
popular, which he characteristically calls also the *moral* sanction
operating through the pains and pleasures arising from the
favour or disfavour of our fellow-creatures.

Such is Bentham's theory of the world. And now, in a
spirit neither of apology nor of censure, but of calm appreciation, we are to inquire how far this view of human
nature and life will carry any one :—how much it will
accomplish in morals, and how much in political and social
philosophy : what it will do for the individual, and what
for society.

It will do nothing for the conduct of the individual,
beyond prescribing some of the more obvious dictates of
worldly prudence, and outward probity and beneficence. There
is no need to expatiate on the deficiencies of a system of
ethics which does not pretend to aid individuals in the
formation of their own character; which recognises no such
wish as that of self-culture, we may even say no such power,
as existing in human nature; and if it did recognise, could
furnish little assistance to that great duty, because it overlooks the existence of about half of the whole number of
mental feelings which human beings are capable of, including
all those of which the direct objects are states of their own
mind.

Morality consists of two parts. One of these is self-
education; the training, by the human being himself, of
his affections and will. That department is a blank in Bentham's system. The other and co-equal part, the regulation
of his outward actions, must be altogether halting and imperfect without the first; for how can we judge in what
manner many an action will affect even the worldly interests.
of ourselves or others, unless we take in, as part of the

question, its influence on the regulation of our, or their,
affections and desires? A moralist on Bentham's principles
may get as far as this, that he ought not to slay, burn, or
steal; but what will be his qualifications for regulating
the nicer shades of human behaviour, or for laying down
even the greater moralities as to those facts in human life
which tend to influence the depths of the character quite
independently of any influence on worldly circumstances—
such, for instance, as the sexual relations, or those of family
in general, or any other social and sympathetic connexions
of an intimate kind? The moralities of these questions depend
essentially on considerations which Bentham never so much
as took into the account; and when he happened to be
in the right, it was always, and necessarily, on wrong or
insufficient grounds.

It is fortunate for the world that Bentham's taste lay
rather in the direction of jurisprudential than of properly
ethical inquiry. Nothing expressly of the latter kind has
been published under his name, except the ' Deontology '—
a book scarcely ever, in our experience, alluded to by any
admirer of Bentham without deep regret that it ever saw the
light. We did not expect from Bentham correct systematic
views of ethics, or a sound treatment of any question the
moralities of which require a profound knowledge of the
human heart; but we did anticipate that the greater moral
questions would have been boldly plunged into, and at least
a searching criticism produced of the received opinions; we
did not expect that the *petite morale* almost alone would
have been treated, and that with the most pedantic minuteness, and on the *quid pro quo* principles which regulate
trade. The book has not even the value which would belong to
an authentic exhibition of the legitimate consequences of an
erroneous line of thought; for the style proves it to have
been so entirely rewritten, that it is impossible to tell how
much or how little of it is Bentham's. The collected edition,
now in progress, will not, it is said, include Bentham's
religious writings; these, although we think most of them
of exceedingly small value, are at least his, and the world
has a right to whatever light they throw upon the con-

stitution of his mind. But the omission of the 'Deontology' would be an act of editorial discretion which we should deem entirely justifiable

If Bentham's theory of life can do so little for the individual, what can it do for society?

It will enable a society which has attained a certain state of spiritual development, and the maintenance of which in that state is otherwise provided for, to prescribe the rules by which it may protect its material interests. It will do nothing (except sometimes as an instrument in the hands of a higher doctrine) for the spiritual interests of society; nor does it suffice of itself even for the material interests. That which alone causes any material interests to exist, which alone enables any body of human beings to exist as a society, is national character: *that* it is, which causes one nation to succeed in what it attempts, another to fail; one nation to understand and aspire to elevated things, another to grovel in mean ones; which makes the greatness of one nation lasting, and dooms another to early and rapid decay. The true teacher of the fitting social arrangements for England, France or America, is the one who can point out how the English, French or American character can be improved, and how it has been made what it is. A philosophy of laws and institutions, not founded on a philosophy of national character, is an absurdity. But what could Bentham's opinion be worth on national character? How could he, whose mind contained so few and so poor types of individual character, rise to that higher generalisation? All he can do is but to indicate means by which, in any given state of the national mind, the material interests of society can be protected; saving the question, of which others must judge, whether the use of those means would have, on the national character, any injurious influence.

We have arrived, then, at a sort of estimate of what a philosophy like Bentham's can do. It can teach the means of organising and regulating the merely *business* part of the social arrangements. Whatever can be understood or whatever done without reference to moral influences, his philosophy is equal to; where those influences require to be taken into account, it is at fault. He committed the mistake of supposing that the business part of human affairs was the whole of them; all at least that the legislator and the moralist had to do with. Not that he disregarded moral influences when he perceived them; but his want of imagination, small experience of human feelings, and ignorance of the filiation and connexion of feelings with one another, made this rarely the case.

The business part is accordingly the only province of human affairs which Bentham has cultivated with any success; into which he has introduced any considerable number of comprehensive and luminous practical principles. That is the field of his greatness; and there he is indeed great. He has swept away the accumulated cobwebs of centuries— he has untied knots which the efforts of the ablest thinkers, age after age, had only drawn tighter; and it is no exaggeration to say of him that over a great part of the field he was the first to shed the light of reason.

We turn with pleasure from what Bentham could not do, to what he did. It is an ungracious task to call a great benefactor of mankind to account for not being a greater— to insist upon the errors of a man who has originated more new truths, has given to the world more sound practical lessons, than it ever received, except in a few glorious instances, from any other individual. The unpleasing part of our work is ended. We are now to show the greatness of the man; the grasp which his intellect took of the subjects with which it was fitted to deal; the giant's task which was before him, and the hero's courage and strength with which he achieved it. Nor let that which he did be deemed of small account because its province was limited: man has but the choice to go a little way in many paths, or a great way in only one. The field of Bentham's labours was like the space between two parallel lines; narrow to excess in one direction, in another it reached to infinity.

Bentham's speculations, as we are already aware, began with law; and in that department he accomplished his greatest triumphs. He found the philosophy of law a chaos, he left it a science: he found the practice of the law an

Augean stable, he turned the river into it which is mining and sweeping away mound after mound of its rubbish.

Without joining in the exaggerated invectives against lawyers, which Bentham sometimes permitted to himself, or making one portion of society alone accountable for the fault of all, we may say that circumstances had made English lawyers in a peculiar degree liable to the reproach of Voltaire, who defines lawyers the 'conservators of ancient barbarous usages.' The basis of the English law was, and still is, the feudal system. That system, like all those which existed as custom before they were established as law, possessed a certain degree of suitableness to the wants of the society among whom it grew up—that is to say, of a tribe of rude soldiers, holding a conquered people in subjection, and dividing its spoils among themselves. Advancing civilisation had, however, converted this armed encampment of barbarous warriors in the midst of enemies reduced to slavery, into an industrious, commercial, rich and free people. The laws which were suitable to the first of these states of society, could have no manner of relation to the circumstances of the second; which could not even have come into existence unless something had been done to adapt those laws to it. But the adaption was not the result of thought and design; it arose not from any comprehensive consideration of the new state of society and its exigencies. What was done, was done by a struggle of centuries between the old barbarism and the new civilisation; between the feudal aristocracy of conquerors, holding fast to the rude system they had established, and the conquered effecting their emancipation. The last was the growing power, but was never strong enough to break its bonds, though ever and anon some weak point gave way. Hence the law came to be like the costume of a full-grown man who had never put off the clothes made for him when he first went to school. Band after band had burst, and, as the rent widened, then, without removing anything except what might drop off of itself, the hole was darned, or patches of fresh law were brought from the nearest shop and stuck on. Hence all ages of English history have given one another rendezvous in

English law; their several products may be seen all together, not interfused, but heaped one upon another, as many different ages of the earth may be read in some perpendicular section of its surface—the deposits of each successive period not substituted but superimposed on those of the preceding. And in the world of law no less than in the physical world, every commotion and conflict of the elements has left its mark behind in some break or irregularity of the strata : every struggle which ever rent the bosom of society is apparent in the disjointed condition of the part of the field of law which covers the spot : nay, the very traps and pitfalls which one contending party set for another are still standing, and the teeth not of hyenas only, but of foxes and all cunning animals, are imprinted on the curious remains found in these antediluvian caves.

In the English law, as in the Roman before it, the adaptations of barbarous laws to the growth of civilised society were made chiefly by stealth. They were generally made by the courts of justice, who could not help reading the new wants of mankind in the cases between man and man which came before them; but who, having no authority to make new laws for those new wants, were obliged to do the work covertly, and evade the jealousy and opposition of an ignorant, prejudiced, and for the most part brutal and tyrannical legislature. Some of the most necessary of these improvements, such as the giving force of law to trusts, and the breaking up of entails, were effected in actual opposition to the strongly-declared will of Parliament, whose clumsy hands, no match for the astuteness of judges, could not, after repeated trials, manage to make any law which the judges could not find a trick for rendering inoperative. The whole history of the contest about trusts may still be read in the words of a conveyance, as could the contest about entails, till the abolition of fine and recovery, by a bill of the present Attorney-General; but dearly did the client pay for the cabinet of historical curiosities which he was obliged to purchase every time that he made a settlement of his estate. The result of this mode of improving social institutions was, that whatever new things were done had to be done in consistency with old forms and names; and the laws were improved with much the same effect as if, in the improvement of agriculture, the plough could only have been introduced by making it look like a spade; or as if, when the primeval practice of ploughing by the horse's tail gave way to the innovation of harness, the tail, for form's sake, had still remained attached to the plough.

When the conflicts were over, and the mixed mass settled down into something like a fixed state, and that state a very profitable and therefore a very agreeable one to lawyers, they, following the natural tendency of the human mind, began to theorise upon it, and, in obedience to necessity, had to digest it and give it a systematic form. It was from this thing of shreds and patches, in which the only part that approached to order or system was the early barbarous part, already more than half superseded, that English lawyers had to construct, by induction and abstraction, their philosophy of law; and without the logical habits and general intellectual cultivation which the lawyers of the Roman empire brought to a similar task. Bentham found the philosophy of law what English practising lawyers had made it; a jumble, in which *real* and *personal* property, *law* and *equity, felony, praemunire, misprision,* and *misdemeanour,* words without a vestige of meaning when detached from the history of English institutions—mere tide-marks to point out the line which the sea and the shore, in their secular struggles, had adjusted as their mutual boundary—all passed for distinctions inherent in the nature of things; in which every absurdity, every lucrative abuse, had a reason found for it—a reason which only now and then even pretended to be drawn from expediency; most commonly a technical reason, one of mere form, derived from the old barbarous system. While the theory of the law was in this state, to describe what the practice of it was would require the pen of a Swift, or of Bentham himself. The whole progress of a suit at law seemed like a series of contrivances for lawyers' profit, in which the suitors were regarded as the prey; and if the poor were not the helpless victims of every Sir Giles Overreach who could pay the price, they might thank opinion and manners for it, not the law.

It may be fancied by some people that Bentham did an easy thing in merely calling all this absurd, and proving it to be so. But he began the contest a young man, and he had grown old before he had any followers. History will one day refuse to give credit to the intensity of the superstition which, till very lately protected this mischievous mess from examination or doubt—passed off the charming representations of Blackstone for a just estimate of the English law, and proclaimed the shame of human reason to be the perfection of it. Glory to Bentham that he has dealt to this superstition its deathblow—that he has been the Hercules of this hydra, the St. George of this pestilent dragon! The honour is all his—nothing but his peculiar qualities could have done it. There were wanted his indefatigable perseverance, his firm self-reliance, needing no support from other men's opinion; his intensely practical turn of mind, his synthetical habits— above all, his peculiar method. Metaphysicians, armed with vague generalities, had often tried their hands at the subject, and left it no more advanced than they found it. Law is a matter of business; means and ends are the things to be considered in it, not abstractions : vagueness was not to be met by vagueness, but by definiteness and precision : details were not to be encountered with generalities, but with details. Nor could any progress be made, on such a subject, by merely showing that existing things were bad; it was necessary also to show how they might be made better. No great man whom we read of was qualified to do this thing except Bentham. He has done it, once and for ever.

Into the particulars of what Bentham has done we cannot enter : many hundred pages would be required to give a tolerable abstract of it. To sum up our estimate under a few heads. First: he has expelled mysticism from the philosophy of law, and set the example of viewing laws in a practical light, as means to certain definite and precise ends. Secondly : he has cleared up the confusion and vagueness attaching to the idea of law in general, to the idea of a body of laws, and the various general ideas therein involved. Thirdly : he demonstrated the necessity and practicability of *codification,* or the conversion of all law into a written and systematically arranged code: not like the Code Napoleon, a code without a single definition, requiring a constant reference to anterior precedent for the meaning of its technical terms; but one containing within itself all that is necessary for its own interpretation, together with a perpetual provision for its own emendation and improvement. He has shown of what parts such a code would consist; the relation of those parts to one another; and by his distinctions and classifications has done very much towards showing what should be, or might be, its nomenclature and arrangement. What he has left undone, he has made it comparatively easy for others to do. Fourthly: he has taken a systematic view[5] of the exigencies of society for which the civil code is intended to provide, and of the principles of human nature by which its provisions are to be tested: and this view, defective (as we have already intimated) wherever spiritual interests require to be taken into account, is excellent for that large portion of the laws of any country which are designed for the protection of material interests. Fifthly: (to say nothing of the subject of punishment, for which something considerable had been done before) he found the philosophy of judicial procedure, including that of judicial establishments and of evidence, in a more wretched state than even any other part of the philosophy of law; he carried it at once almost to perfection. He left it with every one of its principles established, and little remaining to be done even in the suggestion of practical arrangements.

These assertions in behalf of Bentham may be left, without fear for the result, in the hands of those who are competent to judge of them. There are now even in the highest seats of justice, men to whom the claims made for him will not appear extravagant. Principle after principle of those propounded by him is moreover making its way by infiltration into the understandings most shut against his influence, and driving nonsense and prejudice from one corner of them to another. The reform of the laws of any country according to his principles, can only be gradual, and may be long ere it

[5] See the 'Principles of Civil Law,' contained in Part II of his collected works.

is accomplished; but the work is in progress, and both parliament and the judges are every year doing something,
and often something not inconsiderable, towards the forward-
ing of it.

It seems proper here to take notice of an accusation sometimes made both against Bentham and against the principle
of codification—as if they required one uniform suit of ready-
made laws for all times and all states of society. The doctrine
of codification, as the word imports, relates to the form only
of the laws, not their substance; it does not concern itself with
what the laws should be, but declares that whatever they are,
they ought to be systematically arranged, and fixed down to
a determinate form of words. To the accusation, so far as
it affects Bentham, one of the essays in the collection of his
works (then for the first time published in English) is a
complete answer: that ' On the Influence of Time and Place
in Matters of Legislation.' It may there be seen that the
different exigencies of different nations with respect to law,
occupied his attention as systematically as any other portion
of the wants which render laws necessary : with the limitations, it is true, which were set to all his speculations by
the imperfections of his theory of human nature. For, taking,
as we have seen, next to no account of national character
and the causes which form and maintain it, he was pre-
cluded from considering, except to a very limited extent,
the laws of a country as an instrument of national culture :
one of their most important aspects, and in which they
must of course vary according to the degree and kind of
culture already attained; as a tutor gives his pupil different
lessons according to the progress already made in his education. The same laws would not have suited our wild ancestors,
accustomed to rude independence, and a people of Asiatics
bowed down by military despotism : the slave needs to be
trained to govern himself, the savage to submit to the government of others. The same laws will not suit the English, who
distrust everything which emanates from general principles, and
the French, who distrust whatever does not so emanate. Very
different institutions are needed to train to the perfection of
their nature, or to constitute into a united nation and social

polity, an essentially *subjective* people like the Germans, and an essentially *objective* people like those of Northern and Central Italy; the one affectionate and dreamy, the other passionate and worldly; the one trustful and loyal, the other calculating and suspicious; the one not practical enough, the other overmuch; the one wanting individuality, the other fellow-feeling, the one failing for want of exacting enough for itself, the other for want of conceding enough to others. Bentham was little accustomed to look at institutions in their relation to these topics. The effects of this oversight must of course be perceptible throughout his speculations, but we do not think the errors into which it led him very material in the greater part of civil and penal law : it is in the department of constitutional legislation that they were fundamental.

The Benthamic theory of government has made so much noise in the world of late years; it has held such a conspicuous place among Radical philosophies, and Radical modes of thinking have participated so much more largely than any others in its spirit, that many worthy persons imagine there is no other Radical philosophy extant. Leaving such people to discover their mistake as they may, we shall expend a few words in attempting to discriminate between the truth and error of this celebrated theory.

There are three great questions in government. First, to what authority is it for the good of the people that they should be subject? Secondly, how are they to be induced to obey that authority? The answers to these two questions vary indefinitely, according to the degree and kind of civilisation and cultivation already attained by a people, and their peculiar aptitudes for receiving more. Comes next a third question, not liable to so much variation, namely, by what means are the abuses of this authority to be checked? This third question is the only one of the three to which Bentham seriously applies himself, and he gives it the only answer it admits of—Responsibility : responsibility to persons whose interest, whose obvious and recognisable interest, accords with the end in view—good government. This being granted, it is next to be asked, in what body of persons this identity of interest with good government, that is, with the interest

of the whole community, is to be found? In nothing less, says
Bentham, than the numerical majority : nor, say we, even
in the numerical majority itself; of no portion of the community less than all, will the interest coincide, at all times
and in all respects, with the interest of all. But, since power
given to all, by a representative government, is in fact given
to a majority; we are obliged to fall back upon the first of
our three questions, namely, under what authority is it
for the good of the people that they be placed? And if to this
the answer be, under that of a majority among themselves,
Bentham's system cannot be questioned. This one assumption
being made, his ' Constitutional Code' is admirable. That
extraordinary power which he possessed, of at once seizing
comprehensive principles, and scheming out minute details,
is brought into play with surpassing vigour in devising means
for preventing rulers from escaping from the control of the
majority; for enabling and inducing the majority to exercise that control unremittingly; and for providing them with
servants of every desirable endowment, moral and intellectual,
compatible with entire subservience to their will.

But *is* this fundamental doctrine of Bentham's political
philosophy an universal truth? Is it, at all times and places,
good for mankind to be under the absolute authority of the
majority of themselves? We say the authority, not the political
authority merely, because it is chimerical to suppose that
whatever has absolute power over men's bodies will not
arrogate it over their minds—will not seek to control (not
perhaps by legal penalties, but by the persecutions of society)
opinions and feelings which depart from its standard; will
not attempt to shape the education of the young by its model,
and to extinguish all books, all schools, all combinations of
individuals for joint action upon society, which may be
attempted for the purpose of keeping alive a spirit at variance
with its own. Is it, we say, the proper condition of man,
in all ages and nations, to be under the despotism of Public
Opinion?

It is very conceivable that such a doctrine should find
acceptance from some of the noblest spirits, in a time of
reaction against the aristocratic governments of modern Europe;

governments founded on the entire sacrifice (except so far as prudence, and sometimes humane feeling interfere) of the community generally, to the self-interest and ease of a few. European reformers have been accustomed to see the numerical majority everywhere unjustly depressed, everywhere trampled upon, or at the best overlooked, by governments; nowhere possessing power enough to extort redress of their most positive grievances, provision for their mental culture, or even to prevent themselves from being taxed avowedly for the pecuniary profit of the ruling classes. To see these things, and to seek to put an end to them, by means (among other things) of giving more political power to the majority, constitutes Radicalism; and it is because so many in this age have felt this wish, and have felt that the realisation of it was an object worthy of men's devoting their lives to it, that such a theory of government as Bentham's has found favour with them. But, though to pass from one form of bad government to another be the ordinary fate of mankind, philosophers ought not to make themselves parties to it, by sacrificing one portion of important truth to another.

The numerical majority of any society whatever, must consist of persons all standing in the same social position, and having, in the main, the same pursuits, namely, unskilled manual labourers; and we mean no disparagement to them: whatever we say to their disadvantage, we say equally of a numerical majority of shopkeepers, or of squires. Where there is identity of position and pursuits, there also will be identity of partialities, passions, and prejudices; and to give to any one set of partialities, passions, and prejudices, absolute power, without counter-balance from partialities, passions, and prejudices of a different sort, is the way to render the correction of any of those imperfections hopeless; to make one narrow, mean type of human nature universal and perpetual, and to crush every influence which tends to the further improvement of man's intellectual and moral nature. There must, we know, be some paramount power in society; and that the majority should be that power, is on the whole right, not as being just in itself, but as being less unjust than any other footing on which the matter can

be placed. But it is necessary that the institutions of society
should make provision for keeping up, in some form or other,
as a corrective to partial views, and a shelter for freedom
of thought and individuality of character, a perpetual and
standing Opposition to the will of the majority. All countries
which have long continued progressive, or been durably great,
have been so because there has been an organised opposition
to the ruling power, of whatever kind that power was:
plebeians to patricians, clergy to kings, free-thinkers to clergy,
kings to barons, commons to king and aristocracy. Almost all
the greatest men who ever lived have formed part of such
an Opposition. Wherever some such quarrel has not been
going on—wherever it has been terminated by the complete
victory of one of the contending principles, and no new
contest has taken the place of the old—society has either
hardened into Chinese stationariness, or fallen into dissolution.
A centre of resistance, round which all the moral and social
elements which the ruling power views with disfavour may
cluster themselves, and behind whose bulwarks they may
find shelter from the attempts of that power to hunt them
out of existence, is as necessary where the opinion of the
majority is sovereign, as where the ruling power is a hierarchy or an aristocracy. Where no such *point d'appui* exists,
there the human race will inevitably degenerate; and the
question, whether the United States, for instance, will in
time sink into another China (also a most commercial and
industrious nation), resolves itself, to us, into the question,
whether such a centre of resistance will gradually evolve
itself or not.

These things being considered, we cannot think that
Bentham made the most useful employment which might have
been made of his great powers, when, not content with
enthroning the majority as sovereign, by means of universal
suffrage without king or house of lords, he exhausted all
the resources of ingenuity in devising means for riveting
the yoke of public opinion closer and closer round the
necks of all public functionaries, and excluding every possibility of the exercise of the slightest or most temporary

influence either by a minority, or by the functionary's own notions of right. Surely when any power has been made the strongest power, enough has been done for it; care is thenceforth wanted rather to prevent that strongest power from swallowing up all others. Wherever all the forces of society act in one single direction, the just claims of the individual human being are in extreme peril. The power of the majority is salutary so far as it is used defensively, not offensively—as its exertion is tempered by respect for the personality of the individual, and deference to superiority of cultivated intelligence. If Bentham had employed himself in pointing out the means by which institutions fundamentally democratic might be best adapted to the preservation and strengthening of those two sentiments, he would have done something more permanently valuable, and more worthy of his great intellect. Montesquieu, with the lights of the present age, would have done it; and we are possibly destined to receive this benefit from the Montesquieu of our own times, M. de Tocqueville.

Do we then consider Bentham's political speculations useless? Far from it. We consider them only one-sided. He has brought out into a strong light, has cleared from a thousand confusions and misconceptions, and pointed out with admirable skill the best means of promoting, one of the ideal qualities of a perfect government—identity of interest between the trustees and the community for whom they hold their power in trust. This quality is not attainable in its ideal perfection, and must moreover be striven for with a perpetual eye to all other requisites; but those other requisites must still more be striven for without losing sight of this: and when the slightest postponement is made of it to any other end, the sacrifice, often necessary is never unattended with evil. Bentham has pointed out how complete this sacrifice is in modern European societies: how exclusively, partial and sinister interests are the ruling power there, with only such check as is imposed by public opinion—which being thus, in the existing order of things, perpetually apparent as a source of good, he was led by natural partiality to exaggerate its intrinsic excellence. This sinister interest of rulers Bentham hunted through all its disguises, and especially through those which hide it from the men themselves who are influenced by it. The greatest service rendered by him to the philosophy of universal human nature, is, perhaps, his illustration of what he terms ' interest-begotten prejudice '—the common tendency of man to make a duty and a virtue of following his self-interest. The idea, it is true, was far from being peculiarly Bentham's : the artifices by which we persuade ourselves that we are not yielding to our selfish inclinations when we are, had attracted the notice of all moralists, and had been probed by religious writers to a depth as much below Bentham's, as their knowledge of the profundities and windings of the human heart was superior to his. But it is selfish interest in the form of class-interest, and the class morality founded thereon, which Bentham has illustrated : the manner in which any set of persons who mix much together and have a common interest, are apt to make that common interest their standard of virtue, and the social feelings of the members of the class are made to play into the hands of their selfish ones; whence the union so often exemplified in history, between the most heroic personal disinterestedness and the most odious class-selfishness. This was one of Bentham's leading ideas, and almost the only one by which he contributed to the elucidation of history : much of which, except so far as this explained it, must have been entirely inexplicable to him. The idea was given him by Helvetius, whose book, ' De l'Esprit,' is one continued and most acute commentary on it; and, together with the other great idea of Helvetius, the influence of circumstances on character, it will make his name live by the side of Rousseau, when most of the other French metaphysicians of the eighteenth century will be extant as such only in literary history.

In the brief view which we have been able to give of Bentham's philosophy, it may surprise the reader that we have said so little about the first principle of it, with which his name is more identified than with anything else; the ' principle of utility,' or, as he afterwards named it, ' the greatest-happiness principle.' It is a topic on which

much were to be said, if there were room, or if it were in
reality necessary for the just estimation of Bentham. On
an occasion more suitable for a discussion of the metaphysics
of morality, or on which the elucidations necessary to make
an opinion on so abstract a subject intelligible could be
conveniently given, we should be fully prepared to state
what we think on this subject. At present we shall only
say, that while, under proper explanations, we entirely agree
with Bentham in his principle, we do not hold with him that
all right thinking on the details of morals depends on
its express assertion. We think utility, or happiness, much
too complex and indefinite an end to be sought except
through the medium of various secondary ends, concerning
which there may be, and often is, agreement among persons
who differ in their ultimate standard; and about which there
does in fact prevail a much greater unanimity among thinking persons, than might be supposed from their diametrical
divergence on the great questions of moral metaphysics. As
mankind are much more nearly of one nature, than of one
opinion about their own nature, they are more easily brought
to agree in their intermediate principles, *vera illa et media
axiomata,* as Bacon says, than in their first principles : and
the attempt to make the bearings of actions upon the ultimate
end more evident than they can be made by referring them
to the intermediate ends, and to estimate their value by a
direct reference to human happiness, generally terminates
in attaching most importance, not to those effects which are
really the greatest, but to those which can most easily be pointed
to and individually identified. Those who adopt utility as a
standard can seldom apply it truly except through the secondary principles; those who reject it, generally do no more
than erect those secondary principles into first principles.
It is when two or more of the secondary principles conflict,
that a direct appeal to some first principle becomes necessary; and then commences the practical importance of the
utilitarian controversy; which is, in other respects, a
question of arrangement and logical subordination rather than
of practice; important principally in a purely scientific point
of view, for the sake of the systematic unity and coherency

of ethical philosophy. It is probable, however, that to the principle of utility we owe all that Bentham did; that it was necessary to him to find a first principle which he could receive as self-evident, and to which he could attach all his other doctrines as logical consequences : that to him systematic unity was an indispensable condition of his confidence in his own intellect. And there is something further to be remarked. Whether happiness be or be not the end to which morality should be referred—that it be referred to an *end* of some sort, and not left in the dominion of vague feeling or inexplicable internal conviction, that it be made a matter of reason and calculation, and not merely of sentiment, is essential to the very idea of moral philosophy; is, in fact, what renders argument or discussion on moral questions possible. That the morality of actions depends on the consequences which they tend to produce, is the doctrine of rational persons of all schools; that the good or evil of those consequences is measured solely by pleasure or pain, is all of the doctrine of the school of utility, which is peculiar to it.

In so far as Bentham's adoption of the principle of utility induced him to fix his attention upon the consequences of actions as the consideration determining their morality, so far he was indisputably in the right path : though to go far in it without wandering, there was needed a greater knowledge of the formation of character, and of the consequences of actions upon the agent's own frame of mind, than Bentham possessed. His want of power to estimate this class of consequences, together with his want of the degree of modest deference which, from those who have not competent experience of their own, is due to the experience of others on that part of the subject, greatly limit the value of his speculations on questions of practical ethics.

He is chargeable also with another error, which it would be improper to pass over, because nothing has tended more to place him in opposition to the common feelings of mankind, and to give to his philosophy that cold, mechanical, and ungenial air which characterises the popular idea of a Benthamite. This error, or rather one-sidedness, belongs to

him not as a utilitarian, but as a moralist by profession,
and in common with almost all professed moralists, whether
religious or philosophical : it is that of treating the *moral*
view of actions and characters, which is unquestionably the
first and most important mode of looking at them, as if it
were the sole one : whereas it is only one of three, by all
of which our sentiments towards the human being may be,
ought to be, and without entirely crushing our own nature
cannot but be, materially influenced. Every human action
has three aspects : its *moral* aspect, or that of its *right*
and *wrong*; its *aesthetic* aspect, or that of its *beauty;* its
sympathetic aspect, or that of its *loveableness.* The first
addresses itself to our reason and conscience; the second to our
imagination; the third to our human fellow-feeling. According to the first, we approve or disapprove; according to the
second, we admire or despise; according to the third, we
love, pity, or dislike. The morality of an action depends
on its foreseeable consequences; its beauty, and its loveableness, or the reverse, depend on the qualities which it
is evidence of. Thus, a lie is *wrong,* because its effect is
to mislead, and because it tends to destroy the confidence of
man in man; it is also *mean,* because it is cowardly—
because it proceeds from not daring to face the consequences
of telling the truth—or at best is evidence of want of that
power to compass our ends by straightforward means, which
is conceived as properly belonging to every person not deficient in energy or in understanding. The action of Brutus
in sentencing his sons was *right,* because it was executing a
law essential to the freedom of his country, against persons of
whose guilt there was no doubt : it was *admirable,* because it
evinced a rare degree of patriotism, courage, and self-control;
but there was nothing *loveable* in it; it affords either no
presumption in regard to loveable qualities, or a presumption
of their deficiency. If one of the sons had engaged in the
conspiracy from affection for the other, his action would
have been loveable, though neither moral nor admirable. It
is not possible for any sophistry to confound these three
modes of viewing an action; but it is very possible to adhere
to one of them exclusively, and lose sight of the rest.

Sentimentality consists in setting the last two of the three above the first; the error of moralists in general, and of Bentham, is to sink the two latter entirely. This is pre-eminently the case with Bentham : he both wrote and felt as if the moral standard ought not only to be paramount (which it ought), but to be alone; as if it ought to be the sole master of all our actions, and even of all our sentiments; as if either to admire or like, or despise or dislike a person for any action which neither does good nor harm, or which does not do a good or a harm proportioned to the sentiment entertained, were an injustice and a prejudice. He carried this so far, that there were certain phrases which, being expressive of what he considered to be this groundless liking or aversion, he could not bear to hear pronounced in his presence. Among these phrases were those of *good* and *bad taste.* He thought it an insolent piece of dogmatism in one person to praise or condemn another in a matter of taste : as if men's likings and dislikings, on things in themselves indifferent, were not full of the most important inferences as to every point of their character; as if a person's tastes did not show him to be wise or a fool, cultivated or ignorant, gentle or rough, sensitive or callous, generous or sordid, benevolent or selfish, conscientious or depraved.

Connected with the same topic are Bentham's peculiar opinions on poetry. Much more has been said than there is any foundation for, about his contempt for the pleasures of imagination, and for the fine arts. Music was throughout life his favourite amusement; painting, sculpture, and the other arts addressed to the eye, he was so far from holding in any contempt, that he occasionally recognises them as means employable for important social ends; though his ignorance of the deeper springs of human character prevented him (as it prevents most Englishmen) from suspecting how profoundly such things enter into the moral nature of man, and into the education both of the individual and of the race. But towards poetry in the narrower sense, that which employs the language of words, he entertained no favour. Words, he thought, were perverted from their proper office when they were employed in uttering anything but precise logical truth. He says, somewhere in his works, that, 'quantity of pleasure being equal, push-pin is as good as poetry;' but this is only a paradoxical way of stating what he would equally have said of the things which he most valued and admired. Another aphorism is attributed to him, which is much more characteristic of his view of this subject: 'All poetry is misrepresentation.' Poetry, he thought, consisted essentially in exaggeration for effect: in proclaiming some one view of a thing very emphatically, and suppressing all the limitations and qualifications. This trait of character seems to us a curious example of what Mr. Carlyle strikingly calls 'the completeness of limited man.' Here is a philosopher who is happy within his narrow boundary as no man of indefinite range ever was; who flatters himself that he is so completely emancipated from the essential law of poor human intellect, by which it can only see one thing at a time well, that he can even turn round upon the imperfection and lay a solemn interdict upon it. Did Bentham really suppose that it is in poetry only that propositions cannot be exactly true, cannot contain in themselves all the limitations and qualifications with which they require to be taken when applied to practice? We have seen how far his own prose propositions are from realising this Utopia : and even the attempt to approach it would be incompatible not with poetry merely, but with oratory, and popular writing of every kind. Bentham's charge is true to the fullest extent; all writing which undertakes to make men feel truths as well as see them, does take up one point at a time, does seek to impress that, to drive that home, to make it sink into and colour the whole mind of the reader or hearer. It is justified in doing so, if the portion of truth which it thus enforces be that which is called for by the occasion. All writing addressed to the feelings has a natural tendency to exaggeration; but Bentham should have remembered that in this, as in many things, we must aim at too much, to be assured of doing enough.

From the same principle in Bentham came the intricate and involved style, which makes his later writings books for the student only, not the general reader. It was from his perpetually aiming at impracticable precision. Nearly all his earlier, and many parts of his later writings, are models, as we have already observed, of light, playful, and popular style : a Benthamiana might be made of passages worthy of Addison or Goldsmith. But in his later years and more advanced studies, he fell into a Latin or German structure of sentence, foreign to the genius of the English language. He could not bear, for the sake of clearness and the reader's ease, to say, as ordinary men are content to do, a little more than the truth in one sentence, and correct it in the next. The whole of the qualifying remarks which he intended to make, he insisted upon imbedding as parentheses in the very middle of the sentence itself. And thus the sense being so long suspended, and attention being required to the accessory ideas before the principal idea had been properly seized, it became difficult, without some practice, to make out the train of thought. It is fortunate that so many of the most important parts of his writings are free from this defect. We regard it as a *reductio ad absurdum* of his objection to poetry. In trying to write in a manner against which the same objection should not lie, he could stop nowhere short of utter unreadableness, and after all attained no more accuracy than is compatible with opinions as imperfect and one-sided as those of any poet or sentimentalist breathing. Judge then in what state literature and philosophy would be, and what chance they would have of influencing the multitude, if his objection were allowed, and all styles of writing banished which would not stand his test.

We must here close this brief and imperfect view of Bentham and his doctrines; in which many parts of the subject have been entirely untouched, and no part done justice to, but which at least proceeds from an intimate familiarity with his writings, and is nearly the first attempt at an impartial estimate of his character as a philosopher, and of the result of his labours to the world.

After every abatement, and it has been seen whether we have made our abatements sparingly—there remains to Bentham an indisputable place among the great intellectual benefactors of mankind. His writings will long form an indispensable part of the education of the highest order of practical thinkers; and the collected edition of them ought to be in the hands of every one who would either understand his age, or take any beneficial part in the great business of it.[6]

[6] Since the first publication of this paper, Lord Brougham's brilliant series of characters has been published, including a sketch of Bentham. Lord Brougham's view of Bentham's characteristics agrees in the main points, so far as it goes, with the result of our more minute examination, but there is an imputation cast upon Bentham, of a jealous and splenetic disposition in private life, of which we feel called upon to give at once a contradiction and an explanation. It is indispensable to a correct estimate of any of Bentham's dealings with the world, to bear in mind that in everything except abstract speculation he was to the last, what we have called him, essentially a boy. He had the freshness, the simplicity, the confidingness, the liveliness and activity, all the delightful qualities of boyhood, and the weaknesses which are the reverse side of those qualities—the undue importance attached to trifles, the habitual mismeasurement of the practical bearing and value of things, the readiness to be either delighted or offended on inadequate cause. These were the real sources of what was unreasonable in some of his attacks on individuals, and in particular on Lord Brougham, on the subject of his Law Reforms; they were no more the effect of envy or malice, or any really unamiable quality, than the freaks of a pettish child, and are scarcely a fitter subject of censure or criticism.

ON LIBERTY

by John Stuart Mill

CHAPTER I

INTRODUCTORY

The subject of this Essay is not the so-called Liberty of the Will, so unfortunately opposed to the misnamed doctrine of Philosophical Necessity; but Civil, or Social Liberty: the nature and limits of the power which can be legitimately exercised by society over the individual. A question seldom stated, and hardly ever discussed, in general terms, but which profoundly influences the practical controversies of the age by its latent presence, and is likely soon to make itself recognised as the vital question of the future. It is so far from being new, that, in a certain sense, it has divided mankind, almost from the remotest ages; but in the stage of progress into which the more civilised portions of the species have now entered, it presents itself under new conditions, and requires a different and more fundamental treatment.

The struggle between Liberty and Authority is the most conspicuous feature in the portions of history with which we are earliest familiar, particularly in that of Greece, Rome, and England. But in old times this contest was between subjects, or some classes of subjects, and the Government. By liberty, was meant protection against the tyranny of the political rulers. The rulers were conceived (except in some of the popular governments of Greece) as in a necessarily antagonistic position to the people they ruled. They consisted of a governing One, or a governing tribe or caste, who derived their authority from inheritance or conquest, who, at all events, did not hold it at the pleasure of the governed, and whose supremacy men did not venture, perhaps did not desire, to contest, whatever precautions might be taken against its oppressive exercise. Their power was regarded as necessary, but also as highly dangerous; as a weapon which they would attempt to use against their subjects, no less than against external enemies. To prevent the weaker members of the community from being preyed upon by innumerable vultures, it was needful that there should be an animal of prey stronger than the rest, commissioned to keep them down. But as the king of the vultures would be no less bent upon preying on the flock than any of the minor harpies, it was indispensable to be in a perpetual attitude of defence against his beak and claws. The aim, therefore, of patriots was to set limits to the power which the ruler should be suffered to exercise over the community; and this limitation was what they meant by liberty. It was attempted in two ways. First, by obtaining a recognition of certain immunities, called political liberties or rights, which it was to be regarded as a breach of duty in the ruler to infringe, and which if he did infringe, specific resistance, or general rebellion, was held to be justifiable. A second, and generally a later expedient, was the establishment of constitutional checks, by which the consent of the community, or of a body of some sort, supposed to represent its interests, was made a necessary condition to some of the more important acts of the governing power. To the first of these modes of limitation, the ruling power, in most European countries, was compelled, more or less, to submit. It was not so with the second; and, to attain this, or when already in some degree possessed, to attain it more completely, became everywhere the principal object of the lovers of liberty. And so long as mankind were content to combat one enemy by another, and to be ruled by a master, on condition of being guaranteed more or less efficaciously against his tyranny, they did not carry their aspirations beyond this point.

A time, however, came, in the progress of human affairs, when men ceased to think it a necessity of nature that their governors should be an independent power, opposed in interest to themselves. It appeared to them much better that the various magistrates of the State should be their tenants or delegates, revocable at their pleasure. In that way alone, it seemed, could they have complete security that the powers of government would never be abused to their disadvantage. By degrees this new demand for elective and temporary rulers became the prominent object of the exertions of the popular party, wherever any such party existed; and superseded, to a considerable extent, the previous efforts to limit the power of rulers. As the struggle proceeded for making the ruling power emanate from the periodical choice of the ruled, some persons began to think that too much importance had been attached to the limitation of the power itself. *That* (it might seem) was a resource against rulers whose interests were habitually opposed to those of the people. What was now wanted was, that the rulers should be identified with the people; that their interest and will should be the interest and will of the nation. The nation did not need to be protected against its own will. There was no fear of its tyrannising over itself. Let the rulers be effectually responsible to it, promptly removable by it, and it could afford to trust them with power of which it could itself dictate the use to be made. Their power was but the nation's own power, concentrated, and in a form convenient for exercise. This mode of thought, or rather perhaps of feeling, was common among the last generation of European liberalism, in the Continental section of which it still apparently predominates. Those who admit any limit to what a government may do, except in the case of such governments as they think ought not to exist, stand out as brilliant exceptions among the political thinkers of the Continent. A similar tone of sentiment might by this time have been prevalent in our own country, if the circumstances which for a time encouraged it, had continued unaltered.

But, in political and philosophical theories, as well as in persons, success discloses faults and infirmities which failure might have concealed from observation. The notion, that the people have no need to limit their power over themselves, might seem axiomatic, when popular government was a thing only dreamed about, or read of as having existed at some distant period of the past. Neither was that notion necessarily disturbed by such temporary aberrations as those of the French

Revolution, the worst of which were the work of a usurping few, and which, in any case, belonged, not to the permanent working of popular institutions, but to a sudden and convulsive outbreak against monarchical and aristocratic despotism. In time, however, a democratic republic came to occupy a large portion of the earth's surface, and made itself felt as one of the most powerful members of the community of nations; and elective and responsible government became subject to the observations and criticism which wait upon a great existing fact. It was now perceived that such phrases as "self-government," and "the power of the people over themselves," do not express the true state of the case. The "people" who exercise the power are not always the same people with those over whom it is exercised; and the "self-government" spoken of is not the government of each by himself, but of each by all the rest. The will of the people, moreover, practically means the will of the most numerous or the most active *part* of the people; the majority, or those who succeed in making themselves accepted as the majority; the people, consequently *may* desire to oppress a part of their number; and precautions are as much needed against this as against any other abuse of power. The limitation, therefore, of the power of government over individuals loses none of its importance when the holders of power are regularly accountable to the community, that is, to the strongest party therein. This view of things, recommending itself equally to the intelligence of thinkers and to the inclination of those important classes in European society to whose real or supposed interests democracy is adverse, has had no difficulty in establishing itself; and in political speculations "the tyranny of the majority" is now generally included among the evils against which society requires to be on its guard.

Like other tyrannies, the tyranny of the majority was at first, and is still vulgarly, held in dread, chiefly as operating through the acts of the public authorities. But reflecting persons perceived that when society is itself the tyrant— society collectively over the separate individuals who compose it—its means of tyrannising are not restricted to the acts which it may do by the hands of its political functionaries. Society can and does execute its own mandates : and if it issues wrong mandates · instead of right, or any mandates at all in things with which it ought not to meddle, it practises a social tyranny more formidable than many kinds of political oppression, since, though not usually upheld by such extreme penalties, it leaves fewer means of escape, penetrating much more deeply into the details of life, and enslaving the soul itself. Protection, therefore, against the tyranny of the magistrate is not enough : there needs protection also against the tyranny of the prevailing opinion and feeling; against the tendency of society to impose, by other means than civil penalties, its own ideas and practices as rules of conduct on those who dissent from them; to fetter the development, and, if possible, prevent the formation, of any individuality not in harmony with its ways, and compels all characters to fashion themselves upon the model of its own. There is a limit to the legitimate interference of collective opinion with individual independence : and to find that limit, and maintain it against encroachment, is as indispensable to a good condition of human affairs, as protection against political despotism.

But though this proposition is not likely to be contested in general terms, the practical question, where to place the limit —how to make the fitting adjustment between individual independence and social control—is a subject on which nearly everything remains to be done. All that makes existence valuable to any one, depends on the enforcement of restraints upon the actions of other people. Some rules of conduct, therefore, must be imposed, by law in the first place, and by opinion on many things which are not fit subjects for the operation of law. What these rules should be is the principal question in human affairs; but if we except a few of the most obvious cases, it is one of those which least progress has been made in resolving. No two ages, and scarcely any two countries, have decided it alike; and the decision of one age or country is a wonder to another. Yet the people of any given age and country no more suspect any difficulty in it, than if it were a subject on which mankind had always been agreed. The rules which obtain among themselves appear to them self-evident and self-justifying. This all but universal illusion is one of the examples of the magical influence of custom, which is not only, as the proverb says, a second nature, but is continually mistaken for the first. The effect of custom, in preventing any misgivings respecting the rules of conduct which mankind impose on one another, is all the more complete because the subject is one on which it is not generally considered necessary that reasons should be given, either by one person to others or by each to himself. People are accustomed to believe, and have been encouraged in the belief by some who aspire to the character of philosophers, that their feelings, on subjects of this nature, are better than reasons, and render reasons unnecessary. The practical principle which guides them to their opinions on the regulation of human conduct, is the feeling in each person's mind that everybody should be required to act as he, and those with whom he sympathises, would like them to act. No one, indeed, acknowledges to himself that his standard of judgment is his own liking; but an opinion on a point of conduct, not supported by reasons, can only count as one person's preference; and if the reasons, when given, are a mere appeal to a similar preference felt by other people, it is still only many people's liking instead of one. To an ordinary man, however, his own preference, thus supported, is not only a perfectly satisfactory reason, but the only one he generally has for any of his notions of morality, taste, or propriety, which are not expressly written in his religious creed; and his chief guide in the interpretation even of that. Men's opinions, accordingly, on what is laudable or blamable, are affected by all the multifarious causes which influence their wishes in regard to the conduct of others, and which are as numerous as those which determine their wishes on any other subject. Sometimes their reason—at other times their prejudices or superstitions : often their social affections, not seldom their antisocial ones, their envy or jealousy, their arrogance or contemptuousness : but most commonly their desires or fears for themselves—their legitimate or illegitimate self-interest. Wherever there is an ascendant class, a large portion of the morality of the country emanates from its class interests, and its feelings of class superiority. The morality between Spartans and Helots, between planters and negroes, between princes and subjects, between nobles and roturiers, between men and women, has been for the most part the creation of these class interests and feelings : and the sentiments thus generated react in turn upon the moral feelings of the members of the ascendant class, in their relations among themselves. Where, on the other hand, a class, formerly ascendant, has lost its ascendancy, or where it ascendancy is unpopular, the prevailing moral sentiments frequently bear the impress of an impatient dislike of superiority. Another grand determining principle of the rules of conduct, both in act and forbearance, which have been enforced by law or opinion, has been the servility of mankind towards the supposed preferences or aversions of their temporal masters or of their gods. This servility, though essentially selfish, is not hypocrisy; it gives rise to perfectly genuine sentiments of abhorrence; it made men burn magicians and heretics. Among so many baser influences, the general and obvious interests of society have of course had a share, and a large one, in the direction of the moral sentiments : less, however, as a matter of reason, and on their own account, than as a consequence of the sympathies and antipathies which grew out of them : and sympathies and antipathies which had little or nothing to do with the interests of society, have made themselves felt in the establishment of moralities with quite as great force.

The likings and dislikings of society, or of some powerful portion of it, are thus the main thing which has practically determined the rules laid down for general observance, under the penalties of law or opinion. And in general, those who have been in advance of society in thought and feeling, have left this condition of things unassailed in principle, however they may have come into conflict with it in some of its details. They have occupied themselves rather in inquiring what things society ought to like or dislike, than in questioning whether its likings or dislikings should be a law to individuals. They preferred endeavouring to alter the feelings of mankind on the particular points on which they were themselves heretical, rather than make common cause in defence of freedom, with heretics generally. The only case in which the higher ground has been taken on principle and maintained with consistency, by any but an individual here and there, is that of religious belief: a case instructive in many ways, and not least so as forming a most striking instance of the fallibility of what is called the moral sense: for the *odium theologicum,* in a sincere bigot, is one of the most unequivocal cases of moral feeling. Those who first broke the yoke of what called itself the Universal Church, were in general as little willing to permit difference of religious opinion as that church itself. But when the heat of the conflict was over, without giving a complete victory to any party, and each church or sect was reduced to limit its hopes to retaining possession of the ground it already occupied; minorities, seeing that they had no chance of becoming majorities, were under the necessity of pleading to those whom they could not convert, for permission to differ. It is accordingly on this battle field, almost solely, that the rights of the individual against society have been asserted on broad grounds of principle, and the claim of society to exercise authority over dissentients openly controverted. The great writers to whom the world owes what religious liberty it possesses have mostly asserted freedom of conscience as an indefeasible right, and denied absolutely that a human being is accountable to others for his religious belief. Yet so natural to mankind is intolerance in whatever they really care about, that religious freedom has hardly anywhere been practically realised, except where religious indifference, which dislikes to have its peace disturbed by theological quarrels, has added its weight to the scale. In the minds of almost all religious persons, even in the most tolerant countries, the duty of toleration is admitted with tacit reserves. One person will bear with dissent in matters of church government, but not of dogma; another can tolerate everybody, short of a Papist or a Unitarian; another every one who believes in revealed religion; a few extend their charity a little further, but stop at the belief in a God and in a future state. Wherever the sentiment of the majority is still genuine and intense, it is found to have abated little of its claim to be obeyed.

In England, from the peculiar circumstances of our political history, though the yoke of opinion is perhaps heavier, that of law is lighter, than in most other countries of Europe; and there is considerable jealousy of direct interference, by the legislative or the executive power, with private conduct; not so much from any just regard for the independence of the individual, as from the still subsisting habit of looking on the government as representing an opposite interest to the public. The majority have not yet learnt to feel the power of the government their power, or its opinions their opinions. When they do so, individual liberty will probably be as much exposed to invasion from the government, as it already is from public opinion. But, as yet, there is a considerable amount of feeling ready to be called forth against any attempt of the law to control individuals in things in which they have not hitherto been accustomed to be controlled by it; and this with very little discrimination as to whether the matter is, or is not, within the legitimate sphere of legal control; insomuch that the feeling, highly salutary on the whole, is perhaps quite as often misplaced as well grounded in the particular instances of its application. There is, in fact, no recognised principle by which the propriety or impropriety of government interference is customarily tested. People decide according to their personal preferences. Some, whenever they see any good to be done, or evil to be remedied, would willingly instigate the government to undertake the business; while others prefer to bear almost any amount of social evil, rather than add one to the departments of human interests amenable to governmental control. And men range themselves on one or the other side in any particular case, according to this general direction of their sentiments; or according to the degree of interest which they feel in the particular thing which it is proposed that the government should do, or according to the belief they entertain that the government would, or would not, do it in the manner they prefer; but very rarely on account of any opinion to which they consistently adhere, as to what things are fit to be done by a government. And it seems to me that in consequence of this absence of rule or principle, one side is at present as often wrong as the other; the interference of government is, with about equal frequency, improperly invoked and improperly condemned.

The object of this Essay is to assert one very simple principle, as entitled to govern absolutely the dealings of society with the individual in the way of compulsion and control, whether the means used be physical force in the form of legal penalties, or the moral coercion of public opinion. That principle is, that the sole end for which mankind are warranted, individually or collectively, in interfering with the liberty of action of any of their number, is self-protection. That the only purpose for which power can be rightfully exercised over any member of a civilised community, against his will, is to prevent harm to others. His own good, either physical or moral, is not a sufficient warrant. He cannot rightfully be compelled to do or forbear because it will be better for him to do so, because it will make him happier, because, in the opinions of others, to do so would be wise, or even right. These are good reasons for remonstrating with him, or reasoning with him, or persuading him, or entreating him, but not for compelling him, or visiting him with any evil in case he do otherwise. To justify that, the conduct from which it is desired to deter him must be calculated to produce evil to some one else. The only part of the conduct of any one, for which he is amenable to society, is that which concerns others. In the part which merely concerns himself, his independence is, of right, absolute. Over himself, over his own body and mind, the individual is sovereign.

It is, perhaps, hardly necessary to say that this doctrine is meant to apply only to human beings in the maturity of their faculties. We are not speaking of children, or of young persons below the age which the law may fix as that of manhood or womanhood. Those who are still in a state to require being taken care of by others, must be protected against their own actions as well as against external injury. For the same reason, we may leave out of consideration those backward states of

society in which the race itself may be considered as in its
nonage. The early difficulties in the way of spontaneous
progress are so great, that there is seldom any choice of means
for overcoming them; and a ruler full of the spirit of
improvement is warranted in the use of any expedients that
will attain an end, perhaps otherwise unattainable. Despotism
is a legitimate mode of government in dealing with barbarians,
provided the end be their improvement, and the means
justified by actually effecting that end. Liberty, as a principle,
has no application to any state of things anterior to the
time when mankind have become capable of being improved
by free and equal discussion. Until then, there is nothing
for them but implicit obedience to an Akbar or a Charle-
magne, if they are so fortunate as to find one. But as soon
as mankind have attained the capacity of being guided to
their own improvement by conviction or persuasion (a period
long since reached in all nations with whom we need here
concern ourselves), compulsion, either in the direct form or in
that of pains and penalties for non-compliance, is no longer
admissible as a means to their own good, and justifiable only for
the security of others.

It is proper to state that I forego any advantage which could
be derived to my argument from the idea of abstract right,
as a thing independent of utility. I regard utility as the ultimate
appeal on all ethical questions; but it must be utility in the
largest sense, grounded on the permanent interests of a man as
a progressive being. Those interests, I contend, authorise the
subjection of individual spontaneity to external control, only
in respect to those actions of each, which concern the interest
of other people. If any one does an act hurtful to others,
there is a *prima facie* case for punishing him, by law, or, where
legal penalties are not safely applicable, by general disapprobation. There are also many positive acts for the benefit of
others, which he may rightfully be compelled to perform; such
as to give evidence in a court of justice; to bear his fair
share in the common defence, or in any other joint work
necessary to the interest of the society of which he enjoys
the protection; and to perform certain acts of individual
beneficence, such as saving a fellow-creature's life, or inter-

posing to protect the defenceless against ill-usage, things which whenever it is obviously a man's duty to do, he may rightfully be made responsible to society for not doing. A person may cause evil to others not only by his actions but by his inaction, and in either case he is justly accountable to them for the injury. The latter case, it is true, requires a much more cautious exercise of compulsion than the former. To make any one answerable for doing evil to others is the rule; to make him answerable for not preventing evil is, comparatively speaking, the exception. Yet there are many cases clear enough and grave enough to justify that exception. In all things which regard the external relations of the individual, he is *de jure* amenable to those whose interests are concerned, and, if need be, to society as their protector. There are often good reasons for not holding him to the responsibility; but these reasons must arise from the special expediencies of the case: either because it is a kind of case in which he is on the whole likely to act better, when left to his own discretion, than when controlled in any way in which society have it in their power to control him; or because the attempt to exercise control would produce other evils, greater than those which it would prevent. When such reasons as these preclude the enforcement of responsibility, the conscience of the agent himself should step into the vacant judgment seat, and protect those interests of others which have no external protection; judging himself all the more rigidly, because the case does not admit of his being made accountable to the judgment of his fellow-creatures.

But there is a sphere of action in which society, as distinguished from the individual, has, if any, only an indirect interest; comprehending all that portion of a person's life and conduct which affects only himself, or if it also affects others, only with their free, voluntary, and undeceived consent and participation. When I say only himself, I mean directly, and in the first instance; for whatever affects himself, may affect others through himself; and the objection which may be grounded on this contingency, will receive consideration in the sequel. This, then, is the appropriate region of human liberty. It compromises, first, the inward domain of consciousness; demanding liberty of conscience in the most comprehensive sense; liberty of thought and feeling; absolute freedom of opinion and sentiment on all subjects, practical or speculative, scientific, moral, or theological. The liberty of expressing and publishing opinions may seem to fall under a different principle, since it belongs to that part of the conduct of an individual which concerns other people; but, being almost of as much importance as the liberty of thought itself, and resting in great part on the same reasons, is practically inseparable from it. Secondly, the principle requires liberty of tastes and pursuits; of framing the plan of our life to suit our own character; of doing as we like, subject to such consequences as may follow : without impediment from our fellow-creatures, so long as what we do does not harm them, even though they should think our conduct foolish, perverse, or wrong. Thirdly, from this liberty of each individual, follows the liberty, within the same limits, of combination among individuals; freedom to unite, for any purpose not involving harm to others : the persons combining being supposed to be of full age, and not forced or deceived.

No society in which these liberties are not, on the whole, respected, is free, whatever may be its form of government; and none is completely free in which they do not exist absolute and unqualified. The only freedom which deserves the name, is that of pursuing our own good in our own way, so long as we do not attempt to deprive others of theirs, or impede their efforts to obtain it. Each is the proper guardian of his own health, whether bodily, *or* mental and spiritual. Mankind are greater gainers by suffering each other to live as seems good to themselves, than by compelling each to live as seems good to the rest.

Though this doctrine is anything but new, and, to some persons, may have the air of a truism, there is no doctrine which stands more directly opposed to the general tendency of existing opinion and practice. Society has expended fully as much effort in the attempt (according to its lights) to compel people to conform to its notions of personal as of social excellence. The ancient commonwealths thought themselves entitled to practise, and the ancient philosophers countenanced, the regulation of every part of private conduct by public authority, on the ground that the State had a deep interest in the whole bodily and mental discipline of every one of its citizens; a mode of thinking which may have been admissible in small republics surrounded by powerful enemies, in constant peril of being subverted by foreign attack or internal commotion, and to which even a short interval of relaxed energy and self-command might so easily be fatal that they could not afford to wait for the salutary permanent effects of freedom. In the modern world, the greater size of political communities, and, above all, the separation between spiritual and temporal authority (which placed the direction of men's consciences in other hands than those which controlled their worldly affairs), prevented so great an interference by law in the details of private life; but the engines of moral repression have been wielded more strenuously against divergence from the reigning opinion in self-regarding, than even in social matters; religion, the most powerful of the elements which have entered into the formation of moral feeling, having almost always been governed either by the ambition of a hierarchy, seeking control over every department of human conduct, or by the spirit of Puritanism. And some of those modern reformers who have placed themselves in strongest opposition to the religions of the past, have been noway behind either churches or sects in their assertion of the right of spiritual domination : M. Comte, in particular, whose social system, as unfolded in his *Système de Politique Positive,* aims at establishing (though by moral more than by legal appliances) a despotism of society over the individual, surpassing anything contemplated in the political ideal of the most rigid disciplinarian among the ancient philosophers.

Apart from the peculiar tenets of individual thinkers, there is also in the world at large an increasing inclination to stretch unduly the powers of society over the individual, both by the force of opinion and even by that of legislation; and as the tendency of all the changes taking place in the world is to strengthen society, and diminish the power of the

individual, this encroachment is not one of the evils which
tend spontaneously to disappear, but, on the contrary, to
grow more and more formidable. The disposition of mankind,
whether as rulers or as fellow-citizens, to impose their own
opinions and inclinations as a rule of conduct on others, is
so energetically supported by some of the best and by some of
the worst feelings incident to human nature, that it is hardly
ever kept under restraint by anything but want of power;
and as the power is not declining, but growing, unless a strong
barrier of moral conviction can be raised against the mischief,
we must expect, in the present circumstances of the world, to
see it increase.

It will be convenient for the argument, if, instead of at
once entering upon the general thesis, we confine ourselves in
the first instance to a single branch of it, on which the principle
here stated is, if not fully, yet to a certain point, recognised
by the current opinions. This one branch is the Liberty of
Thought: from which it is impossible to separate the cognate
liberty of speaking and of writing. Although these liberties,
to some considerable amount, form part of the political morality
of all countries which profess religious toleration and free
institutions, the grounds, both philosophical and practical, on
which they rest, are perhaps not so familiar to the general
mind, nor so thoroughly appreciated by many even of the
leaders of opinion, as might have been expected. Those
grounds, when rightly understood, are of much wider application than to only one division of the subject, and a thorough
consideration of this part of the question will be found the
best introduction to the remainder. Those to whom nothing
which I am about to say will be new, may therefore, I hope,
excuse me, if on a subject which for now three centuries has
been so often discussed, I venture on one discussion more.

CHAPTER II

OF THE LIBERTY OF THOUGHT AND DISCUSSION

The time, it is to be hoped, is gone by, when any defence would be necessary of the "liberty of the press" as one of the securities against corrupt or tyrannical government. No argument, we may suppose, can now be needed, against permitting a legislature or an executive, not identified in interest with the people, to prescribe opinions to them, and determine what doctrines or what arguments they shall be allowed to hear. This aspect of the question, besides, has been so often and so triumphantly enforced by preceding writers, that it needs not be specially insisted on in this place. Though the law of England, on the subject of the press, is as servile to this day as it was in the time of the Tudors, there is little danger of its being actually put in force against political discussion, except during some temporary panic, when fear of insurrection drives ministers and judges from their propriety;[1]

---

[1] These words had scarcely been written, when, as if to give them an emphatic contradiction, occurred the Government Press Prosecutions of 1858. That ill-judged interference with the liberty of public discussion has not, however, induced me to alter a single word in the text, nor has it at all weakened my conviction that, moments of panic excepted, the era of pains and penalties for political discussion has, in our own country, passed away. For, in the first place, the prosecutions were not persisted in; and, in the second, they were never, properly speaking, political prosecutions. The offence charged was not that of criticising institutions, or the acts or persons of rulers, but of circulating what was deemed an immoral doctrine, the lawfulness of Tyrannicide.

If the arguments of the present chapter are of any validity, there ought to exist the fullest liberty of professing and discussing, as a matter of ethical conviction, any doctrine, however immoral it may be considered. It would, therefore, be irrelevant and out of place to examine here, whether the doctrine of Tyrannicide deserves that title. I shall content myself with saying that the subject has been at all times one of the open questions of morals; that the

and, speaking generally, it is not, in constitutional countries, to be apprehended, that the government, whether completely responsible to the people or not, will often attempt to control the expression of opinion, except when in doing so it makes itself the organ of the general intolerance of the public. Let us suppose, therefore, that the government is entirely at one with the people, and never thinks of exerting any power of coercion unless in agreement with what it conceives to be their voice. But I deny the right of the people to exercise such coercion, either by themselves or by their government. The power itself is illegitimate. The best government has no more title to it than the worst. It is as noxious, or more noxious, when exerted in accordance with public opinion, than when in opposition to it. If all mankind minus one were of one opinion, and only one person were of the contrary opinion, mankind would be no more justified in silencing that one person, than he, if he had the power, would be justified in silencing mankind. Were an opinion a personal possession of no value except to the owner; if to be obstructed in the enjoyment of it were simply a private injury, it would make some difference whether the injury was inflicted only on a few persons or on many. But the peculiar evil of silencing the expression of an opinion is, that it is robbing the human race; posterity as well as the existing generation; those who dissent from the opinion, still more than those who hold it. If the opinion is right, they are deprived of the opportunity of exchanging error for truth: if wrong,

---

act of a private citizen in striking down a criminal, who, by raising himself above the law, has placed himself beyond the reach of legal punishment or control, has been accounted by whole nations, and by some of the best and wisest of men, not a crime, but an act of exalted virtue; and that, right or wrong, it is not of the nature of assassination, but of civil war. As such, I hold that the instigation to it, in a specific case, may be a proper subject of punishment, but only if an overt act has followed, and at least a probable connection can be established between the act and the instigation. Even then, it is not a foreign government, but the very government assailed, which alone, in the exercise of self-defence, can legitimately punish attacks directed against its own existence.

they lose, what is almost as great a benefit, the clearer perception and livelier impression of truth, produced by its collision with error.

It is necessary to consider separately these two hypotheses, each of which has a distinct branch of the argument corresponding to it. We can never be sure that the opinion we are endeavouring to stifle is a false opinion; and if we were sure, stifling it would be an evil still.

First: the opinion which it is attempted to suppress by authority may possibly be true. Those who desire to suppress it, of course deny its truth; but they are not infallible. They have no authority to decide the question for all mankind, and exclude every other person from the means of judging. To refuse a hearing to an opinion, because they are sure that it is false, is to assume that *their* certainty is the same thing as *absolute* certainty. All silencing of discussion is an assumption of infallibility. Its condemnation may be allowed to rest on this common argument, not the worse for being common.

Unfortunately for the good sense of mankind, the fact of their fallibility is far from carrying the weight in their practical judgment which is always allowed to it in theory; for while every one well knows himself to be fallible, few think it necessary to take any precautions against their own fallibility, or admit the supposition that any opinion, of which they feel very certain, may be one of the examples of the error to which they acknowledge themselves to be liable. Absolute princes, or others who are accustomed to unlimited deference, usually feel this complete confidence in their own opinions on nearly all subjects. People more happily situated, who sometimes hear their opinions disputed, and are not wholly unused to be set right when they are wrong, place the same unbounded reliance only on such of their opinions as are shared by all who surround them, or to whom they habitually defer; for in proportion to a man's want of confidence in his own solitary judgment, does he usually repose, with implicit trust, on the infallibility of "the world" in general. And the world, to each individual, means the part of it with which he comes in contact; his party, his sect, his church, his class of society; the man may be called, by comparison, almost liberal and large-minded to whom it means anything so comprehensive as his own country or his own age. Nor is his faith in this collective authority at all shaken by his being aware that other ages, countries, sects, churches, classes, and parties have thought, and even now think, the exact reverse. He devolves upon his own world the responsibility of being in the right against the dissentient worlds of other people; and it never troubles him that mere accident has decided which of these numerous worlds is the object of his reliance, and that the same causes which make him a Churchman in London, would have made him a Buddhist or a Confucian in Pekin. Yet it is as evident in itself, as any amount of argument can make it, that ages are no more infallible than individuals; every age having held many opinions which subsequent ages have deemed not only false but absurd; and it is as certain that many opinions now general will be rejected by future ages, as it is that many, once general, are rejected by the present.

The objection likely to be made to this argument would probably take some such form as the following. There is no greater assumption of infallibility in forbidding the propagation of error, than in any other thing which is done by public authority on its own judgment and responsibility. Judgment is given to men that they may use it. Because it may be used erroneously, are men to be told that they ought not to use it at all? To prohibit what they think pernicious, is not claiming exemption from error, but fulfilling the duty incumbent on them, although fallible, of acting on their conscientious conviction. If we were never to act on our opinions, because those opinions may be wrong, we should leave all our interests uncared for, and all our duties unperformed. An objection which applies to all conduct can be no valid objection to any conduct in particular. It is the duty of governments, and of individuals, to form the truest opinions they can; to form them carefully, and never impose them upon others unless they are quite sure of being right. But when they are sure (such reasoners may say), it is not conscientiousness but cowardice to shrink from acting on their opinions, and allow doctrines which they honestly think dangerous to the welfare of mankind, either in this life or in another, to be scattered abroad without restraint, because other people, in less enlightened times, have persecuted opinions now believed to be true. Let us take care, it may be said, not to make the same mistake : but governments and nations have made mistakes in other things, which are not denied to be fit subjects for the exercise of authority : they have laid on bad taxes, made unjust wars. Ought we therefore to lay on no taxes, and, under whatever provocation, make no wars? Men, and governments, must act to the best of their ability. There is no such thing as absolute certainty, but there is assurance sufficient for the purposes of human life. We may, and must, assume our opinion to be true for the guidance of our own conduct : and it is assuming no more when we forbid bad men to pervert society by the propagation of opinions which we regard as false and pernicious.

I answer, that it is assuming very much more. There is the greatest difference between presuming an opinion to be true, because, with every opportunity for contesting it, it has not been refuted, and assuming its truth for the purpose of not permitting its refutation. Complete liberty of contradicting and disproving our opinion is the very condition which justifies us in assuming its truth for purposes of action; and on no other terms can a being with human faculties have any rational assurance of being right.

When we consider either the history of opinion, or the ordinary conduct of human life, to what is it to be ascribed that the one and the other are no worse than they are? Not certainly to the inherent force of the human understanding; for, on any matter not self-evident, there are ninety-nine persons totally incapable of judging of it for one who is capable; and the capacity of the hundredth person is only comparative; for the majority of the eminent men of every past generation held many opinions now known to be erroneous, and did or approved numerous things which no one will now justify. Why is it, then, that there is on the whole a preponderance among mankind of rational opinions and rational conduct? If there really is this preponderance—

which there must be unless human affairs are, and have always
been, in an almost desperate state—it is owing to a quality of
the human mind, the source of everything respectable in man
either as an intellectual or as a moral being, namely, that his
errors are corrigible. He is capable of rectifying his mistakes,
by discussion and experience. Not by experience alone. There
must be discussion, to show how experience is to be interpreted. Wrong opinions and practices gradually yield to fact
and argument; but facts and arguments, to produce any effect
on the mind, must be brought before it. Very few facts are
able to tell their own story, without comments to bring out
their meaning. The whole strength and value, then, of human
judgment, depending on the one property, that it can be set
right when it is wrong, reliance can be placed on it only when
the means of setting it right are kept constantly at hand. In
the case of any person whose judgment is really deserving of
confidence, how has it become so? Because he has kept his
mind open to criticism of his opinions and conduct. Because
it has been his practice to listen to all that could be said
against him; to profit by as much of it as was just, and expound
to himself, and upon occasion to others, the fallacy of what
was fallacious. Because he has felt, that the only way in which
a human being can make some approach to knowing the
whole of a subject, is by hearing what can be said about it
by persons of every variety of opinion, and studying all
modes in which it can be looked at by every character of
mind. No wise man ever acquired his wisdom in any mode
but this; nor is it in the nature of human intellect to
become wise in any other manner. The steady habit of
correcting and completing his own opinion by collating it with
those of others, so far from causing doubt and hesitation in
carrying it into practice, is the only stable foundation for a
just reliance on it: for, being cognisant of all that can,
at least obviously, be said against him, and having taken
up his position against all gainsayers—knowing that he has
sought for objections and difficulties, instead of avoiding
them, and has shut out no light which can be thrown upon the
subject from any quarter—he has a right to think his judg-

ment better than that of any person, or any multitude, who have not gone through a similar process.

It is not too much to require that what the wisest of mankind, those who are best entitled to trust their own judgment, find necessary to warrant their relying on it, should be submitted to by that miscellaneous collection of a few wise and many foolish individuals, called the public. The most intolerant of churches, the Roman Catholic Church, even at the canonisation of a saint, admits, and listens patiently to, a " devil's advocate." The holiest of men, it appears, cannot be admitted to posthumous honours, until all that the devil could say against him is known and weighed. If even the Newtonian philosophy were not permitted to be questioned, mankind could not feel as complete assurance of its truth as they now do. The beliefs which we have most warrant for have no safeguard to rest on, but a standing invitation to the whole world to prove them unfounded. If the challenge is not accepted, or is accepted and the attempt fails, we are far enough from certainty still; but we have done the best that the existing state of human reason admits of; we have neglected nothing that could give the truth a chance of reaching us: if the lists are kept open, we may hope that if there be a better truth, it will be found when the human mind is capable of receiving it; and in the meantime we may rely on having attained such approach to truth as is possible in our own day. This is the amount of certainty attainable by a fallible being, and this the sole way of attaining it.

Strange it is, that men should admit the validity of the arguments for free discussion, but object to their being " pushed to an extreme;" not seeing that unless the reasons are good for an extreme case, they are not good for any case. Strange that they should imagine that they are not assuming infallibility, when they acknowledge that there should be free discussion on all subjects which can possibly be *doubtful,* but think that some particular principle or doctrine should be forbidden to be questioned because it is so *certain,* that is, because *they are certain* that it is certain. To call any pro-

position certain, while there is any one who would deny
its certainty if permitted, but who is not permitted, is to
assume that we ourselves, and those who agree with us,
are the judges of certainty, and judges without hearing the
other side.

In the present age—which has been described as " destitute
of faith, but terrified at scepticism "—in which people feel
sure, not so much that their opinions are true, as that they
should not know what to do without them—the claims of
an opinion to be protected from public attack are rested not
so much on its truth, as on its importance to society. There
are, it is alleged, certain beliefs so useful, not to say indispensable, to well-being that it is as much the duty of
governments to uphold those beliefs, as to protect any other of
the interests of society. In a case of such necessity, and so
directly in the line of their duty, something less than infallibility may, it is maintained, warrant, and even bind, governments to act on their own opinion, confirmed by the general
opinion of mankind. It is also often argued, and still oftener
thought, that none but bad men would desire to weaken these
salutary beliefs; and there can be nothing wrong, it is
thought, in restraining bad men, and prohibiting what only
such men would wish to practise. This mode of thinking
makes the justification of restraints on discussion not a question of the truth of doctrines, but of their usefulness; and
flatters itself by that means to escape the responsibility of
claiming to be an infallible judge of opinions. But those who
thus satisfy themselves, do not perceive that the assumption
of infallibility is merely shifted from one point to another.
The usefulness of an opinion is itself matter of opinion : as
disputable, as open to discussion, and requiring discussion as
much as the opinion itself. There is the same need of an
infallible judge of opinions to decide an opinion to be noxious,
as to decide it to be false, unless the opinion condemned
has full opportunity of defending itself. And it will not do
to say that the heretic may be allowed to maintain the utility
or harmlessness of his opinion, though forbidden to maintain
its truth. The truth of an opinion is part of its utility.
If we would know whether or not it is desirable that a

proposition should be believed, is it possible to exclude the consideration of whether or not it is true? In the opinion, not of bad men, but of the best men, no belief which is contrary to truth can be really useful : and can you prevent such men from urging that plea, when they are charged with culpability for denying some doctrine which they are told is useful, but which they believe to be false? Those who are on the side of received opinions never fail to take all possible advantage of this plea; you do not find *them* handling the question of utility as if it could be completely abstracted from that of truth : on the contrary, it is, above all, because their doctrine is " the truth," that the knowledge or the belief of it is held to be so indispensable. There can be no fair discussion of the question of usefulness when an argument so vital may be employed on one side, but not on the other. And in point of fact, when law or public feeling do not permit the truth of an opinion to be disputed, they are just as little tolerant of a denial of its usefulness. The utmost they allow is an extenu-ation of its absolute necessity, or of the positive guilt of rejecting it.

In order more fully to illustrate the mischief of denying a hearing to opinions because we, in our own judgment, have condemned them, it will be desirable to fix down the dis-cussion to a concrete case; and I choose, by preference, the cases which are least favourable to me—in which the argu-ment against freedom of opinion, both on the score of truth and on that of utility, is considered the strongest. Let the opinions impugned be the belief in a God and in a future state, or any of the commonly received doctrines of morality. To fight the battle on such ground gives a great advantage to an unfair antagonist; since he will be sure to say (and many who have no desire to be unfair will say it internally), Are these the doctrines which you do not deem sufficiently certain to be taken under the protection of law? Is the belief in a God one of the opinions to feel sure of which you hold to be assuming infallibility? But I must be per-mitted to observe, that it is not the feeling sure of a doctrine (be it what it may) which I call an assumption of infallibility. It is the undertaking to decide that question *for others*, without

allowing them to hear what can be said on the contrary side.
And I denounce and reprobate this pretension not the less,
if put forth on the side of my most solemn convictions.
However positive any one's persuasion may be, not only of the
falsity but of the pernicious consequences—not only of the
pernicious consequences, but (to adopt expressions which I
altogether condemn) the immorality and impiety of an opinion;
yet if, in pursuance of that private judgment, though backed
by the public judgment of his country or his contemporaries,
he prevents the opinion from being heard in its defence, he
assumes infallibility.   And so far from the assumption
being less objectionable or less dangerous because the
opinion is called immoral or impious, this is the case
of all others in which it is most fatal.   These are exactly
the occasions on which the men of one generation commit
those dreadful mistakes which excite the astonishment and
horror of posterity.   It is among such that we find the
instances memorable in history, when the arm of the law has
been employed to root out the best men and the noblest
doctrines; with deplorable success as to the men, though
some of the doctrines have survived to be (as if in mockery)
invoked in defence of similar conduct towards those who
dissent from *them,* or from their received interpretation.

Mankind can hardly be too often reminded, that there was
once a man named Socrates, between whom and the legal
authorities and public opinion of his time there took place a
memorable collision. Born in an age and country abounding
in individual greatness, this man has been handed down to us
by those who best knew both him and the age, as the most
virtuous man in it; while *we* know him as the head and
prototype of all subsequent teachers of virtue, the source
equally of the lofty inspiration of Plato and the judicious
utilitarianism of Aristotle, "*i maestri di color che sanno,*"
the two headsprings of ethical as of all other philosophy.
This acknowledged master of all the eminent thinkers who
have since lived—whose fame, still growing after more than
two thousand years, all but outweighs the whole remainder
of the names which make his native city illustrious—was
put to death by his countrymen, after a judicial conviction,

for impiety and immorality. Impiety, in denying the gods recognised by the State; indeed his accuser asserted (see the " Apologia ") that he believed in no gods at all. Immorality, in being, by his doctrines and instructions, a " corruptor of youth." Of these charges the tribunal, there is every ground for believing, honestly found him guilty, and condemned the man who probably of all then born had deserved best of mankind to be put to death as a criminal.

To pass from this to the only other instance of judicial iniquity, the mention of which, after the condemnation of Socrates, would not be an anti-climax: the event which took place on Calvary rather more than eighteen hundred years ago. The man who left on the memory of those who witnessed his life and conversation such an impression of his moral grandeur that eighteen subsequent centuries have done homage to him as the Almighty in person, was ignominiously put to death, as what? As a blasphemer. Men did not merely mistake their benefactor; they mistook him for the exact contrary of what he was, and treated him as that prodigy of impiety which they themselves are now held to be for their treatment of him. The feelings with which mankind now regard these lamentable transactions, especially the later of the two, render them extremely unjust in their judgment of the unhappy actors. These were, to all appearance, not bad men—not worse than men commonly are, but rather the contrary; men who possessed in a full, or somewhat more than a full measure, the religious, moral, and patriotic feelings of their time and people : the very kind of men who, in all times, our own included, have every chance of passing through life blameless and respected. The high-priest who rent his garments when the words were pronounced, which, according to all the ideas of his country, constituted the blackest guilt, was in all probability quite as sincere in his horror and indignation as the generality of respectable and pious men now are in the religious and moral sentiments they profess; and most of those who now shudder at his conduct, if they had lived in his time, and been born Jews, would have acted precisely as he did. Orthodox Christians who are tempted to think that those who stoned to death the first martyrs must have been worse men than they themselves are, ought to remember that one of those persecutors was Saint Paul.

Let us add one more example, the most striking of all, if the impressiveness of an error is measured by the wisdom and virtue of him who falls into it. If ever any one, possessed of power, had grounds for thinking himself the best and most enlightened among his contemporaries, it was the Emperor Marcus Aurelius. Absolute monarch of the whole civilised world, he preserved through life not only the most unblemished justice, but what was less to be expected from his Stoical breeding, the tenderest heart. The few failings which are attributed to him were all on the side of indulgence : while his writings, the highest ethical product of the ancient mind, differ scarcely perceptibly, if they differ at all, from the most characteristic teachings of Christ. This man, a better Christian in all but the dogmatic sense of the word than almost any of the ostensibly Christian sovereigns who have since reigned, persecuted Christianity. Placed at the summit of all the previous attainments of humanity, with an open, unfettered intellect, and a character which led him of himself to embody in his moral writings the Christian ideal, he yet failed to see that Christianity was to be a good and not an evil to the world, with his duties to which he was so deeply penetrated. Existing society he knew to be in a deplorable state. But such as it was, he saw, or thought he saw, that it was held together, and prevented from being worse, by belief and reverence of the received divinities. As a ruler of mankind, he deemed it his duty not to suffer society to fall in pieces ; and saw not how, if its existing ties were removed, any others could be formed which could again knit it together. The new religion openly aimed at dissolving these ties : unless, therefore, it was his duty to adopt that religion, it seemed to be his duty to put it down. Inasmuch then as the theology of Christianity did not appear to him true or of divine origin; inasmuch as this strange history of a crucified God was not credible to him, and a system which purported to rest entirely upon a foundation to him so wholly unbelievable, could not be foreseen by him to be that renovating agency which, after all abatements, it has in fact proved to be; the gentlest and most amiable of philosophers and rulers, under a solemn sense of duty, authorised the persecution of Christianity. To my mind this is one of the most tragical facts in all history. It is a bitter thought, how different a thing the Christianity of the world might have been, if the Christian faith had been adopted as the religion of the empire under the auspices of Marcus Aurelius instead of those of Constantine. But it would be equally unjust to him and false to truth to deny, that no one plea which can be urged for punishing anti-Christian teaching was wanting to Marcus Aurelius for punishing, as he did, the propagation of Christianity. No Christian more firmly believes that Atheism is false, and tends to the dissolution of society, than Marcus Aurelius believed the same things of Christianity; he who, of all men then living, might have been thought the most capable of appreciating it. Unless any one who approves of punishment for the promulgation of opinions, flatters himself that he is a wiser and better man than Marcus Aurelius—more deeply versed in the wisdom of his time, more elevated in his intellect above it —more earnest in his search for truth, or more single-minded in his devotion to it when found; let him abstain from that assumption of the joint infallibility of himself and the multitude, which the great Antoninus made with so unfortunate a result.

Aware of the impossibility of defending the use of punishment for restraining irreligious opinions by any argument which will not justify Marcus Antoninus, the enemies of religious freedom, when hard pressed, occasionally accept this consequence, and say, with Dr. Johnson, that the persecutors of Christianity were in the right; that persecution is an ordeal through which truth ought to pass, and always passes successfully, legal penalties being, in the end, powerless against truth, though sometimes beneficially effective against mischievous errors. This is a form of the argument for religious intolerance sufficiently remarkable not to be passed without notice.

A theory which maintains that truth may justifiably be persecuted because persecution cannot possibly do it any

harm, cannot be charged with being intentionally hostile
to the reception of new truths; but we cannot commend
the generosity of its dealing with the persons to whom mankind are indebted for them. To discover to the world something which deeply concerns it, and of which it was previously
ignorant; to prove to it that it had been mistaken on some
vital point of temporal or spiritual interest, is as important a
service as a human being can render to his fellow-creatures,
and in certain cases, as in those of the early Christians and
of the Reformers, those who think with Dr. Johnson believe
it to have been the most precious gift which could be bestowed
on mankind. That the authors of such splendid benefits should
be requited by martyrdom; that their reward should be to
be dealt with as the vilest of criminals, is not, upon this
theory, a deplorable error and misfortune, for which humanity
should mourn in sackcloth and ashes, but the normal and justifiable state of things. The propounder of a new truth, according to this doctrine, should stand, as stood, in the legislation
of the Locrians, the proposer of a new law, with a halter
round his neck, to be instantly tightened if the public assembly
did not, on hearing his reasons, then and there adopt his proposition. People who defend this mode of treating benefactors cannot be supposed to set much value on the benefit;
and I believe this view of the subject is mostly confined
to the sort of persons who think that new truths may have been
desirable once, but that we have had enough of them now.

But, indeed, the dictum that truth always triumphs over
persecution is one of those pleasant falsehoods which men
repeat after one another till they pass into commonplace, but
which all experience refutes. History teems with instances of
truth put down by persecution. If not suppressed for ever,
it may be thrown back for centuries. To speak only of
religious opinions : the Reformation broke out at least twenty
times before Luther, and was put down. Arnold of Brescia
was put down. Fra Dolcino was put down. Savonarola was
put down. The Albigeois were put down. The Vaudois
were put down. The Lollards were put down. The Hussites
were put down. Even after the era of Luther, wherever
persecution was persisted in, it was successful. In Spain,

Italy, Flanders, the Austrian empire, Protestantism was rooted out; and, most likely, would have been so in England, had Queen Mary lived, or Queen Elizabeth died. Persecution has always succeeded, save where the heretics were too strong a party to be effectually persecuted. No reasonable person can doubt that Christianity might have been extirpated in the Roman Empire. It spread, and became predominant, because the persecutions were only occasional, lasting but a short time, and separated by long intervals of almost undisturbed propagandism. It is a piece of idle sentimentality that truth, merely as truth, has any inherent power denied to error of prevailing against the dungeon and the stake. Men are not more zealous for truth than they often are for error, and a sufficient application of legal or even of social penalties will generally succeed in stopping the propagation of either. The real advantage which truth has consists in this, that when an opinion is true, it may be extinguished once, twice, or many times, but in the course of ages there will generally be found persons to rediscover it, until some one of its reappearances falls on a time when from favourable circumstances it escapes persecution until it has made such head as to withstand all subsequent attempts to suppress it.

It will be said, that we do not now put to death the introducers of new opinions : we are not like our fathers who slew the prophets, we even build sepulchres to them. It is true we no longer put heretics to death; and the amount of penal infliction which modern feeling would probably tolerate, even against the most obnoxious opinions, is not sufficient to extirpate them. But let us not flatter ourselves that we are yet free from the stain even of legal persecution. Penalties for opinion, or at least for its expression, still exist by law; and their enforcement is not, even in these times, so unexampled as to make it at all incredible that they may some day be revived in full force. In the year 1857, at the summer assizes of the county of Cornwall, an unfortunate man,[2] said to be of unexceptionable conduct in all relations of life, was sentenced to twenty-one months' imprisonment, for uttering, and writing

[2] Thomas Pooley, Bodmin Assizes, July 31, 1857. In December following, he received a free pardon from the Crown.

on a gate, some offensive words concerning Christianity. Within a month of the same time, at the Old Bailey, two persons, on two separate occasions,[3] were rejected as jurymen, and one of them grossly insulted by the judge and by one of the counsel, because they honestly declared that they had no theological belief; and a third, a foreigner,[4] for the same reason, was denied justice against a thief. This refusal of redress took place in virtue of the legal doctrine, that no person can be allowed to give evidence in a court of justice who does not profess belief in a God (any god is sufficient) and in a future state; which is equivalent to declaring such persons to be outlaws, excluded from the protection of the tribunals; who may not only be robbed or assaulted with impunity, if no one but themselves, or persons of similar opinions, be present, but any one else may be robbed or assaulted with impunity, if the proof of the fact depends on their evidence. The assumption on which this is grounded is that the oath is worthless of a person who does not believe in a future state; a proposition which betokens much ignorance of history in those who assent to it (since it is historically true that a large proportion of infidels in all ages have been persons of distinguished integrity and honour); and would be maintained by no one who had the smallest conception how many of the persons in greatest repute with the world, both for virtues and attainments, are well known, at least to their intimates, to be unbelievers. The rule, besides, is suicidal, and cuts away its own foundation. Under pretence that atheists must be liars, it admits the testimony of all atheists who are willing to lie, and rejects only those who brave the obloquy of publicly confessing a detested creed rather than affirm a falsehood. A rule thus self-convicted of absurdity so far as regards its professed purpose, can be kept in force only as a badge of hatred, a relic of persecution; a persecution, too, having the peculiarity that the qualification for undergoing it is the being clearly proved not to deserve

[3] George Jacob Holyoake, August 17, 1857; Edward Truelove, July, 1857.
[4] Baron de Gleichen, Marlborough Street Police Court, August 4, 1857.

it. The rule, and the theory it implies, are hardly less insulting to believers than to infidels. For if he who does not believe in a future state necessarily lies, it follows that they who do believe are only prevented from lying, if prevented they are, by the fear of hell. We will not do the authors and abettors of the rule the injury of supposing that the conception which they have formed of Christian virtue is drawn from their own consciousness.

These, indeed, are but rags and remnants of persecution, and may be thought to be not so much an indication of the wish to persecute, as an example of that very frequent infirmity of English minds, which makes them take a preposterous pleasure in the assertion of a bad principle, when they are no longer bad enough to desire to carry it really into practice. But unhappily there is no security in the state of the public mind that the suspension of worse forms of legal persecution, which has lasted for about the space of a generation, will continue. In this age the quiet surface of routine is as often ruffled by attempts to resuscitate past evils, as to introduce new benefits. What is boasted of at the present time as the revival of religion, is always, in narrow and uncultivated minds, at least as much the revival of bigotry; and where there is the strong permanent leaven of intolerance in the feelings of a people, which at all times abides in the middle classes of this country, it needs but little to provoke them into actively persecuting those whom they have never ceased to think proper objects of persecution.[5] For it is this—it is

[5] Ample warning may be drawn from the large infusion of the passions of a persecutor, which mingled with the general display of the worst parts of our national character on the occasion of the Sepoy insurrection. The ravings of fanatics or charlatans from the pulpit may be unworthy of notice; but the heads of the Evangelical party have announced as their principle for the government of Hindoos and Mahomedans, that no schools be supported by public money in which the Bible is not taught, and by necessary consequence that no public employment be given to any but real or pretended Christians. An Under-Secretary of State, in a speech delivered to his constituents on the 12th of November, 1857, is reported to have said: " Toleration of their faith " (the faith of a hundred millions of British subjects), " the superstition which they

the opinions men entertain, and the feelings they cherish, respecting those who disown the beliefs they deem important, which makes this country not a place of mental freedom. For a long time past, the chief mischief of the legal penalties is that they strengthen the social stigma. It is that stigma which is really effective, and so effective is it, that the profession of opinions which are under the ban of society is much less common in England than is, in many other countries, the avowal of those which incur risk of judicial punishment. In respect to all persons but those whose pecuniary circumstances make them independent of the good will of other people, opinion, on this subject, is as efficacious as law; men might as well be imprisoned, as excluded from the means of earning their bread. Those whose bread is already secured, and who desire no favours from men in power, or from bodies of men, or from the public, have nothing to fear from the open avowal of any opinions, but to be ill-thought of and ill-spoken of, and this it ought not to require a very heroic mould to enable them to bear. There is no room for any appeal *ad misericordiam* in behalf of such persons. But though we do not now inflict so much evil on those who think differently from us as it was formerly our custom to do, it may be that we do ourselves as much evil as ever by our treatment of them. Socrates was put to death, but Socratic philosophy rose like the sun in heaven, and spread its illumination over the whole intellectual firmament. Christians were

---

called religion, by the British Government, had had the effect of retarding the ascendancy of the British name, and preventing the salutary growth of Christianity. . . . Toleration was the great cornerstone of the religious liberties of this country; but do not let them abuse that precious word toleration. As he understood it, it meant the complete liberty to all, freedom of worship, *among Christians, who worshipped upon the same foundation*. It meant toleration of all sects and denominations of *Christians who believed in the one mediation.*" I desire to call attention to the fact, that a man who has been deemed fit to fill a high office in the government of this country under a liberal ministry, maintains the doctrine that all who do not believe in the divinity of Christ are beyond the pale of toleration. Who, after this imbecile display, can indulge the illusion that religious persecution has passed away, never to return?

cast to the lions, but the Christian church grew up a stately and spreading tree, overtopping the older and less vigorous growths, and stifling them by its shade. Our merely social intolerance kills no one, roots out no opinions, but induces men to disguise them, or to abstain from any active effort for their diffusion. With us, heretical opinions do not perceptibly gain, or even lose, ground in each decade or generation; they never blaze out far and wide, but continue to smoulder in the narrow circles of thinking and studious persons among whom they originate, without ever lighting up the general affairs of mankind with either a true or a deceptive light. And thus is kept up a state of things very satisfactory to some minds, because, without the unpleasant process of fining or imprisoning anybody, it maintains all prevailing opinions outwardly undisturbed, while it does not absolutely interdict the exercise of reason by dissentients afflicted with the malady of thought. A convenient plan for having peace in the intellectual world, and keeping all things going on therein very much as they do already. But the price paid for this sort of intellectual pacification is the sacrifice of the entire moral courage of the human mind. A state of things in which a large portion of the most active and inquiring intellects find it advisable to keep the general principles and grounds of their convictions within their own breasts, and attempt, in what they address to the public, to fit as much as they can of their own conclusions to premises which they have internally renounced, cannot send forth the open, fearless characters, and logical, consistent intellects who once adorned the thinking world. The sort of men who can be looked for under it, are either mere conformers to commonplace, or time-servers for truth, whose arguments on all great subjects are meant for their hearers, and are not those which have convinced themselves. Those who avoid this alternative, do so by narrowing their thoughts and interest to things which can be spoken of without venturing within the region of principles, that is, to small practical matters, which would come right of themselves, if but the minds of mankind were strengthened and enlarged, and which will never be made effectually right until then: while that which would strengthen and enlarge men's minds, free and daring speculation on the highest subjects, is abandoned.

Those in whose eyes this reticence on the part of heretics is no evil should consider, in the first place, that in consequence of it there is never any fair and thorough discussion of heretical opinions; and that such of them as could not stand such a discussion, though they may be prevented from spreading, do not disappear. But it is not the minds of heretics that are deteriorated most by the ban placed on all inquiry which does not end in the orthodox conclusions. The greatest harm done is to those who are not heretics, and whose whole mental development is cramped, and their reason cowed, by the fear of heresy. Who can compute what the world loses in the multitude of promising intellects combined with timid characters, who dare not follow out any bold, vigorous, independent train of thought, lest it should land them in something which would admit of being considered irreligious or immoral? Among them we may occasionally see some man of deep conscientiousness, and subtle and refined understanding, who spends a life in sophisticating with an intellect which he cannot silence, and exhausts the resources of ingenuity in attempting to reconcile the promptings of his conscience and reason with orthodoxy, which yet he does not, perhaps, to the end succeed in doing. No one can be a great thinker who does not recognise, that as a thinker it is his first duty to follow his intellect to whatever conclusions it may lead. Truth gains more even by the errors of one who, with due study and preparation, thinks for himself, than by the true opinions of those who only hold them because they do not suffer themselves to think. Not that it is solely, or chiefly, to form great thinkers, that freedom of thinking is required. On the contrary, it is as much and even more indispensable to enable average human beings to attain the mental stature which they are capable of. There have been, and may again be, great individual thinkers in a general atmosphere of mental slavery. But there never has been, nor ever will be, in that atmosphere an intellectually active people. Where any people has made a temporary approach to such a character, it has been because the dread of heterodox speculation was for a time suspended. Where there is a tacit convention that principles are not to be disputed; where the discussion of the greatest questions which can occupy humanity is considered to be closed, we cannot hope to find that generally high scale of mental activity which has made some periods of history so remarkable. Never when controversy avoided the subjects which are large and important enough to kindle enthusiasm, was the mind of a people stirred up from its foundations, and the impulse given which raised even persons of the most ordinary intellect to something of the dignity of thinking beings. Of such we have had an example in the condition of Europe during the times immediately following the Reformation; another, though limited to the Continent and to a more cultivated class, in the speculative movement of the latter half of the eighteenth century; and a third, of still briefer duration, in the intellectual fermentation of Germany during the Goethian and Fichtean period. These periods differed widely in the particular opinions which they developed; but were alike in this, that during all three the yoke of authority was broken. In each, an old mental despotism had been thrown off, and no new one had yet taken its place. The impulse given at these three periods has made Europe what it now is. Every single improvement which has taken place either in the human mind or in institutions, may be traced distinctly to one or other of them. Appearances have for some time indicated that all three impulses are well nigh spent; and we can expect no fresh start until we again assert our mental freedom.

Let us now pass to the second division of the argument, and dismissing the supposition that any of the received opinions may be false, let us assume them to be true, and examine into the worth of the manner in which they are likely to be held, when their truth is not freely and openly canvassed. However unwillingly a person who has a strong opinion may admit the possibility that his opinion may be false, he ought to be moved by the consideration that, however true it may be, if it is not fully, frequently, and fearlessly discussed, it will be held as a dead dogma, not a living truth.

There is a class of persons (happily not quite so numerous

as formerly) who think it enough if a person assents undoubt-
ingly to what they think true, though he has no knowledge
whatever of the grounds of the opinion, and could not make
a tenable defence of it against the most superficial objections.
Such persons, if they can once get their creed taught from authority, naturally think that no good, and some harm, comes of
its being allowed to be questioned. Where their influence prevails, they make it nearly impossible for the received opinion to
be rejected wisely and considerately, though it may still be
rejected rashly and ignorantly; for to shut out discussion
entirely is seldom possible, and when it once gets in, beliefs
not grounded on conviction are apt to give way before the
slightest semblance of an argument. Waiving, however, this
possibility—assuming that the true opinion abides in the
mind, but abides as a prejudice, a belief independent of,
and proof against, argument—this is not the way in which
truth ought to be held by a rational being. This is not
knowing the truth. Truth, thus held, is but one superstition
the more, accidentally clinging to the words which enunciate
a truth.

If the intellect and judgment of mankind ought to be cultivated, a thing which Protestants at least do not deny, on
what can these faculties be more appropriately exercised by
any one, than on the things which concern him so much that
it is considered necessary for him to hold opinions on them?
If the cultivation of the understanding consists in one thing
more than in another, it is surely in learning the grounds of
one's own opinions. Whatever people believe, on subjects on
which it is of the first importance to believe rightly, they
ought to be able to defend against at least the common
objections. But, some one may say, " Let them be *taught*
the grounds of their opinions. It does not follow that opinions
must be merely parroted because they are never heard controverted. Persons who learn geometry do not simply commit
the theorems to memory, but understand and learn likewise the
demonstrations; and it would be absurd to say that they
remain ignorant of the grounds of geometrical truths, because
they never hear any one deny, and attempt to disprove
them." Undoubtedly: and such teaching suffices on a subject

like mathematics, where there is nothing at all to be said
on the wrong side of the question. The peculiarity of the
evidence of mathematical truths is that all the argument is on
one side. There are no objections, and no answers to objections. But on every subject on which difference of opinion
is possible, the truth depends on a balance to be struck
between two sets of conflicting reasons. Even in natural
philosophy, there is always some other explanation possible
of the same facts; some geocentric theory instead of helio-
centric, some phlogiston instead of oxygen; and it has to be
shown why that other theory cannot be the true one: and
until this is shown, and until we know how it is shown, we
do not understand the grounds of our opinion. But when
we turn to subjects infinitely more complicated, to morals,
religion, politics, social relations, and the business of life,
three-fourths of the arguments for every disputed opinion consists in dispelling the appearances which favour some opinion
different from it. The greatest orator, save one, of antiquity,
has left it on record that he always studied his adversary's case
with as great, if not still greater, intensity than even his own.
What Cicero practised as the means of forensic success requires
to be imitated by all who study any subject in order to arrive
at the truth. He who knows only his own side of the case,
knows little of that. His reasons may be good, and no one
may have been able to refute them. But if he is equally
unable to refute the reasons on the opposite side; if he does
not so much as know what they are, he has no ground for
preferring either opinion. The rational position for him would
be suspension of judgment, and unless he contents himself
with that, he is either led by authority, or adopts, like the
generality of the world, the side to which he feels most
inclination. Nor is it enough that he should hear the arguments of adversaries from his own teachers, presented as
they state them, and accompanied by what they offer as
refutations. That is not the way to do justice to the arguments, or bring them into real contact with his own mind.
He must be able to hear them from persons who actually
believe them; who defend them in earnest, and do their very
utmost for them. He must know them in their most plausible

and persuasive form; he must feel the whole force of the difficulty which the true view of the subject has to encounter and dispose of; else he will never really possess himself of the portion of truth which meets and removes that difficulty. Ninety-nine in a hundred of what are called educated men are in this condition; even of those who can argue fluently for their opinions. Their conclusion may be true, but it might be false for anything they know : they have never thrown themselves into the mental position of those who think differently from them, and considered what such persons may have to say; and consequently they do not, in any proper sense of the word, know the doctrine which they themselves profess. They do not know those parts of it which explain and justify the remainder; the considerations which show that a fact which seemingly conflicts with another is reconcilable with it, or that, of two apparently strong reasons, one and not the other ought to be preferred. All that part of the truth which turns the scale, and decides the judgment of a completely informed mind, they are strangers to; nor is it ever really known, but to those who have attended equally and impartially to both sides, and endeavoured to see the reasons of both in the strongest light. So essential is this discipline to a real understanding of moral and human subjects, that if opponents of all important truths do not exist, it is indispensable to imagine them, and supply them with the strongest arguments which the most skilful devil's advocate can conjure up.

To abate the force of these considerations, an enemy of free discussion may be supposed to say, that there is no necessity for mankind in general to know and understand all that can be said against or for their opinions by philosophers and theologians. That it is not needful for common men to be able to expose all the misstatements or fallacies of an ingenious opponent. That it is enough if there is always somebody capable of answering them, so that nothing likely to mislead uninstructed persons remains unrefuted. That simple minds, having been taught the obvious grounds of the truths inculcated on them, may trust to authority for the rest, and being aware that they have neither knowledge nor talent to resolve every difficulty which can be raised, may repose in the assurance that all those which have been raised have been or can be answered, by those who are specially trained to the task.

Conceding to this view of the subject the utmost that can be claimed for it by those most easily satisfied with the amount of understanding of truth which ought to accompany the belief of it; even so, the argument for free discussion is no way weakened. For even this doctrine acknowledges that mankind ought to have a rational assurance that all objections have been satisfactorily answered; and how are they to be answered if that which requires to be answered is not spoken? or how can the answer be known to be satisfactory, if the objectors have no opportunity of showing that it is unsatisfactory? If not the public, at least the philosophers and theologians who are to resolve the difficulties, must make themselves familiar with those difficulties in their most puzzling form; and this cannot be accomplished unless they are freely stated, and placed in the most advantageous light which they admit of. The Catholic Church has its own way of dealing with this embarrassing problem. It makes a broad separation between those who can be permitted to receive its doctrines on conviction, and those who must accept them on trust. Neither, indeed, are allowed any choice as to what they will accept; but the clergy, such at least as can be fully confided in, may admissibly and meritoriously make themselves acquainted with the arguments of opponents, in order to answer them, and may, therefore, read heretical books; the laity, not unless by special permission, hard to be obtained. This discipline recognises a knowledge of the enemy's case as beneficial to the teachers, but finds means, consistent with this, of denying it to the rest of the world : thus giving to the *élite* more mental culture, though not more mental freedom, than it allows to the mass. By this device it succeeds in obtaining the kind of mental superiority which its purposes require; for though culture without freedom never made a large and liberal mind, it can make a clever *nisi prius* advocate of a cause. But in countries professing Protestantism, this resource is denied; since Protestants hold, at least in theory, that the responsibility for the choice of a religion must be borne by each for himself, and cannot be thrown off upon teachers. Besides, in the present state of the world, it is practically impossible that writings which are read by the instructed can be kept from the uninstructed. If the teachers of mankind are to be cognisant of all that they ought to know, everything must be free to be written and published without restraint.

If, however, the mischievous operation of the absence of free discussion, when the received opinions are true, were confined to leaving men ignorant of the grounds of those opinions, it might be thought that this, if an intellectual, is no moral evil, and does not affect the worth of the opinions, regarded in their influence on the character. The fact, however, is, that not only the grounds of the opinion are forgotten in the absence of discussion, but too often the meaning of the opinion itself. The words which convey it cease to suggest ideas, or suggest only a small portion of those they were originally employed to communicate. Instead of a vivid conception and a living belief, there remain only a few phrases retained by rote; or, if any part, the shell and husk only of the meaning is retained, the finer essence being lost. The great chapter in human history which this fact occupies and fills, cannot be too earnestly studied and meditated on.

It is illustrated in the experience of almost all ethical doctrines and religious creeds. They are all full of meaning and vitality to those who originate them, and to the direct disciples of the originators. Their meaning continues to be felt in undiminished strength, and is perhaps brought out into even fuller consciousness, so long as the struggle lasts to give the doctrine or creed an ascendancy over other creeds. At last it either prevails, and becomes the general opinion, or its progress stops; it keeps possession of the ground it has gained, but ceases to spread further. When either of these results has become apparent, controversy on the subject flags, and gradually dies away. The doctrine has taken its place, if not as a received opinion, as one of the admitted sects or divisions of opinion: those who hold it have generally inherited, not adopted it; and conversion from one of these doctrines to another, being now an exceptional fact, occupies little place in the thoughts of their professors. Instead of being, as at first, constantly on the alert either to defend themselves against the world, or to bring the world over to them, they have subsided into acquiescence, and neither listen, when they can help it, to arguments against their creed, nor trouble dissentients (if there be such) with arguments in its favour. From this time may usually be dated the decline in the living power of the doctrine. We often hear the teachers of all creeds lamenting the difficulty of keeping up in the minds of believers a lively apprehension of the truth which they nominally recognise, so that it may penetrate the feelings, and acquire a real mastery over the conduct. No such difficulty is complained of while the creed is still fighting for its existence : even the weaker combatants then know and feel what they are fighting for, and the difference between it and other doctrines; and in that period of every creed's existence, not a few persons may be found, who have realised its fundamental principles in all the forms of thought, have weighed and considered them in all their important bearings, and have experienced the full effect on the character which belief in that creed ought to produce in a mind thoroughly imbued with it. But when it has come to be an hereditary creed, and to be received passively, not actively—when the mind is no longer compelled, in the same degree as at first, to exercise its vital powers on the questions which its belief presents to it, there is a progressive tendency to forget all of the belief except the formularies, or to give it a dull and torpid assent, as if accepting it on trust dispensed with the necessity of realising it in consciousness, or testing it by personal experience, until it almost ceases to connect itself at all with the inner life of the human being. Then are seen the cases, so frequent in this age of the world as almost to form the majority, in which the creed remains as it were outside the mind, incrusting and petrifying it against all other influences addressed to the higher parts of our nature; manifesting its power by not suffering any fresh and living conviction to get in, but itself doing nothing for the mind or heart, except standing sentinel over them to keep them vacant.

To what an extent doctrines intrinsically fitted to make the deepest impression upon the mind may remain in it as dead beliefs, without being ever realised in the imagination, the feelings, or the understanding, is exemplified by the manner in which the majority of believers hold the doctrines of Christianity. By Christianity I here mean what is accounted such by all churches and sects—the maxims and precepts contained in the New Testament. These are considered sacred, and accepted as laws, by all professing Christians. Yet it is scarcely too much to say that not one Christian in a thousand guides or tests his individual conduct by reference to those laws. The standard to which he does refer it, is the custom of his nation, his class, or his religious profession. He has thus, on the one hand, a collection of ethical maxims, which he believes to have been vouchsafed to him by infallible wisdom as rules for his government; and on the other a set of every-day judgments and practices, which go a certain length with some of those maxims, not so great a length with others, stand in direct opposition to some, and are, on the whole, a compromise between the Christian creed and the interests and suggestions of worldly life. To the first of these standards he gives his homage; to the other his real allegiance. All Christians believe that the blessed are the poor and humble, and those who are ill-used by the world; that it is easier for a camel to pass through the eye of a needle than for a rich man to enter the kingdom of heaven; that they should judge not, lest they be judged; that they should swear not at all; that they should love their neighbour as themselves; that if one take their cloak, they should give him their coat also; that they should take no thought for the morrow; that if they would be perfect they should sell all that they have and give it to the poor. They are not insincere when they say that they believe these things. They do believe them, as people believe what they have always heard lauded and never discussed. But in the sense of that living belief which regulates conduct, they believe these doctrines just up to the point to which it is usual to act upon them. The doctrines in their integrity are serviceable to pelt adversaries with; and it is understood that they are to be put forward (when possible) as the reasons for whatever people do that they think laudable. But any one who reminded them that the maxims require an infinity of things which they never even think of doing, would gain nothing but to be classed among those very unpopular characters who affect to be better than other people. The doctrines have no hold on ordinary believers— are not a power in their minds. They have an habitual respect for the sound of them, but no feeling which spreads from the words to the things signified, and forces the mind to take *them* in, and make them conform to the formula. Whenever conduct is concerned, they look round for Mr. A and B to direct them how far to go in obeying Christ.

Now we may be well assured that the case was not thus, but far otherwise, with the early Christians. Had it been thus, Christianity never would have expanded from an obscure sect of the despised Hebrews into the religion of the Roman empire. When their enemies said, " See how these Christians love one another " (a remark not likely to be made by anybody now), they assuredly had a much livelier feeling of the meaning of their creed than they have ever had since. And to this cause, probably, it is chiefly owing that Christianity now makes so little progress in extending its domain, and after eighteen centuries is still nearly confined to Europeans and the descendants of Europeans. Even with the strictly religious, who are much in earnest about their doctrines, and attach a greater amount of meaning to many of them than people in general, it commonly happens that the part which is thus comparatively active in their minds is that which was made by Calvin, or Knox, or some such person much nearer in character to themselves. The sayings of Christ coexist passively in their minds, producing hardly any effect beyond what is caused by mere listening to words so amiable and bland. There are many reasons, doubtless, why doctrines which are the badge of a sect retain more of their vitality than those common to all recognised sects, and why more pains are taken by teachers to keep their meaning alive; but one reason certainly is, that the peculiar doctrines are more questioned, and have to be oftener defended against open gainsayers. Both teachers and learners go to sleep at their post, as soon as there is no enemy in the field.

The same thing holds true, generally speaking, of all traditional doctrines—those of prudence and knowledge of life, as well as of morals or religion. All languages and literatures are full of general observations on life, both as to what it is, and how to conduct oneself in it; observations which everybody knows, which everybody repeats, or hears with acquiescence, which are received as truisms, yet of which most people first truly learn the meaning when experience, generally of a painful kind, has made it a reality to them. How often, when smarting under some unforeseen misfortune or disappointment, does a person call to mind some proverb or common saying, familiar to him all his life, the meaning of which, if he had ever before felt it as he does now, would have saved him from the calamity. There are indeed reasons for this, other than the absence of discussion; there are many truths of which the full meaning *cannot* be realised until personal experience has brought it home. But much more of the meaning even of these would have been understood, and what was understood would have been far more deeply impressed on the mind, if the man had been accustomed to hear it argued *pro* and *con* by people who did understand it. The fatal tendency of mankind to leave off thinking about a thing when it is no longer doubtful, is the cause of half their errors. A contemporary author has well spoken of "the deep slumber of a decided opinion."

But what! (it may be asked) Is the absence of unanimity an indispensable condition of true knowledge? Is it necessary that some part of mankind should persist in error to enable any to realise the truth? Does a belief cease to be real and vital as soon as it is generally received—and is a proposition never thoroughly understood and felt unless some doubt of it remains? As soon as mankind have unanimously accepted a truth, does the truth perish within them? The highest aim and best result of improved intelligence, it has hitherto been thought, is to unite mankind more and more in the acknowledgment of all important truths; and does the intelligence only last as long as it has not achieved its object? Do the fruits of conquest perish by the very completeness of the victory?

I affirm no such thing. As mankind improve, the number of doctrines which are no longer disputed or doubted will be constantly on the increase: and the well-being of mankind may almost be measured by the number and gravity of the truths which have reached the point of being uncontested. The cessation, on one question after another, of serious controversy, is one of the necessary incidents of the consolidation of opinion; a consolidation as salutary in the case of true opinions, as it is dangerous and noxious when the opinions are erroneous. But though this gradual narrowing of the bounds of diversity of opinion is necessary in both senses of the term, being at once inevitable and indispensable, we are not therefore obliged to conclude that all its consequences must be beneficial. The loss of so important an aid to the intelligent and living apprehension of a truth, as is afforded by the necessity of explaining it to, or defending it against, opponents, though not sufficient to outweigh, is no trifling drawback from, the benefit of its universal recognition. Where this advantage can no longer be had, I confess I should like to see the teachers of mankind endeavouring to provide a substitute for it; some contrivance for making the difficulties of the question as present to the learner's consciousness, as if they were pressed upon him by a dissentient champion, eager for his conversion.

But instead of seeking contrivances for this purpose, they have lost those they formerly had. The Socratic dialectics, so magnificently exemplified in the dialogues of Plato, were a contrivance of this description. They were essentially a negative discussion of the great question of philosophy and life, directed with consummate skill to the purpose of convincing any one who had merely adopted the commonplaces of received opinion that he did not understand the subject —that he as yet attached no definite meaning to the doctrines he professed; in order that, becoming aware of his ignorance, he might be put in the way to obtain a stable belief resting on a clear apprehension both of the meaning of doctrines and of their evidence. The school disputations of the Middle Ages had a somewhat similar object. They were intended to make sure that the pupil understood his own opinion, and (by necessary correlation) the opinion opposed to it, and could enforce the grounds of the one and confute those of the other. These last-mentioned contests had indeed the incurable defect, that the premises appealed to were taken from authority, not from reason; and, as a discipline to the mind, they were in every respect inferior to the powerful dialectics which formed the intellects of the " Socratici viri;" but the modern mind owes far more to both than it is generally willing to admit, and the present modes of education contain nothing which in the smallest degree supplies the place either of the one or of the other. A person who derives all his instructions from teachers or books, even if he escape the besetting temptation of contenting himself with cram, is under no compulsion to hear both sides; accordingly it is far from a frequent accomplishment, even among thinkers, to know both sides; and the weakest part of what everybody says in defence of his opinion is what he intends as a reply to antagonists. It is the fashion of the present time to disparage negative logic —that which points out weaknesses in theory or errors in practice, without establishing positive truths. Such negative criticism would indeed be poor enough as an ultimate result; but as a means to attaining any positive knowledge or conviction worthy the name, it cannot be valued too highly; and until people are again systematically trained to it, there will be a few great thinkers, and a low general average of intellect, in any but the mathematical and physical departments of speculation. On any other subject no one's opinions deserve the name of knowledge, except so far as he has either had forced upon him by others, or gone through of himself, the same mental process which would have been required of him in carrying on an active controversy with opponents. That, therefore, which when absent, it is so indispensable, but so difficult, to create, how worse than absurd it is to forego, when spontaneously offering itself! If there are any persons who contest a received opinion, or who will do so if law or opinion will let them, let us thank them for it, open our minds to listen to them, and rejoice that there is some one to do for us what we otherwise ought, if we have any regard for either the certainty or the vitality of our convictions, to do with much greater labour for ourselves.

It still remains to speak of one of the principal causes which make diversity of opinion advantageous, and will continue to do so until mankind shall have entered a stage of intellectual advancement which at present seems at an incalculable distance. We have hitherto considered only two possibilities : that the received opinion may be false, and some other opinion, consequently, true; or that, the received opinion being true, a conflict with the opposite error is essential to a clear apprehension and deep feeling of its truth. But there is a commoner case than either of these; when the conflicting doctrines, instead of being one true and the other false, share the truth between them; and the nonconforming opinion is needed to supply the remainder of the truth, of which the received doctrine embodies only a part. Popular opinions, on subjects not palpable to sense, are often true, but seldom or never the whole truth. They are a part of the truth; sometimes a greater, sometimes a smaller part, but exaggerated, distorted, and disjointed from the truths by which they ought to be accompanied and limited. Heretical opinions, on the other hand, are generally some of these suppressed and neglected truths, bursting the bonds which kept them down, and either seeking reconciliation with the truth contained in the common opinion, or fronting it as enemies, and setting themselves up, with similar exclusiveness, as the whole truth. The latter case is hitherto the most frequent, as, in the human mind, one-sidedness has always been the rule, and many-sidedness the exception. Hence, even in revolutions of opinion, one part of the truth usually sets while another rises. Even progress, which ought to superadd, for the most part only substitutes, one partial and incomplete truth for another; improvement consisting chiefly in this, that the new fragment of truth is more wanted, more adapted to the

needs of the time, than that which it displaces. Such being the
partial character of prevailing opinions, even when resting on
a true foundation, every opinion which embodies somewhat
of the portion of truth which the common opinion omits,
ought to be considered precious, with whatever amount of error
and confusion that truth may be blended. No sober judge
of human affairs will feel bound to be indignant because
those who force on our notice truths which we should otherwise have overlooked, overlook some of those which we see.
Rather, he will think that so long as popular truth is one-
sided, it is more desirable than otherwise that unpopular truth
should have one-sided assertors too; such being usually the
most energetic, and the most likely to compel reluctant attention to the fragment of wisdom which they proclaim as if
it were the whole.

Thus, in the eighteenth century, when nearly all the instructed, and all those of the uninstructed who were led
by them, were lost in admiration of what is called civilisation,
and of the marvels of modern science, literature, and philosophy, and while greatly overrating the amount of unlikeness between the men of modern and those of ancient times,
indulged the belief that the whole of the difference was in
their own favour; with what a salutary shock did the
paradoxes of Rousseau explode like bombshells in the midst,
dislocating the compact mass of one-sided opinion, and forcing
its element to recombine in a better form and with additional
ingredients. Not that the current opinions were on the whole
farther from the truth than Rousseau's were; on the contrary, they were nearer to it; they contained more of positive
truth, and very much less of error. Nevertheless there lay
in Rousseau's doctrine, and has floated down the stream
of opinion along with it, a considerable amount of exactly
those truths which the popular opinion wanted; and these
are the deposit which was left behind when the flood
subsided. The superior worth of simplicity of life, the ener-
vating and demoralising effect of the trammels and hypocrisies
of artificial society, are ideas which have never been entirely
absent from cultivated minds since Rousseau wrote; and they
will in time produce their due effect, though at present need-

ing to be asserted as much as ever, and to be asserted by
deeds, for words, on this subject, have nearly exhausted their
power.

In politics, again, it is almost a commonplace, that a party
of order or stability, and a party of progress or reform, are
both necessary elements of a healthy state of political life;
until the one or the other shall have so enlarged its mental
grasp as to be a party equally of order and of progress, knowing and distinguishing what is fit to be preserved from what
ought to be swept away. Each of these modes of thinking
derives its utility from the deficiencies of the other; but it
is in a great measure the opposition of the other that keeps
each within the limits of reason and sanity. Unless opinions
favourable to democracy and to aristocracy, to property and to
equality, to co-operation and to competition, to luxury and
to abstinence, to sociality and individuality, to liberty and
discipline, and all the other standing antagonisms of practical
life, are expressed with equal freedom, and enforced and
defended with equal talent and energy, there is no chance of
both elements obtaining their due; one scale is sure to go up,
and the other down. Truth, in the great practical concerns of
life, is so much a question of the reconciling and combining
of opposites, that very few have minds sufficiently capacious
and impartial to make the adjustment with an approach to
correctness, and it has to be made by the rough process of
a struggle between combatants fighting under hostile banners.
On any of the great open questions just enumerated, if
either of the two opinions has a better claim than the
other, not merely to be tolerated, but to be encouraged and
countenanced, it is the one which happens at the particular
time and place to be in a minority. That is the opinion which,
for the time being, represents the neglected interests, the
side of human well-being which is in danger of obtaining
less than its share. I am aware that there is not, in this
country, any intolerance of differences of opinion on most of
these topics. They are adduced to show, by admitted and
multiplied examples, the universality of the fact, that only
through diversity of opinion is there, in the existing state
of human intellect, a chance of fair play to all sides of

the truth. When there are persons to be found who form an exception to the apparent unanimity of the world on any subject, even if the world is in the right, it is always probable that dissentients have something worth hearing to say for themselves, and that truth would lose something by their silence.

It may be objected, " But *some* received principles, especially on the highest and most vital subjects, are more than half-truths. The Christian morality, for instance, is the whole truth on that subject, and if any one teaches a morality which varies from it, he is wholly in error." As this is of all cases the most important in practice, none can be fitter to test the general maxim. But before pronouncing what Christian morality is or is not, it would be desirable to decide what is meant by Christian morality. If it means the morality of the New Testament, I wonder that any one who derives his knowledge of this from the book itself, can suppose that it was announced, or intended, as a complete doctrine of morals. The Gospel always refers to a pre-existing morality, and confines its precepts to the particulars in which that morality was to be corrected, or superseded by a wider and higher; expressing itself, moreover, in terms most general, often impossible to be interpreted literally, and possessing rather the impressiveness of poetry or eloquence than the precision of legislation. To extract from it a body of ethical doctrine, has never been possible without eking it out from the Old Testament, that is, from a system elaborate indeed, but in many respects barbarous, and intended only for a barbarous people. St. Paul, a declared enemy to this Judaical mode of interpreting the doctrine and filling up the scheme of his Master, equally assumes a pre-existing morality, namely that of the Greeks and Romans; and his advice to Christians is in a great measure a system of accommodation to that; even to the extent of giving an apparent sanction to slavery. What is called Christian, but should rather be termed theological, morality, was not the work of Christ or the Apostles, but is of much later origin, having been gradually built up by the Catholic church of the first five centuries, and though not implicitly adopted by moderns and Protestants, has been much less modified by them than might have been expected. For the most part, indeed, they have contented themselves with cutting off the additions which had been made to it in the Middle Ages, each sect supplying the place by fresh additions, adapted to its own character and tendencies. That mankind owe a great debt to this morality, and to its early teachers, I should be the last person to deny; but I do not scruple to say of it that it is, in many important points, incomplete and one-sided, and that unless ideas and feelings, not sanctioned by it, had contributed to the formation of European life and character, human affairs would have been in a worse condition than they now are. Christian morality (so called) has all the characters of a reaction; it is, in great part, a protest against Paganism. Its ideal is negative rather than positive; passive rather than active; Innocence rather than Nobleness; Abstinence from Evil, rather than energetic Pursuit of Good; in its precepts (as has been well said) "thou shalt not" predominates unduly over "thou shalt." In its horror of sensuality, it made an idol of asceticism, which has been gradually compromised away into one of legality. It holds out the hope of heaven and the threat of hell, as the appointed and appropriate motives to a virtuous life: in this falling far below the best of the ancients, and doing what lies in it to give to human morality an essentially selfish character, by disconnecting each man's feelings of duty from the interests of his fellow-creatures, except so far as a self-interested inducement is offered to him for consulting them. It is essentially a doctrine of passive obedience; it inculcates submission to all authorities found established; who indeed are not to be actively obeyed when they command what religion forbids, but who are not to be resisted, far less rebelled against, for any amount of wrong to ourselves. And while, in the morality of the best Pagan nations, duty to the State holds even a disproportionate place, infringing on the just liberty of the individual; in purely Christian ethics, that grand department of duty is scarcely noticed or acknowledged. It is in the Koran, not the New Testament, that we read the maxim—" A ruler who appoints any man to an office, when there is in his dominions another man better qualified for it, sins against God and against the State." What little recognition the idea of obligation to the public obtains in modern morality is derived from Greek and Roman sources, not from Christian; as, even in the morality of private life, whatever exists of magnanimity, highmindedness, personal dignity, even the sense of honour, is derived from the purely human, not the religious part of our education, and never could have grown out of a standard of ethics in which the only worth, professedly recognised, is that of obedience.

I am as far as any one from pretending that these defects are necessarily inherent in the Christian ethics in every manner in which it can be conceived, or that the many requisites of a complete moral doctrine which it does not contain do not admit of being reconciled with it. Far less would I insinuate this of the doctrines and precepts of Christ himself. I believe that the sayings of Christ are all that I can see any evidence of their having been intended to be; that they are irreconcilable with nothing which a comprehensive morality requires; that everything which is excellent in ethics may be brought within them, with no greater violence to their language than has been done to it by all who have attempted to deduce from them any practical system of conduct whatever. But it is quite consistent with this to believe that they contain, and were meant to contain, only a part of the truth; that many essential elements of the highest morality are among the things which are not provided for, nor intended to be provided for, in the recorded deliverances of the Founder of Christianity, and which have been entirely thrown aside in the system of ethics erected on the basis of those deliverances by the Christian Church. And this being so, I think it a great error to persist in attempting to find in the Christian doctrine that complete rule for our guidance which its author intended it to sanction and enforce, but only partially to provide. I believe, too, that this narrow theory is becoming a grave practical evil, detracting greatly from the moral training and instruction which so many well-meaning persons are now at length exerting themselves to promote. I much fear that by attempting to form the mind and feelings on an exclusively religious type, and discarding those secular standards (as for want of a better name they may be called) which heretofore co-existed with and supplemented the Christian ethics, receiving some of its spirit, and infusing into it some of theirs, there will result, and is even now resulting, a low, abject, servile type of character, which, submit itself as it may to what it deems the Supreme Will, is incapable of rising to or sympathising in the conception of Supreme Goodness. I believe that other ethics than any which can be evolved from exclusively Christian source, must exist side by side with Christian ethics to produce the moral regeneration of mankind; and that the Christian system is no exception to the rule, that in an imperfect state of the human mind the interests of truth require a diversity of opinions. It is not necessary that in ceasing to ignore the moral truths not contained in Christianity men should ignore any of those which it does contain. Such prejudice, or oversight, when it occurs, is altogether an evil; but it is one from which we cannot hope to be always exempt, and must be regarded as the price paid for an inestimable good. The exclusive pretension made by a part of the truth to be the whole, must and ought to be protested against; and if a reactionary impulse should make the protestors unjust in their turn, this one-sidedness, like the other, may be lamented, but must be tolerated. If Christians would teach infidels to be just to Christianity, they should themselves be just to infidelity. It can do truth no service to blink the fact, known to all who have the most ordinary acquaintance with literary history, that a large portion of the noblest and most valuable moral teaching has been the work, not only of men who did not know, but of men who knew and rejected, the Christian faith.

I do not pretend that the most unlimited use of the freedom of enunciating all possible opinions would put an end to the evils of religious or philosophical sectarianism. Every truth which men of narrow capacity are in earnest about, is sure to be asserted, inculcated, and in many ways even acted on, as if no other truth existed in the world, or at all events none that could limit or qualify the first. I acknowledge that the tendency of all opinions to become sectarian is not cured by the freest discussion, but is often heightened and exacerbated thereby; the truth which ought to have been, but was not, seen, being rejected all the more violently because proclaimed by persons regarded as opponents. But it is not on the impassioned partisan, it is on the calmer and more disinterested bystander, that this collision of opinions works its salutary effect. Not the violent conflict between parts of the truth, but the quiet suppression of half of it, is the formidable evil; there is always hope when people are forced to listen to both sides; it is when they attend only to one that errors harden into prejudices, and truth itself ceases to have the effect of truth, by being exaggerated into falsehood. And since there are few mental attributes more rare than the judicial faculty which can sit in intelligent judgment between two sides of a question, of which only one is represented by an advocate before it, truth has no chance but in proportion as every side of it, every opinion which embodies any fraction of the truth, not only finds advocates, but is so advocated as to be listened to.

We have now recognised the necessity to the mental well-being of mankind (on which all their other well-being depends) of freedom of opinion, and freedom of the expression of opinion, on four distinct grounds; which we will now briefly recapitulate.

First, if any opinion is compelled to silence, that opinion may, for aught we can certainly know, be true. To deny this is to assume our own infallibility.

Secondly, though the silenced opinion be an error, it may, and very commonly does, contain a portion of truth; and since the general or prevailing opinion on any subject is rarely or never the whole truth, it is only by the collision of adverse opinions that the remainder of the truth has any chance of being supplied.

Thirdly, even if the received opinion be not only true, but the whole truth, unless it is suffered to be, and actually is, vigorously and earnestly contested, it will, by most of those who receive it, be held in the manner of a prejudice, with little comprehension or feeling of its rational grounds. And not only this, but, fourthly, the meaning of the doctrine itself will be in danger of being lost, or enfeebled, and deprived of its vital effect on the character and conduct : the dogma becoming a mere formal profession, inefficacious for good, but cumbering the ground, and preventing the growth of any real and heartfelt conviction, from reason or personal experience.

Before quitting the subject of freedom of opinion, it is fit to take some notice of those who say that the free expression of all opinions should be permitted, on condition that the manner be temperate, and do not pass the bounds of fair discussion. Much might be said on the impossibility of fixing where these supposed bounds are to be placed; for if the test be offence to those whose opinions are attacked, I think experience testifies that this offence is given whenever the attack is telling and powerful, and that every opponent who pushes them hard, and whom they find it difficult to answer, appears to them, if he shows any strong feeling on the subject, an intemperate opponent. But this, though an important consideration in a practical point of view, merges in a more fundamental objection. Undoubtedly the manner of asserting an opinion, even though it be a true one, may be very objectionable, and may justly incur severe censure. But the principal offences of the kind are such as it is mostly impossible, unless by accidental self-betrayal, to bring home to conviction. The gravest of them is, to argue sophistically, to suppress facts or arguments, to misstate the elements of the case, or misrepresent the opposite opinion. But all this even to the most aggravated degree, is so continually done in perfect good faith, by persons who are not considered, and in many other respects may not deserve to be considered, ignorant or incompetent, that it is rarely possible, on adequate grounds, conscientiously to stamp the misrepresentation as morally culpable; and still less could law presume to interfere with this kind of controversial misconduct. With regard to what is commonly meant by intemperate discussion, namely invective, sarcasm, personality, and the like, the denunciation of these weapons would deserve more sympathy

if it were ever proposed to interdict them equally to both
sides; but it is only desired to restrain the employment of
them against the prevailing opinion : against the unprevailing
they may not only be used without general disapproval, but
will be likely to obtain for him who uses them the praise
of honest zeal and righteous indignation. Yet whatever mischief arises from their use is greatest when they are employed
against the comparatively defenceless; and whatever unfair
advantage can be derived by any opinion from this mode of
asserting it, accrues almost exclusively to received opinions.
The worst offence of this kind which can be committed by
a polemic is to stigmatise those who hold the contrary opinion
as bad and immoral men. To calumny of this sort, those
who hold any unpopular opinion are peculiarly exposed,
because they are in general few and uninfluential, and nobody
but themselves feels much interested in seeing justice done
them; but this weapon is, from the nature of the case,
denied to those who attack a prevailing opinion : they can
neither use it with safety to themselves, nor, if they could,
would it do anything but recoil on their own cause. In general,
opinions contrary to those commonly received can only obtain
a hearing by studied moderation of language, and the most
cautious avoidance of unnecessary offence, from which they
hardly ever deviate even in a slight degree without losing
ground : while unmeasured vituperation employed on the
side of the prevailing opinion really does deter people from
professing contrary opinions, and from listening to those who
profess them. For the interest, therefore, of truth and justice,
it is far more important to restrain this employment of
vituperative language than the other; and, for example, if
it were necessary to choose, there would be much more need to
discourage offensive attacks on infidelity than on religion.
It is, however, obvious that law and authority have no business
with restraining either, while opinion ought, in every instance,
to determine its verdict by the circumstances of the individual
case; condemning every one, on whichever side of the argument he places himself, in whose mode of advocacy either
want of candour, or malignity, bigotry, or intolerance of
feeling manifest themselves; but not inferring these vices

from the side which a person takes, though it be the contrary side of the question to our own; and giving merited honour to every one, whatever opinion he may hold, who has calmness to see and honesty to state what his opponents and their opinions really are, exaggerating nothing to their discredit, keeping nothing back which tells, or can be supposed to tell, in their favour. This is the real morality of public discussion: and if often violated, I am happy to think that there are many controversialists who to a great extent observe it, and a still greater number who conscientiously strive towards it.

CHAPTER III

OF INDIVIDUALITY, AS ONE OF THE ELEMENTS OF WELL-BEING

Such being the reasons which make it imperative that human beings should be free to form opinions, and to express their opinions without reserve; and such the baneful consequences to the intellectual, and through that to the moral nature of man, unless this liberty is either conceded, or asserted in spite of prohibition; let us next examine whether the same reasons do not require that men should be free to act upon their opinions—to carry these out in their lives, without hindrance, either physical or moral, from their fellow-men, so long as it is at their own risk and peril. This last proviso is of course indispensable. No one pretends that actions should be as free as opinions. On the contrary, even opinions lose their immunity when the circumstances in which they are expressed are such as to constitute their expression a positive instigation to some mischievous act. An opinion that corn-dealers are starvers of the poor, or that private property is robbery, ought to be unmolested when simply circulated through the press, but may justly incur punishment when delivered orally to an excited mob assembled before the house of a corn-dealer, or when handed about among the same mob in the form of a placard. Acts, of whatever kind, which, without justifiable cause, do harm to others, may be, and in the more important cases absolutely require to be, controlled by the unfavourable sentiments, and, when needful, by the active interference of mankind. The liberty of the individual must be thus far limited; he must not make himself a nuisance to other people. But if he refrains from molesting others in what concerns them, and merely acts according to his own inclination and judgment in things which concern himself, the same reasons which show that opinion should be free, prove also that he should be allowed, without molestation, to carry his opinions into practice at his own cost. That mankind are not infallible; that their truths, for the most part, are only half-truths; that unity of opinion, unless resulting from the fullest and freest comparison of opposite opinions, is not desirable, and diversity not an evil, but a good, until mankind are much more capable than at present of recognising all sides of the truth, are principles applicable to men's modes of action, not less than to their opinions. As it is useful that while mankind are imperfect there should be different opinions, so it is that there should be different experiments of living; that free scope should be given to varieties of character, short of injury to others; and that the worth of different modes of life should be proved practically, when any one thinks fit to try them. It is desirable, in short, that in things which do not primarily concern others, individuality should assert itself. Where, not the person's own character, but the traditions or customs of other people are the rule of conduct, there is wanting one of the principal ingredients of human happiness, and quite the chief ingredient of individual and social progress.

In maintaining this principle, the greatest difficulty to be encountered does not lie in the appreciation of means towards an acknowledged end, but in the indifference of persons in general to the end itself. If it were felt that the free development of individuality is one of the leading essentials of well-being; that it is not only a co-ordinate element with all that is designated by the terms civilisation, instruction, education, culture, but is itself a necessary part and condition of all those things; there would be no danger that liberty should be undervalued, and the adjustment of the boundaries between it and social control would present no extraordinary difficulty. But the evil is, that individual spontaneity is hardly recognised by the common modes of thinking as having any intrinsic worth, or deserving any regard on its own account. The majority, being satisfied with the ways of mankind as they now are (for it is they who make them what they are), cannot comprehend why those ways should not be good enough for everybody; and what is more, spontaneity forms no part of the ideal of the majority of moral and social reformers, but is rather looked on with jealousy, as a troublesome and perhaps rebellious obstruction to the general acceptance of what these reformers, in their own judgment, think would be best for mankind. Few persons, out of Germany, even comprehend the meaning of the doctrine which Wilhelm von Humboldt, so eminent both as a *savant* and as a politician, made the text of a treatise—that "the end of man, or that which is prescribed by the eternal or immutable dictates of reason, and not suggested by vague and transient desires, is the highest and most harmonious development of his powers to a complete and consistent whole;" that, therefore, the object "towards which every human being must ceaselessly direct his efforts, and on which especially those who design to influence their fellow-men must ever keep their eyes, is the individuality of power and development;" that for this there are two requisites, "freedom, and variety of situations;" and that from the union of these arise "individual vigour and manifold diversity," which combine themselves in "originality."[1]

Little, however, as people are accustomed to a doctrine like that of von Humboldt, and surprising as it may be to them to find so high a value attached to individuality, the question, one must nevertheless think, can only be one of degree. No one's idea of excellence in conduct is that people should do absolutely nothing but copy one another. No one would assert that people ought not to put into their mode of life, and into the conduct of their concerns, any impress whatever of their own judgment, or of their own individual character. On the other hand, it would be absurd to pretend that people ought to live as if nothing whatever had been known in the world before they came into it; as if experience had as yet done nothing towards showing that one mode of existence, or of conduct, is preferable to another. Nobody denies that people should be so taught and trained in youth as to know and benefit by the ascertained results of human experience. But it is the privilege and proper condition of a human being, arrived at the maturity of his faculties, to use and interpret experience in his own way.

[1] *The Sphere and Duties of Government,* from the German of Baron Wilhelm von Humboldt, pp. 11-13.

It is for him to find out what part of recorded experience is properly applicable to his own circumstances and character. The traditions and customs of other people are, to a certain extent, evidence of what their experience has taught *them*; presumptive evidence, and as such, have a claim to his deference : but, in the first place, their experience may be too narrow; or they may not have interpreted it rightly. Secondly, their interpretation of experience may be correct, but unsuitable to him. Customs are made for customary circumstances and customary characters; and his circumstances or his character may be uncustomary. Thirdly, though the customs be both good as customs, and suitable to him, yet to conform to custom, merely *as* custom, does not educate or develop in him any of the qualities which are the distinctive endowment of a human being. The human faculties of perception, judgment, discriminative feeling, mental activity, and even moral preference, are exercised only in making a choice. He who does anything because it is the custom makes no choice. He gains no practice either in discerning or in desiring what is best. The mental and moral, like the muscular powers, are improved only by being used. The faculties are called into no exercise by doing a thing merely because others do it, no more than by believing a thing only because others believe it. If the grounds of an opinion are not conclusive to the person's own reason, his reason cannot be strengthened, but is likely to be weakened, by his adopting it : and if the inducements to an act are not such as are consentaneous to his own feelings and character (where affection, or the rights of others, are not concerned) it is so much done towards rendering his feelings and character inert and torpid, instead of active and energetic.

He who lets the world, or his own portion of it, choose his plan of life for him, has no need of any other faculty than the ape-like one of imitation. He who chooses his plan for himself, employs all his faculties. He must use observation to see, reasoning and judgment to foresee, activity to gather materials for decision, discrimination to decide, and when he has decided, firmness and self-control to hold to his deliberate decision. And these qualities he requires and exercises exactly in proportion as the part of his conduct which he determines according to his own judgment and feelings is a large one. It is possible that he might be guided in some good path, and kept out of harm's way, without any of these things. But what will be his comparative worth as a human being? It really is of importance, not only what men do, but also what manner of men they are that do it. Among the works of man, which human life is rightly employed in perfecting and beautifying, the first in importance surely is man himself. Supposing it were possible to get houses built, corn grown, battles fought, causes tried, and even churches erected and prayers said, by machinery—by automatons in human form—it would be a considerable loss to exchange for these automatons even the men and women who at present inhabit the more civilised parts of the world, and who assuredly are but starved specimens of what nature can and will produce. Human nature is not a machine to be built after a model, and set to do exactly the work prescribed for it, but a tree, which requires to grow and develop itself on all sides, according to the tendency of the inward forces which make it a living thing.

It will probably be conceded that it is desirable people should exercise their understandings, and that an intelligent following of custom, or even occasionally an intelligent deviation from custom, is better than a blind and simply mechanical adhesion to it. To a certain extent it is admitted that our understanding should be our own : but there is not the same willingness to admit that our desires and impulses should be our own likewise; or that to possess impulses of our own, and of any strength, is anything but a peril and a snare. Yet desires and impulses are as much a part of a perfect human being as beliefs and restraints : and strong impulses are only perilous when not properly balanced; when one set of aims and inclinations is developed into strength, while others, which ought to co-exist with them, remain weak and inactive. It is not because men's desires are strong that they act ill; it is because their consciences are weak. There is no natural connection between strong impulses and a weak conscience. The natural connection is the other way. To say that one person's desires and feelings are stronger and more various than those of another, is merely to say that he has more of the raw material of human nature, and is therefore capable, perhaps of more evil, but certainly of more good. Strong impulses are but another name for energy. Energy may be turned to bad uses; but more good may always be made of an energetic nature, than of an indolent and impassive one. Those who have most natural feeling are always those whose cultivated feelings may be made the strongest. The same strong susceptibilities which make the personal impulses vivid and powerful, are also the source from whence are generated the most passionate love of virtue, and the sternest self-control. It is through the cultivation of these that society both does its duty and protects its interests: not by rejecting the stuff of which heroes are made, because it knows not how to make them. A person whose desires and impulses are his own—are the expression of his own nature, as it has been developed and modified by his own culture—is said to have a character. One whose desires and impulses are not his own, has no character, no more than a steam-engine has a character. If, in addition to being his own, his impulses are strong, and are under the government of a strong will, he has an energetic character. Whoever thinks that individuality of desires and impulses should not be encouraged to unfold itself, must maintain that society has no need of strong natures—is not the better for containing many persons who have much character—and that a high general average of energy is not desirable.

In some early states of society, these forces might be, and were, too much ahead of the power which society then possessed of disciplining and controlling them. There has been a time when the element of spontaneity and individuality was in excess, and the social principle had a hard struggle with it. The difficulty then was to induce men of strong bodies or minds to pay obedience to any rules which required them to control their impulses. To overcome this difficulty, law and discipline, like the Popes struggling against the Emperors, asserted a power over the whole man, claiming to control all his life in order to control his character—which society

had not found any other sufficient means of binding. But
society has now fairly got the better of individuality; and
the danger which threatens human nature is not the excess,
but the deficiency, of personal impulses and preferences.
Things are vastly changed since the passions of those who
were strong by station or by personal endowment were in a
state of habitual rebellion against laws and ordinances, and
required to be rigorously chained up to enable the persons
within their reach to enjoy any particle of security. In our
times, from the highest class of society down to the lowest,
every one lives as under the eye of a hostile and dreaded
censorship. Not only in what concerns others, but in what
concerns only themselves, the individual or the family do
not ask themselves—what do I prefer? or, what would
suit my character and disposition? or, what would allow the
best and highest in me to have fair play, and enable it to
grow and thrive? They ask themselves, what is suitable to my
position? what is usually done by persons of my station and
pecuniary circumstances? or (worse still) what is usually
done by persons of a station and circumstances superior to
mine? I do not mean that they choose what is customary in
preference to what suits their own inclination. It does not
occur to them to have any inclination, except for what is
customary. Thus the mind itself is bowed to the yoke : even
in what people do for pleasure, conformity is the first thing
thought of; they like in crowds; they exercise choice only
among things commonly done : peculiarity of taste, eccentricity of conduct, are shunned equally with crimes : until by
dint of not following their own nature they have no nature to
follow : their human capacities are withered and starved :
they become incapable of any strong wishes or native pleasures,
and are generally without either opinions or feelings of home
growth, or properly their own. Now is this, or is it not,
the desirable condition of human nature?

It is so, on the Calvinistic theory. According to that,
the one great offence of man is self-will. All the good of
which humanity is capable is comprised in obedience. You
have no choice; thus you must do, and no otherwise :
" whatever is not a duty, is a sin." Human nature being

radically corrupt, there is no redemption for any one until human nature is killed within him. To one holding this theory of life, crushing out any of the human faculties, capacities, and susceptibilities, is no evil : man needs no capacity, but that of surrendering himself to the will of God : and if he uses any of his faculties for any other purpose but to do that supposed will more effectually, he is better without them. This is the theory of Calvinism; and it is held, in a mitigated form, by many who do not consider themselves Calvinists; the mitigation consisting in giving a less ascetic interpretation to the alleged will of God; asserting it to be his will that mankind should gratify some of their inclinations; of course not in the manner they themselves prefer, but in the way of obedience, that is, in a way prescribed to them by authority; and, therefore, by the necessary condition of the case, the same for all.

In some such insidious form there is at present a strong tendency to this narrow theory of life, and to the pinched and hidebound type of human character which it patronises. Many persons, no doubt, sincerely think that human beings thus cramped and dwarfed are as their Maker designed them to be; just as many have thought that trees are a much finer thing when clipped into pollards, or cut out into figures of animals, than as nature made them. But if it be any part of religion to believe that man was made by a good Being, it is more consistent with that faith to believe that this Being gave all human faculties that they might be cultivated and unfolded, not rooted out and consumed, and that he takes delight in every nearer approach made by his creatures to the ideal, conception embodied in them, every increase in any of their capabilities of comprehension, of action, or of enjoyment. There is a different type of human excellence from the Calvinistic : a conception of humanity as having its nature bestowed on it for other purposes than merely to be abnegated. " Pagan self-assertion " is one of the elements of human worth, as well as " Christian self-denial."[2] There is a Greek ideal of self-development, which the Platonic and Christian ideal of self-government blends with, but

[2] Sterling's *Essays*.

does not supersede. It may be better to be a John Knox than an Alcibiades, but it is better to be a Pericles than either; nor would a Pericles, if we had one in these days, be without anything good which belonged to John Knox.

It is not by wearing down into uniformity all that is individual in themselves, but by cultivating it, and calling it forth, within the limits imposed by the rights and interests of others, that human beings become a noble and beautiful object of contemplation; and as the works partake the character of those who do them, by the same process human life also becomes rich, diversified, and animating, furnishing more abundant aliment to high thoughts and elevating feelings, and strengthening the tie which binds every individual to the race, by making the race infinitely better worth belonging to. In proportion to the development of his individuality, each person becomes more valuable to himself, and is therefore capable of being more valuable to others. There is a greater fulness of life about his own existence, and when there is more life in the units there is more in the mass which is composed of them. As much compression as is necessary to prevent the stronger specimens of human nature from encroaching on the rights of others cannot be dispensed with; but for this there is ample compensation even in the point of view of human development. The means of development which the individual loses by being prevented from gratifying his inclinations to the injury of others, are chiefly obtained at the expense of the development of other people. And even to himself there is a full equivalent in the better development of the social part of his nature, rendered possible by the restraint put upon the selfish part. To be held to rigid rules of justice for the sake of others, develops the feelings and capacities which have the good of others for their object. But to be restrained in things not affecting their good, by their mere displeasure, develops nothing valuable, except such force of character as may unfold itself in resisting the restraint. If acquiesced in, it dulls and blunts the whole nature. To give any fair play to the nature of each, it is essential that different persons should be allowed to lead different lives. In proportion as this latitude has been exercised in any age, has that age been noteworthy to posterity. Even despotism does not produce its worst effects, so long as individuality exists under it; and whatever crushes individuality is despotism, by whatever name it may be called, and whether it professes to be enforcing the will of God or the injunctions of men.

Having said that the individuality is the same thing with development, and that it is only the cultivation of individuality which produces, or can produce, well-developed human beings, I might here close the argument: for what more or better can be said of any condition of human affairs than that it brings human beings themselves nearer to the best thing they can be? or what worse can be said of any obstruction to good than that it prevents this? Doubtless, however, these considerations will not suffice to convince those who most need convincing; and it is necessary further to show, that these developed human beings are of some use to the undeveloped—to point out to those who do not desire liberty, and would not avail themselves of it, that they may be in some intelligible manner rewarded for allowing other people to make use of it without hindrance.

In the first place, then, I would suggest that they might possibly learn something from them. It will not be denied by anybody, that originality is a valuable element in human affairs. There is always need of persons not only to discover new truths, and point out when what were once truths are true no longer, but also to commence new practices, and set the example of more enlightened conduct, and better taste and sense in human life. This cannot well be gainsaid by anybody who does not believe that the world has already attained perfection in all its ways and practices. It is true that this benefit is not capable of being rendered by everybody alike: there are but few persons, in comparison with the whole of mankind, whose experiments, if adopted by others, would be likely to be any improvement on established practice. But these few are the salt of the earth; without them, human life would become a stagnant pool. Not only is it they who introduce good things which did not before exist; it is they who keep the life in those which already exist.

If there were nothing to be done, would human intellect cease to be necessary? Would it be a reason why those who do the old things should forget why they are done, and do them like cattle, not like human beings? There is only too great a tendency in the best beliefs and practices to degenerate into the mechanical; and unless there were a succession of persons whose ever-recurring originality prevents the grounds of those beliefs and practices from becoming merely traditional, such dead matter would not resist the smallest shock from anything really alive, and there would be no reason why civilisation should not die out, as in the Byzantine Empire. Persons of genius, it is true, are, and are always likely to be, a small minority; but in order to have them, it is necessary to preserve the soil in which they grow. Genius can only breathe freely in an *atmosphere* of freedom. Persons of genius are, *ex vi termini,* more individual than any other people—less capable, consequently, of fitting themselves, without hurtful compression, into any of the small number of moulds which society provides in order to save its members the trouble of forming their own character. If from timidity they consent to be forced into one of these moulds, and to let all that part of themselves which cannot expand under the pressure remain unexpanded, society will be little the better for their genius. If they are of a strong character, and break their fetters, they become a mark for the society which has not succeeded in reducing them to commonplace, to point out with solemn warning as "wild," "erratic," and the like; much as if one should complain of the Niagara river for not flowing smoothly between its banks like a Dutch canal.

I insist thus emphatically on the importance of genius, and the necessity of allowing it to unfold itself freely both in thought and in practice, being well aware that no one will deny the position in theory, but knowing also that almost every one, in reality, is totally indifferent to it. People think genius a fine thing if it enables a man to write an exciting poem, or paint a picture. But in its true sense, that of originality in thought and action, though no one says that it is not a thing to be admired, nearly all, at heart, think that they can do very well without it. Unhappily this is too natural to be wondered at. Originality is the one thing which unoriginal minds cannot feel the use of. They cannot see what it is to do for them : how should they? If they could see what it would do for them, it would not be originality. The first service which originality has to render them, is that of opening their eyes : which being once fully done, they would have a chance of being themselves original. Meanwhile, recollecting that nothing was ever yet done which some one was not the first to do, and that all good things which exist are the fruits of originality, let them be modest enough to believe that there is something still left for it to accomplish, and assure themselves that they are more in need of originality, the less they are conscious of the want.

In sober truth, whatever homage may be professed, or even paid, to real or supposed mental superiority, the general tendency of things throughout the world is to render mediocrity the ascendant power among mankind. In ancient history, in the Middle Ages, and in a diminishing degree through the long transition from feudality to the present time, the individual was a power in himself; and if he had either great talents or a high social position, he was a considerable power. At present individuals are lost in the crowd. In politics it is almost a triviality to say that public opinion now rules the world. The only power deserving the name is that of masses, and of governments while they make themselves the organ of the tendencies and instincts of masses. This is as true in the moral and social relations of private life as in public transactions. Those whose opinions go by the name of public opinion are not always the same sort of public : in America they are the whole white population; in England, chiefly the middle class. But they are always a mass, that is to say, collective mediocrity. And what is a still greater novelty, the mass do not now take their opinions from dignitaries in Church or State, from ostensible leaders, or from books. Their thinking is done for them by men much like themselves, addressing them or speaking in their name, on the spur of the moment, through the newspapers. I am not complaining of all this. I do not assert that anything better is compatible, as a general rule, with the present low state of the human mind. But that does not hinder the government of mediocrity from being mediocre government. No government by a democracy or a numerous aristocracy, either in its political acts or in the opinions, qualities, and tone of mind which it fosters, ever did or could rise above mediocrity, except in so far as the sovereign many have let themselves be guided (which in their best times they always have done) by the counsels and influence of a more highly gifted and instructed One or Few. The initiation of all wise or noble things comes and must come from the individuals; generally at first from some one individual. The honour and glory of the average man is that he is capable of following that initiative; that he can respond internally to wise and noble things, and be led to them with his eyes open. I am not countenancing the sort of " hero-worship " which applauds the strong man of genius for forcibly seizing on the government of the world and making it do his bidding in spite of itself. All he can claim is, freedom to point out the way. The power of compelling others into it is not only inconsistent with the freedom and development of all the rest, but corrupting to the strong man himself. It does seem, however, that when the opinions of masses of merely average men are everywhere become or becoming the dominant power, the counterpoise and corrective to that tendency would be the more and more pronounced individuality of those who stand on the higher eminences of thought. It is in these circumstances most especially, that exceptional individuals, instead of being deterred, should be encouraged in acting differently from the mass. In other times there was no advantage in their doing so, unless they acted not only differently but better. In this age, the mere example of non-conformity, the mere refusal to bend the knee to custom, is itself a service. Precisely because the tyranny of opinion is such as to make eccentricity a reproach, it is desirable, in order to break through that tyranny, that people should be eccentric. Eccentricity has always abounded when and where strength of character has abounded; and the amount of eccentricity in a society has generally been proportional to the amount of genius, mental vigour, and moral courage it contained. That so few now dare to be eccentric marks the chief danger of the time.

I have said that it is important to give the freest scope possible to uncustomary things, in order that it may in time appear which of these are fit to be converted into customs. But independence of action, and disregard of custom, are not solely deserving of encouragement for the chance they afford that better modes of action, and customs more worthy of general adoption, may be struck out; nor is it only persons of decided mental superiority who have a just claim to carry on their lives in their own way. There is no reason that all human existence should be constructed on some one or some small number of patterns. If a person possesses any tolerable amount of common sense and experience, his own mode of laying out his existence is the best, not because it is the best in itself, but because it is his own mode. Human beings are not like sheep; and even sheep are not undistinguishably alike. A man cannot get a coat or a pair of boots to fit him unless they are either made to his measure, or he has a whole warehouseful to choose from: and is it easier to fit him with a life than with a coat, or are human beings more like one another in their whole physical and spiritual conformation than in the shape of their feet? If it were only that people have diversities of taste, that is reason enough for not attempting to shape them all after one model. But different persons also require different conditions for their spiritual development; and can no more exist healthily in the same moral, than all the variety of plants can in the same physical, atmosphere and climate. The same things which are helps to one person towards the cultivation of his higher nature are hindrances to another. The same mode of life is a healthy excitement to one, keeping all his faculties of action and enjoyment in their best order, while to another it is a distracting burthen, which suspends or crushes all internal life. Such are the differences among human beings in their sources of pleasure, their susceptibilities of pain, and the operation on them of different physical and moral agencies, that unless there is a corresponding diversity in their modes of life, they neither obtain their fair share of happiness, nor grow up to the mental, moral, and æsthetic stature of which their nature is capable. Why then should tolerance, as far as the public sentiment is concerned, extend only to tastes and modes of life which extort acquiescence by the multitude of their adherents? Nowhere (except in some monastic institutions) is diversity of taste entirely unrecognised; a person may, without blame, either like or dislike rowing, or smoking, or music, or athletic exercises, or chess, or cards, or study, because both those who like each of these things, and those who dislike them, are too numerous to be put down. But the man, and still more the woman, who can be accused either of doing " what nobody does," or of not doing " what everybody does," is the subject of as much depreciatory remark as if he or she had committed some grave moral delinquency. Persons require to possess a title, or some other badge of rank, or of the consideration of people of rank, to be able to indulge somewhat in the luxury of doing as they like without detriment to their estimation. To indulge somewhat, I repeat : for whoever allow themselves much of that indulgence, incur the risk of something worse than disparaging speeches— they are in peril of a commission *de lunatico,* and of having their property taken from them and given to their relations.[8]

[8] There is something both contemptible and frightful in the sort of evidence on which, of late years, any person can be judicially declared unfit for the management of his affairs; and after his death, his disposal of his property can be set aside, if there is enough of it to pay the expenses of litigation—which are charged on the property itself. All the minute details of his daily life are pried into, and whatever is found which, seen through the medium of the perceiving and describing faculties of the lowest of the low, bears an appearance unlike absolute commonplace, is laid before the jury as evidence of insanity, and often with success; the jurors being little, if at all, less vulgar and ignorant than the witnesses; while the judges, with that extraordinary want of knowledge of human nature and life which continually astonishes us in English lawyers, often help to mislead them. These trials speak volumes as to the state of feeling and opinion among the vulgar with regard to human liberty. So far from setting any value on individuality—so far from respecting the right of each individual to act, in things indifferent, as seems good to his own judgment and

There is one characteristic of the present direction of public opinion peculiarly calculated to make it intolerant of any marked demonstration of individuality. The general average of mankind are not only moderate in intellect, but also moderate in inclinations : they have no tastes or wishes strong enough to incline them to do anything unusual, and they consequently do not understand those who have, and class all such with the wild and intemperate whom they are accustomed to look down upon. Now, in addition to this fact which is general, we have only to suppose that a strong movement has set in towards the improvement of morals, and it is evident what we have to expect. In these days such a movement has set in; much has actually been effected in the way of increased regularity of conduct and discouragement of excesses; and there is a philanthropic spirit abroad, for the exercise of which there is no more inviting field than the moral and prudential improvement of our fellow-creatures. These tendencies of the times cause the public to be more disposed than at most former periods to prescribe general rules of conduct, and endeavour to make every one conform to the approved standard. And that standard, express or tacit, is to desire nothing strongly. Its ideal of character is to be without any marked character; to maim by compression, like a Chinese lady's foot, every part of human nature which stands out prominently, and tends to make the person markedly dissimilar in outline to commonplace humanity.

As is usually the case with ideals which exclude one-half of what is desirable, the present standard of approbation produces only an inferior imitation of the other half. Instead of

---

inclinations, judges and juries cannot even conceive that a person in a state of sanity can desire such freedom. In former days, when it was proposed to burn atheists, charitable people used to suggest putting them in a madhouse instead: it would be nothing surprising now-a-days were we to see this done, and the doers applauding themselves, because, instead of persecuting for religion, they had adopted so humane and Christian a mode of treating these unfortunates, not without a silent satisfaction at their having thereby obtained their deserts.

great energies guided by vigorous reason, and strong feelings strongly controlled by a conscientious will, its result is weak feelings and weak energies, which therefore can be kept in outward conformity to rule without any strength either of will or of reason. Already energetic characters on any large scale are becoming merely traditional. There is now scarcely any outlet for energy in this country except business. The energy expended in this may still be regarded as considerable. What little is left from that employment is expended on some hobby; which may be a useful, even a philanthropic hobby, but is always some one thing, and generally a thing of small dimensions. The greatness of England is now all collective; individually small, we only appear capable of anything great by our habit of combining; and with this our moral and religious philanthropists are perfectly contented. But it was men of another stamp than this that made England what it has been; and men of another stamp will be needed to prevent its decline.

The despotism of custom is everywhere the standing hindrance to human advancement, being in unceasing antagonism to that disposition to aim at something better than customary, which is called, according to circumstances, the spirit of liberty, or that of progress or improvement. The spirit of improvement is not always a spirit of liberty, for it may aim at forcing improvements on an unwilling people; and the spirit of liberty, in so far as it resists such attempts, may ally itself locally and temporarily with the opponents of improvement; but the only unfailing and permanent source of improvement is liberty, since by it there are as many possible independent centres of improvement as there are individuals. The progressive principle, however, in either shape, whether as the love of liberty or of improvement, is antagonistic to the sway of Custom, involving at least emancipation from that yoke; and the contest between the two constitutes the chief interest of the history of mankind. The greater part of the world has, properly speaking, no history, because the despotism of Custom is complete. This is the case over the whole East. Custom is there, in all things, the final appeal; justice and right mean conformity to custom; the argument of custom no one, unless some tyrant intoxicated with power, thinks of resisting. And we see the result. Those nations must once have had originality; they did not start out of the ground populous, lettered, and versed in many of the arts of life; they made themselves all this, and were then the greatest and most powerful nations of the world. What are they now? The subjects or dependents of tribes whose forefathers wandered in the forests when theirs had magnificent palaces and gorgeous temples, but over whom custom exercised only a divided rule with liberty and progress. A people, it appears, may be progressive for a certain length of time, and then stop : when does it stop? When it ceases to possess individuality. If a similar change should befall the nations of Europe, it will not be in exactly the same shape : the despotism of custom with which these nations are threatened is not precisely stationariness. It proscribes singularity, but it does not preclude change, provided all change together. We have discarded the fixed costumes of our forefathers; every one must still dress like other people, but the fashion may change once or twice a year. We thus take care that when there is a change, it shall be for change's sake, and not from any idea of beauty or convenience; for the same idea of beauty or convenience would not strike all the world at the same moment, and be simultaneously thrown aside by all at another moment. But we are progressive as well as changeable : we continually make new inventions in mechanical things, and keep them until they are again superseded by better; we are eager for improvement in politics, in education, even in morals, though in this last our idea of improvement chiefly consists in persuading or forcing other people to be as good as ourselves. It is not progress that we object to; on the contrary, we flatter ourselves that we are the most progressive people who ever lived. It is individuality that we war against : we should think we had done wonders if we had made ourselves all alike; forgetting that the unlikeness of one person to another is generally the first thing which draws the attention of either to the imperfection of his own type, and the superiority of another, or the possibility, by combining the advantages of both, of producing something better than either. We have a warning example in China—a nation of much talent, and, in some respects, even wisdom, owing to the rare good fortune of having been provided at an early period with a particularly good set of customs, the work, in some measure, of men to whom even the most enlightened European must accord, under certain limitations, the title of sages and philosophers. They are remarkable, too, in the excellence of their apparatus for impressing, as far as possible, the best wisdom they possess upon every mind in the community, and securing that those who have appropriated most of it shall occupy the posts of honour and power. Surely the people who did this have discovered the secret of human progressiveness, and must have kept themselves steadily at the head of the movement of the world. On the contrary, they have become stationary—have remained so for thousands of years; and if they are ever to be further improved, it must be by foreigners. They have succeeded beyond all hope in what English philanthropists are so industriously working at—in making a people all alike, all governing their thoughts and conduct by the same maxims and rules; and these are the fruits. The modern *régime* of public opinion is, in an unorganised form, what the Chinese educational and political systems are in an organised; and unless individuality shall be able successfully to assert itself against this yoke, Europe, notwithstanding its noble ante-cedents and its professed Christianity, will tend to become another China.

What is it that has hitherto preserved Europe from this lot? What has made the European family of nations an improving, instead of a stationary portion of mankind? Not any superior excellence in them, which, when it exists, exists as the effect not as the cause; but their remarkable diversity of character and culture. Individuals, classes, nations, have been extremely unlike one another : they have struck out a great variety of paths, each leading to something valuable; and although at every period those who travelled in different paths have been intolerant of one another, and each would have thought it an excellent thing if all the rest could have been compelled to travel his road, their attempts to thwart each other's development have rarely had any permanent success, and each has in time endured to receive the good which the others have offered. Europe is, in my judgment, wholly indebted to this plurality of paths for its progressive and many-sided development. But it already begins to possess this benefit in a considerably less degree. It is decidedly advancing towards the Chinese ideal of making all people alike. M. de Tocqueville, in his last important work, remarks how much more the Frenchmen of the present day resemble one another than did those even of the last generation. The same remark might be made of Englishmen in a far greater degree. In a passage already quoted from Wilhelm von Humboldt, he points out two things as necessary conditions of human development, because necessary to render people unlike one another; namely, freedom, and variety of situations. The second of these two conditions is in this country every day diminishing. The circumstances which surround different classes and individuals, and shape their characters, are daily becoming more assimilated. Formerly, different ranks, different neighbourhoods, different trades and professions, lived in what might be called different worlds; at present to a great degree in the same. Comparatively speaking, they now read the same things, listen to the same things, see the same things, go to the same places, have their hopes and fears directed to the same objects, have the same rights and liberties, and the same means of asserting them. Great as are the differences of position which remain, they are nothing to those which have ceased. And the assimilation is still proceeding. All the political changes of the age promote it, since they all tend to raise the low and to lower the high. Every extension of education promotes it, because education brings people under common influences, and gives them access to the general stock of facts and sentiments. Improvements in the means of communication promotes it, by bringing the inhabitants of distant places into personal contact, and keeping up a rapid flow of changes of residence between one place and another. The increase of commerce and manufactures promotes it, by diffusing more widely the advantages of easy circumstances, and opening all objects of ambition, even the highest, to general competition, whereby the desire of rising becomes no longer the character of a particular class, but of all classes. A more powerful agency than all these, in bringing about a general similarity among mankind, is the complete establishment, in this and other free countries, of the ascendancy of public opinion in the State. As the various social eminences which enabled persons entrenched on them to disregard the opinion of the multitude gradually become levelled; as the very idea of resisting the will of the public, when it is positively known that they have a will, disappears more and more from the minds of practical politicians; there ceases to be any social support for non-conformity—any substantive power in society which, itself opposed to the ascendancy of numbers, is interested in taking under its protection opinions and tendencies at variance with those of the public.

The combination of all these causes forms so great a mass of influences hostile to Individuality, that it is not easy to see how it can stand its ground. It will do so with increasing difficulty, unless the intelligent part of the public can be made to feel its value—to see that it is good there should be differences, even though not for the better, even though, as it may appear to them, some should be for the worse. If the claims of Individuality are ever to be asserted, the time is now, while much is still wanting to complete the enforced assimiliation. It is only in the earlier stages that any stand can be successfully made against the encroachment. The demand that all other people shall resemble ourselves grows by what it feeds on. If resistance waits till life is reduced *nearly* to one uniform type, all deviations from that type will come to be considered impious, immoral, even monstrous and contrary to nature. Mankind speedily become unable to conceive diversity, when they have been for some time unaccustomed to see it.

CHAPTER IV

OF THE LIMITS TO THE AUTHORITY OF SOCIETY OVER THE INDIVIDUAL

What, then, is the rightful limit to the sovereignty of the individual over himself? Where does the authority of society begin? How much of human life should be assigned to individuality, and how much to society?

Each will receive its proper share, if each has that which more particularly concerns it. To individuality should belong the part of life in which it is chiefly the individual that is interested; to society, the part which chiefly interests society. Though society is not founded on a contract, and though no good purpose is answered by inventing a contract in order to deduce social obligations from it, every one who receives the protection of society owes a return for the benefit, and the fact of living in society renders it indispensable that each should be bound to observe a certain line of conduct towards the rest. This conduct consists, first, in not injuring the interests of one another; or rather certain interests, which, either by express legal provision or by tacit understanding, ought to be considered as rights; and secondly, in each person's bearing his share (to be fixed on some equitable principle) of the labours and sacrifices incurred for defending the society or its members from injury and molestation. These conditions society is justified in enforcing, at all costs to those who endeavour to withhold fulfilment. Nor is this all that society may do. The acts of an individual may be hurtful to others, or wanting in due consideration for their welfare, without going to the length of violating any of their constituted rights. The offender may then be justly punished by opinion, though not by law. As soon as any part of a person's conduct affects prejudicially the interests of others, society has jurisdiction over it, and the question whether the general welfare will or will not be promoted by interfering with it, becomes open to discussion. But there is no room for entertaining any such

question when a person's conduct affects the interests of
no persons besides himself, or needs not affect them unless
they like (all the persons concerned being of full age, and
the ordinary amount of understanding). In all such cases,
there should be perfect freedom, legal and social, to do
the action and stand the consequences.

It would be a great misunderstanding of this doctrine to
suppose that it is one of selfish indifference, which pretends
that human beings have no business with each other's conduct in life, and that they should not concern themselves about
the well-doing or well-being of one another, unless their
own interest is involved. Instead of any diminution, there is
need of a great increase of disinterested exertion to promote
the good of others. But disinterested benevolence can find
other instruments to persuade people to their good than whips
and scourges, either of the literal or the metaphorical sort. I
am the last person to undervalue the self-regarding virtues;
they are only second in importance, if even second, to the
social. It is equally the business of education to cultivate both.
But even education works by conviction and persuasion as
well as by compulsion, and it is by the former only that,
when the period of education is passed, the self-regarding
virtues should be inculcated. Human beings owe to each
other help to distinguish the better from the worse, and
encouragement to choose the former and avoid the latter. They
should be for ever stimulating each other to increased exercise
of their higher faculties, and increased direction of their
feelings and aims towards wise instead of foolish, elevating
instead of degrading, objects and contemplations. But neither
one person, nor any number of persons, is warranted in
saying to another human creature of ripe years, that he shall
not do with his life for his own benefit what he chooses to do
with it. He is the person most interested in his own well-
being: the interest which any other person, except in cases
of strong personal attachment, can have in it, is trifling,
compared with that which he himself has; the interest which
society has in him individually (except as to his conduct to
others) is fractional, and altogether indirect; while with
respect to his own feelings and circumstances, the most

ordinary man or woman has means of knowledge immeasurably surpassing those that can be possessed by any one else. The interference of society to overrule his judgment and purposes in what only regards himself must be grounded on general presumptions; which may be altogether wrong, and even if right, are as likely as not to be misapplied to individual cases, by persons no better acquainted with the circumstances of such cases than those are who look at them merely from without. In this department, therefore, of human affairs, Individuality has its proper field of action. In the conduct of human beings towards one another it is necessary that general rules should for the most part be observed, in order that people may know what they have to expect : but in each person's own concerns his individual spontaneity is entitled to free exercise. Considerations to aid his judgment, exhortations to strengthen his will, may be offered to him, even obtruded on him, by others : but he himself is the final judge. All errors which he is likely to commit against advice and warning are far outweighed by the evil of allowing others to constrain him to what they deem his good.

I do not mean that the feelings with which a person is regarded by others ought not to be in any way affected by his self-regarding qualities or deficiencies. This is neither possible nor desirable. If he is eminent in any of the qualities which conduce to his own good, he is, so far, a proper object of admiration. He is so much the nearer to the ideal perfection of human nature. If he is grossly deficient in those qualities, a sentiment the opposite of admiration will follow. There is a degree of folly, and a degree of what may be called (though the phrase is not unobjectionable) lowness or depravation of taste, which, though it cannot justify doing harm to the person who manifests it, renders him necessarily and properly a subject of distaste, or, in extreme cases, even of contempt : a person could not have the opposite qualities in due strength without entertaining these feelings. Though doing no worse to any one, a person may so act as to compel us to judge him, and feel to him, as a fool, or as a being of an inferior order : and since this judgment and feeling are a fact which he would prefer to avoid, it is doing him a service to warn him of it beforehand, as of any other disagreeable consequence to which he exposes himself. It would be well, indeed, if this good office were much more freely rendered than the common notions of politeness at present permit, and if one person could honestly point out to another that he thinks him in fault, without being considered unmannerly or presuming. We have a right, also, in various ways, to act upon our unfavourable opinion of any one, not to the oppression of his individuality, but in the exercise of ours. We are not bound, for example, to seek his society; we have a right to avoid it (though not to parade the avoidance), for we have a right to choose the society most acceptable to us. We have a right, and it may be our duty, to caution others against him, if we think his example or conversation likely to have a pernicious effect on those with whom he associates. We may give others a preference over him in optional good offices, except those which tend to his improvement. In these various modes a person may suffer very severe penalties at the hands of others for faults which directly concern only himself; but he suffers these penalties only in so far as they are the natural and, as it were, the spontaneous consequences of the faults themselves, not because they are purposely inflicted on him for the sake of punishment. A person who shows rashness, obstinacy, self-conceit—who cannot live within moderate means—who cannot restrain himself from hurtful indulgences—who pursues animal pleasures at the expense of those of feeling and intellect—must expect to be lowered in the opinion of others, and to have a less share of their favourable sentiments; but of this he has no right to complain, unless he has merited their favour by special excellence in his social relations, and has thus established a title to their good offices, which is not affected by his demerits towards himself.

What I contend for is, that the inconveniences which are strictly inseparable from the unfavourable judgment of others, are the only ones to which a person should ever be subjected for that portion of his conduct and character which concerns his own good, but which does not affect the interest of others in their relations with him. Acts injurious to others require a totally different treatment. Encroachment on their rights; infliction on them of any loss or damage not justified by his own rights; falsehood or duplicity in dealing with them; unfair or ungenerous use of advantages over them; even selfish abstinence from defending them against injury —these are fit objects of moral reprobation, and, in grave cases, of moral retribution and punishment. And not only these acts, but the dispositions which lead to them, are properly immoral, and fit subjects of disapprobation which may rise to abhorrence. Cruelty of disposition; malice and ill-nature; that most anti-social and odious of all passions, envy; dissimulation and insincerity, irascibility on insufficient cause, and resentment disproportioned to the provocation; the love of domineering over others; the desire to engross more than one's share of advantages (the πλεονεξία of the Greeks); the pride which derives gratification from the abasement of others; the egotism which thinks self and its concerns more important than everything else, and decides all doubtful questions in its own favour;—these are moral vices, and constitute a bad and odious moral character: unlike the self-regarding faults previously mentioned, which are not properly immoralities, and to whatever pitch they may be carried, do not constitute wickedness. They may be proofs of any amount of folly, or want of personal dignity and self-respect; but they are only a subject of moral reprobation when they involve a breach of duty to others, for whose sake the individual is bound to have care for himself. What are called duties to ourselves are not socially obligatory, unless circumstances render them at the same time duties to others. The term duty to oneself, when it means anything more than prudence, means self-respect or self-development, and for none of these is any one accountable to his fellow-creatures, because for none of them is it for the good of mankind that he be held accountable to them.

The distinction between the loss of consideration which a person may rightly incur by defect of prudence or of personal dignity, and the reprobation which is due to him for an offence against the rights of others, is not a merely nominal dis-

tinction. It makes a vast difference both in our feelings and
in our conduct towards him whether he displeases us in
things in which we think we have a right to control him, or
in things in which we know that we have not. If he displeases us, we may express our distaste, and we may stand
aloof from a person as well as from a thing that displeases
us; but we shall not therefore feel called on to make his
life uncomfortable. We shall reflect that he already bears,
or will bear, the whole penalty of his error; if he spoils
his life by mismanagement, we shall not, for that reason,
desire to spoil it still further : instead of wishing to punish
him, we shall rather endeavour to alleviate his punishment,
by showing him how he may avoid or cure the evils his
conduct tends to bring upon him. He may be to us an object
of pity, perhaps of dislike, but not of anger or resentment;
we shall not treat him like an enemy of society : the worst
we shall think ourselves justified in doing is leaving him
to himself, if we do not interfere benevolently by showing
interest or concern for him. It is far otherwise if he has
infringed the rules necessary for the protection of his fellow-
creatures, individually or collectively. The evil consequences
of his acts do not then fall on himself, but on others; and
society, as the protector of all its members, must retaliate
on him; must inflict pain on him for the express purpose of
punishment, and must take care that it be sufficiently severe.
In the one case, he is an offender at our bar, and we are called
on not only to sit in judgment on him, but, in one shape or
another, to execute our own sentence : in the other case, it
is not our part to inflict any suffering on him, except what
may incidentally follow from our using the same liberty in
the regulation of our own affairs, which we allow to him
in his.

The distinction here pointed out between the part of a
person's life which concerns only himself, and that which
concerns others, many persons will refuse to admit. How
(it may be asked) can any part of the conduct of a member of
society be a matter of indifference to the other members? No
person is an entirely isolated being; it is impossible for a
person to do anything seriously or permanently hurtful to

himself, without mischief reaching at least to his near connections, and often far beyond them. If he injures his property, he does harm to those who directly or indirectly derived support from it, and usually diminishes, by a greater or less amount, the general resources of the community. If he deteriorates his bodily or mental faculties, he not only brings evil upon all who depended on him for any portion of their happiness, but disqualifies himself for rendering the services which he owes to his fellow-creatures generally; perhaps becomes a burthen on their affection or benevolence; and if such conduct were very frequent, hardly any offence that is committed would detract more from the general sum of good. Finally, if by his vices or follies a person does no direct harm to others, he is nevertheless (it may be said) injurious by his example; and ought to be compelled to control himself, for the sake of those whom the sight or knowledge of his conduct might corrupt or mislead.

And even (it will be added) if the consequences of misconduct could be confined to the vicious or thoughtless individual, ought society to abandon to their own guidance those who are manifestly unfit for it? If protection against themselves is confessedly due to children and persons under age, is not society equally bound to afford it to persons of mature years who are equally incapable of self-government? If gambling, or drunkenness, or incontinence, or idleness, or uncleanliness, are as injurious to happiness, and as great a hindrance to improvement, as many or most of the acts prohibited by law, why (it may be asked) should not law, so far as is consistent with practicability and social convenience, endeavour to repress these also? And as a supplement to the unavoidable imperfections of law, ought not opinion at least to organise a powerful police against these vices, and visit rigidly with social penalties those who are known to practise them? There is no question here (it may be said) about restricting individuality, or impeding the trial of new and original experiments in living. The only things it is sought to prevent are things which have been tried and condemned from the beginning of the world until now; things which experience has shown not to be useful or suitable to any person's individuality. There must be some length of time and amount of experience after which a moral or prudential truth may be regarded as established : and it is merely desired to prevent generation after generation from falling over the same precipice which has been fatal to their predecessors.

I fully admit that the mischief which a person does to himself may seriously affect, both through their sympathies and their interests, those nearly connected with him and, in a minor degree, society at large. When, by conduct of this sort, a person is led to violate a distinct and assignable obligation to any other person or persons, the case is taken out of the self-regarding class, and becomes amenable to moral disapprobation in the proper sense of the term. If, for example, a man, through intemperance or extravagance, becomes unable to pay his debts, or, having undertaken the moral responsibility of a family, becomes from the same cause incapable of supporting or educating them, he is deservedly reprobated, and might be justly punished; but it is for the breach of duty to his family or creditors, not for the extravagance. If the resources which ought to have been devoted to them, had been diverted from them for the most prudent investment, the moral culpability would have been the same. George Barnwell murdered his uncle to get money for his mistress, but if he had done it to set himself up in business, he would equally have been hanged. Again, in the frequent case of a man who causes grief to his family by addiction to bad habits, he deserves reproach for his unkindness or ingratitude; but so he may for cultivating habits not in themselves vicious, if they are painful to those with whom he passes his life, or who from personal ties are dependent on him for their comfort. Whoever fails in the consideration generally due to the interests and feelings of others, not being compelled by some more imperative duty, or justified by allowable self-preference, is a subject of moral disapprobation for that failure, but not for the cause of it, nor for the errors, merely personal to himself, which may have remotely led to it. In like manner, when a person disables himself, by conduct purely self-regarding, from the performance of some definite duty incumbent on him to the public, he is guilty of a social offence. No person ought to be punished simply for being drunk; but a soldier or a policeman should be punished for being drunk on duty. Whenever, in short, there is a definite damage, or a definite risk of damage, either to an individual or to the public, the case is taken out of the province of liberty, and placed in that of morality or law.

But with regard to the merely contingent, or, as it may be called, constructive injury which a person causes to society, by conduct which neither violates any specific duty to the public, nor occasions perceptible hurt to any assignable individual except himself; the inconvenience is one which society can afford to bear, for the sake of the greater good of human freedom. If grown persons are to be punished for not taking proper care of themselves, I would rather it were for their own sake, than under pretence of preventing them from impairing their capacity or rendering to society benefits which society does not pretend it has a right to exact. But I cannot consent to argue the point as if society had no means of bringing its weaker members up to its ordinary standard of rational conduct, except waiting till they do something irrational, and then punishing them, legally or morally, for it. Society has had absolute power over them during all the early portion of their existence: it has had the whole period of childhood and nonage in which to try whether it could make them capable of rational conduct in life. The existing generation is master both of the training and the entire circumstances of the generation to come; it cannot indeed make them perfectly wise and good, because it is itself lamentably deficient in goodness and wisdom; and its best efforts are not always, in individual cases, its most successful ones; but it is perfectly well able to make the rising generation, as a whole, as good as, and a little better than, itself. If society lets any considerable number of its members grow up mere children, incapable of being acted on by rational consideration of distant motives, society has itself to blame for the consequences. Armed not only with all the powers of education, but with the ascendancy which the authority of a received opinion always exercises over the minds who are least fitted to judge for themselves; and aided by the *natural* penalties which cannot be prevented from falling on those who incur the distaste or the contempt of those who know them; let not society pretend that it needs, besides all this, the power to issue commands and enforce obedience in the personal concerns of individuals, in which, on all principles of justice and policy, the decision ought to rest with those who are to abide the consequences. Nor is there anything which tends more to discredit and frustrate the better means of influencing conduct than a resort to the worse. If there be among those whom it is attempted to coerce into prudence or temperance any of the material of which vigorous and independent characters are made, they will infallibly rebel against the yoke. No such person will ever feel that others have a right to control him in his concerns, such as they have to prevent him from injuring them in theirs; and it easily comes to be considered a mark of spirit and courage to fly in the face of such usurped authority, and do with ostentation the exact opposite of what it enjoins; as in the fashion of grossness which succeeded, in the time of Charles II, to the fanatical moral intolerance of the Puritans. With respect to what is said of the necessity of protecting society from the bad example set to others by the vicious or the self-indulgent; it is true that bad example may have a pernicious effect, especially the example of doing wrong to others with impunity to the wrong-doer. But we are now speaking of conduct which, while it does no wrong to others, is supposed to do great harm to the agent himself : and I do not see how those who believe this can think otherwise than that the example, on the whole, must be more salutary than hurtful, since, if it displays the misconduct, it displays also the painful or degrading consequences which, if the conduct is justly censured, must be supposed to be in all or most cases attendant on it.

But the strongest of all the arguments against the interference of the public with purely personal conduct is that, when it does interfere, the odds are that it interferes wrongly, and in the wrong place. On questions of social morality, of duty to others, the opinion of the public, that is, of an overruling majority, though often wrong, is likely to be still oftener right; because on such questions they are only required to judge of their own interests; of the manner in which some mode of conduct, if allowed to be practised, would effect themselves. But the opinion of a similar majority, imposed as a law on the minority, on questions of self-regarding conduct, is quite as likely to be wrong as right; for in these cases public opinion means, at the best, some people's opinion of what is good or bad for other people; while very often it does not even mean that; the public, with the most perfect indifference, passing over the pleasure or convenience of those whose conduct they censure, and considering only their own preference. There are many who consider as an injury to themselves any conduct which they have a distaste for, and resent it as an outrage to their feelings; as a religious bigot, when charged with disregarding the religious feelings of others, has been known to retort that they disregard his feelings, by persisting in their abominable worship or creed. But there is no parity between the feeling of a person for his own opinion, and the feeling of another who is offended at his holding it; no more than between the desire of a thief to take a purse, and the desire of the right owner to keep it. And a person's taste is as much his own peculiar concern as his opinion or his purse. It is easy for any one to imagine an ideal public which leaves the freedom and choice of individuals in all uncertain matters undisturbed, and only requires them to abstain from modes of conduct which universal experience has condemned. But where has there been seen a public which set any such limit to its censorship? or when does the public trouble itself about universal experience? In its interferences with personal conduct it is seldom thinking of anything but the enormity of acting or feeling differently from itself; and this standard of judgment, thinly disguised, is held up to mankind as the dictate of religion and philosophy, by nine-tenths of all moralists and speculative writers. These teach that things are right because they are right; because we feel them to be so. They tell us to search in our own minds and hearts for laws of conduct binding on ourselves and on all others.

What can the poor public do but apply these instructions, and make their own personal feelings of good and evil, if they are tolerably unanimous in them, obligatory on all the world?

The evil here pointed out is not one which exists only in theory; and it may perhaps be expected that I should specify the instances in which the public of this age and country improperly invests its own preferences with the character of moral laws. I am not writing an essay on the aberrations of existing moral feeling. That is too weighty a subject to be discussed parenthetically, and by way of illustration. Yet examples are necessary to show that the principle I maintain is of serious and practical moment, and that I am not endeavouring to erect a barrier against imaginary evils. And it is not difficult to show, by abundant instances, that to extend the bounds of what may be called moral police, until it encroaches on the most unquestionably legitimate liberty of the individual, is one of the most universal of all human propensities.

As a first instance, consider the antipathies which men cherish on no better grounds than that persons whose religious opinions are different from theirs do not practise their religious observances, especially their religious abstinences. To cite a rather trivial example, nothing in the creed or practice of Christians does more to envenom the hatred of Mahomedans against them than the fact of their eating pork. There are few acts which Christians and Europeans regard with more unaffected disgust than Mussulmans regard this particular mode of satisfying hunger. It is, in the first place, an offence against their religion; but this circumstance by no means explains either the degree or the kind of their repugnance; for wine also is forbidden by their religion, and to partake of it is by all Mussulmans accounted wrong, but not disgusting. Their aversion to the flesh of the "unclean beast" is, on the contrary, of that peculiar character, resembling an instinctive antipathy, which the idea of uncleanness, when once it thoroughly sinks into the feelings, seems always to excite even in those whose personal habits are anything but scrupulously cleanly and of which the sentiment of religious impurity, so intense in the Hindoos, is a remarkable example. Suppose now that in a people, of whom the majority were Mussulmans, that majority should insist upon not permitting pork to be eaten within the limits of the country. This would be nothing new in Mahomedan countries.[1] Would it be a legitimate exercise of the moral authority of public opinion? and if not, why not? The practice is really revolting to such a public. They also sincerely think that it is forbidden and abhorred by the Deity. Neither could the prohibition be censured as religious persecution. It might be religious in its origin, but it would not be persecution for religion, since nobody's religion makes it a duty to eat pork. The only tenable ground of condemnation would be that with the personal tastes and self-regarding concerns of individuals the public has no business to interfere.

To come somewhat nearer home : the majority of Spaniards consider it a gross impiety, offensive in the highest degree to the Supreme Being, to worship him in any other manner than the Roman Catholic; and no other public worship is lawful on Spanish soil. The people of all Southern Europe look upon a married clergy as not only irreligious, but unchaste, indecent, gross, disgusting. What do Protestants think of these perfectly sincere feelings, and of the attempt to enforce them against non-Catholics? Yet, if mankind are justified in interfering with each other's liberty in things which do not concern the interests of others, on what principle is it possible consistently to exclude these cases? or who can blame people for desiring to suppress what they regard as a scandal in the sight of God and man? No stronger case can be shown

[1] The case of the Bombay Parsees is a curious instance in point. When this industrious and enterprising tribe, the descendants of the Persian fire-worshippers, flying from their native country before the Caliphs, arrived in Western India, they were admitted to toleration by the Hindoo sovereigns, on condition of not eating beef. When those regions afterwards fell under the dominion of Mahomedan conquerors, the Parsees obtained from them a continuance of indulgence, on condition of refraining from pork. What was at first obedience to authority became a second nature, and the Parsees to this day abstain both from beef and pork. Though not required by their religion, the double abstinence has had time to grow into a custom of their tribe; and custom, in the East, is a religion.

for prohibiting anything which is regarded as a personal immorality, than is made out for suppressing these practices in the eyes of those who regard them as impieties; and unless we are willing to adopt the logic of persecutors, and to say that we may persecute others because we are right, and that they must not persecute us because they are wrong, we must beware of admitting a principle of which we should resent as a gross injustice the application to ourselves.

The preceding instances may be objected to, although unreasonably, as drawn from contingencies impossible among us : opinion, in this country, not being likely to enforce abstinence from meats, or to interfere with people for worshipping, and for either marrying or not marrying, according to their creed or inclination. The next example, however, shall be taken from an interference with liberty which we have by no means passed all danger of. Wherever the Puritans have been sufficiently powerful, as in New England, and in Great Britain at the time of the Commonwealth, they have endeavoured, with considerable success, to put down all public, and nearly all private, amusements : especially music, dancing, public games, or other assemblages for purposes of diversion, and the theatre. There are still in this country large bodies of persons by whose notions of morality and religion these recreations are condemned; and those persons belonging chiefly to the middle class, who are the ascendant power in the present social and political condition of the kingdom, it is by no means impossible that persons of these sentiments may at some time or other command a majority in Parliament. How will the remaining portion of the community like to have the amusements that shall be permitted to them regulated by the religious and moral sentiments of the stricter Calvinists and Methodists? Would they not, with considerable peremptoriness, desire these intrusively pious members of society to mind their own business? This is precisely what should be said to every government and every public, who have the pretension that no person shall enjoy any pleasure which they think wrong. But if the principle of the pretension be admitted, no one can reasonably object to its being acted on in the sense of the majority, or other preponderating power in the country; and all persons must be ready to conform to the idea of a Christian commonwealth, as understood by the early settlers in New England, if a religious profession similiar to theirs should ever succeed in regaining its lost ground, as religions supposed to be declining have so often been known to do.

To imagine another contingency, perhaps more likely to be realised than the one last mentioned. There is confessedly a strong tendency in the modern world towards a democratic constitution of society, accompanied or not by popular political institutions. It is affirmed that in the country where this tendency is most completely realised—where both society and the government are most democratic—the United States—the feeling of the majority, to whom any appearance of a more showy or costly style of living than they can hope to rival is disagreeable, operates as a tolerably effectual sumptuary law, and that in many parts of the Union it is really difficult for a person possessing a very large income to find any mode of spending it which will not incur popular disapprobation. Though such statements as these are doubtless much exaggerated as a representation of existing facts, the state of things they describe is not only a conceivable and possible, but a probable result of democratic feeling, combined with the notion that the public has a right to a veto on the manner in which individuals shall spend their incomes. We have only further to suppose a considerable diffusion of Socialist opinions, and it may become infamous in the eyes of the majority to possess more property than some very small amount, or any income not earned by manual labour. Opinions similar in principle to these already prevail widely among the artisan class, and weigh oppressively on those who are amenable to the opinion chiefly of that class, namely, its own members. It is known that the bad workmen who form the majority of the operatives in many branches of industry, are decidedly of opinion that bad workmen ought to receive the same wages as good, and that no one ought to be allowed, through piecework or otherwise, to earn by superior skill or industry more than others can without it. And they employ a moral police, which occasionally becomes a physical one, to deter skilful workmen from receiving, and employers from giving, a larger remuneration for a more useful service. If the public have any jurisdiction over private concerns, I cannot see that these people are in fault, or that any individual's particular public can be blamed for asserting the same authority over his individual conduct which the general public asserts over people in general.

But, without dwelling upon supposititious cases, there are, in our own day, gross usurpations upon the liberty of private life actually practised, and still greater ones threatened with some expectation of success, and opinions propounded which assert an unlimited right in the public not only to prohibit by law everything which it thinks wrong, but, in order to get at what it thinks wrong, to prohibit a number of things which it admits to be innocent.

Under the name of preventing intemperance, the people of one English colony, and of nearly half the United States, have been interdicted by law from making any use whatever of fermented drinks, except for medical purposes : for prohibition of their sale is in fact, as it is intended to be, prohibition of their use. And though the impracticability of executing the law has caused its repeal in several of the States which had adopted it, including the one from which it derives its name, an attempt has notwithstanding been commenced, and is prosecuted with considerable zeal by many of the professed philanthropists, to agitate for a similar law in this country. The association, or " Alliance " as it terms itself, which has been formed for this purpose, has acquired some notoriety through the publicity given to a correspondence between its secretary and one of the very few English public men who hold that a politician's opinions ought to be founded on principles. Lord Stanley's share in this correspondence is calculated to strengthen the hopes already built on him, by those who know how rare such qualities as are manifested in some of his public appearances unhappily are among those who figure in political life. The organ of the Alliance, who would " deeply deplore the recognition of any principle which could be wrested to justify bigotry and persecution," undertakes to point out the " broad and impassable barrier " which divides such principles from those of the association. "All matters relating to thought, opinion, conscience, appear to me," he says, "to be without the sphere of legislation; all pertaining to social act, habit, relation, subject only to a discretionary power vested in the State itself, and not in the individual, to be within it." No mention is made of a third class, different from either of these, viz., acts and habits which are not social, but individual; although it is to this class, surely, that the act of drinking fermented liquors belongs. Selling fermented liquors, however, is trading, and trading is a social act. But the infringement complained of is not on the liberty of the seller, but on that of the buyer and consumer; since the State might just as well forbid him to drink wine as purposely make it impossible for him to obtain it. The secretary, however, says, "I claim, as a citizen, a right to legislate whenever my social rights are invaded by the social act of another." And now for the definition of these "social rights." "If anything invades my social rights, certainly the traffic in strong drink does. It destroys my primary right of security, by constantly creating and stimulating social disorder. It invades my right of equality, by deriving a profit from the creation of a misery I am taxed to support. It impedes my right to free moral and intellectual development, by surrounding my path with dangers, and by weakening and demoralising society, from which I have a right to claim mutual aid and intercourse." A theory of "social rights" the like which probably never before found its way into distinct language : being nothing short of this—that it is the absolute social right of every individual, that every other individual shall act in every respect exactly as he ought; that whosoever fails thereof in the smallest particular violates my social right, and entitles me to demand from the legislature the removal of the grievance. So monstrous a principle is far more dangerous than any single interference with liberty; there is no violation of liberty which it would not justify; it acknowledges no right to any freedom whatever, except perhaps to that of holding opinions in secret, without ever disclosing them : for, the moment an opinion which I consider noxious passes any one's lips, it invades all the "social rights" attributed to me by the Alliance. The doctrine ascribes to all mankind a vested interest in each other's moral, intellectual, and even physical perfection, to be defined by each claimant according to his own standard.

Another important example of illegitimate interference with the rightful liberty of the individual, not simply threatened, but long since carried into triumphant effect, is Sabbatarian legislation. Without doubt, abstinence on one day in the week, so far as the exigencies of life permit, from the usual daily occupation, though in no respect religiously binding on any except Jews, is a highly beneficial custom. And inasmuch as this custom cannot be observed without a general consent to that effect among the industrious classes, therefore, in so far as some persons by working may impose the same necessity on others, it may be allowable and right that the law should guarantee to each the observance by others of the custom, by suspending the greater operations of industry on a particular day. But this justification, grounded on the direct interest which others have in each individual's observance of the practice, does not apply to the self-chosen occupations in which a person may think fit to employ his leisure; nor does it hold good, in the smallest degree, for legal restrictions on amusements. It is true that the amusement of some is the day's work of others; but the pleasure, not to say the useful recreation, of many, is worth the labour of a few, provided the occupation is freely chosen, and can be freely resigned. The operatives are perfectly right in thinking that if all worked on Sunday, seven days' work would have to be given for six days' wages; but so long as the great mass of employments are suspended, the small number who for the enjoyment of others must still work, obtain a proportional increase of earnings; and they are not obliged to follow those occupations if they prefer leisure to emolument. If a further remedy is sought, it might be found in the establishment by custom of a holiday on some other day of the week for those particular classes of persons. The only ground, therefore, on which restrictions on Sunday amusements can be defended, must be that they are religiously wrong; a motive of legislation which can never be too earnestly protested against.

" Deorum injuriæ Diis curæ." It remains to be proved that society or any of its officers holds a commission from on high to avenge any supposed offence to Omnipotence, which is not also a wrong to our fellow-creatures. The notion that it is one man's duty that another should be religious, was the foundation of all the religious persecutions ever perpetuated, and, if admitted, would fully justify them. Though the feeling which breaks out in the repeated attempts to stop railway travelling on Sunday, in the resistance to the opening of Museums, and the like, has not the cruelty of the old persecutors, the state of mind indicated by it is fundamentally the same. It is a determination not to tolerate others in doing what is permitted by their religion, because it is not permitted by the persecutor's religion. It is a belief that God not only abominates the act of the misbeliever, but will not hold us guiltless if we leave him unmolested.

I cannot refrain from adding to these examples of the little account commonly made of human liberty, the language of downright persecution which breaks out from the press of this country whenever it feels called on to notice the remarkable phenomenon of Mormonism. Much might be said on the unexpected and instructive fact that an alleged new revelation, and a religion founded on it, the product of palpable imposture, not even supported by the *prestige* of extraordinary qualities in its founder, is believed by hundreds of thousands, and has been made the foundation of a society, in the age of newspapers, railways, and the electric telegraph. What here concerns us is, that this religion, like other and better religions, has its martyrs : that its prophet and founder was, for his teaching, put to death by a mob; that others of its adherents lost their lives by the same lawless violence; that they were forcibly expelled, in a body, from the country in which they first grew up; while now that they have been chased into a solitary recess in the midst of a desert, many in this country openly declare that it would be right (only that it is not convenient) to send an expedition against them, and compel them by force to conform to the opinions of other people. The article of the Mormonite doctrine which is the chief provocative to the antipathy which thus breaks through the ordinary restraints of religious tolerance, is its sanction of polygamy; which, though permitted to Mahomedans, and Hindoos, and Chinese, seems to excite unquenchable animosity when practised by persons who speak English and profess to be a kind of Christian. No one has a deeper disapprobation than I have of this Mormon institution; both for other reasons, and because, far from being in any way countenanced by the principle of liberty, it is a direct infraction of that principle, being a mere riveting of the chains of one half of the community, and an emancipation of the other from reciprocity of obligation towards them. Still, it must be remembered that this relation is as much voluntary on the part of the women concerned in it, and who may be deemed the sufferers by it, as is the case with any other form of the marriage institution; and however surprising this fact may appear, it has its explanation in the common ideas and customs of the world, which teaching women to think marriage the one thing needful, make it intelligible that many a woman should prefer being one of several wives, to not being a wife at all. Other countries are not asked to recognise such unions, or release any portion of their inhabitants from their own laws on the score of Mormonite opinions. But when the dissentients have conceded to the hostile sentiments of others far more than could justly be demanded; when they have left the countries to which their doctrines were unacceptable, and established themselves in a remote corner of the earth, which they have been the first to render habitable to human beings; it is difficult to see on what principles but those of tyranny they can be prevented from living there under what laws they please, provided they commit no aggression on other nations, and allow perfect freedom of departure to those who are dissatisfied with their ways. A recent writer, in some respects of considerable merit, proposes (to use his own words) not a crusade, but a *civilisade,* against this polygamous community, to put an end to what seems to him a retrograde step in civilisation. It also appears so to me, but I am not aware that any community has a right to force another to be civilised. So long as the sufferers by the bad law do not invoke assistance from other communities, I cannot admit that persons entirely unconnected with them ought to step in and require that a condition of things with which all who are directly interested appear to be satisfied, should be put an end to because it is a scandal to persons some thousands of miles distant, who have no part or concern in it. Let them send missionaries, if they please, to preach against it; and let them, by any fair means (of which silencing the teachers is not one), oppose the progress of similar doctrines among their own people. If civilisation has got the better of barbarism when barbarism had the world to itself, it is too much to profess to be afraid lest barabarism, after having been fairly got under, should revive and conquer civilisation. A civilisation that can thus succumb to its vanquished enemy, must first have become so degenerate, that neither its appointed priests and teachers, nor anybody else, has the capacity, or will take the trouble, to stand up for it. If this be so, the sooner such a civilisation receives notice to quit the better. It can only go on from bad to worse, until destroyed and regenerated (like the Western Empire) by energetic barbarians.

CHAPTER V

APPLICATIONS

The principles asserted in these pages must be more generally admitted as the basis for discussion of details, before a consistent application of them to all the various departments of government and morals can be attempted with any prospect of advantage. The few observations I propose to make on questions of detail are designed to illustrate the principles, rather than to follow them out to their consequences. I offer, not so much applications, as specimens of application; which may serve to bring into greater clearness the meaning and limits of the two maxims which together form the entire doctrine of this Essay, and to assist the judgment in holding the balance between them, in the cases where it appears doubtful which of them is applicable to the case.

The maxims are, first, that the individual is not accountable to society for his actions, in so far as these concern the interests of no person but himself. Advice, instruction, persuasion, and avoidance by other people if thought necessary by them for their own good, are the only measures by which society can justifiably express its dislike or disapprobation of his conduct. Secondly, that for such actions as are prejudicial to the interests of others, the individual is accountable, and may be subjected either to social or to legal punishment, if society is of opinion that the one or the other is requisite for its protection.

In the first place, it must by no means be supposed, because damage, or probability of damage, to the interests of others, can alone justify the interference of society, that therefore it always does justify such interference. In many cases, an individual, in pursuing a legitimate object, necessarily and therefore legitimately causes pain or loss to others, or intercepts a good which they had a reasonable hope of obtaining. Such oppositions of interest between individuals often arise from bad social institutions, but are unavoidable while those institutions last; and some would be unavoidable under any institutions. Whoever succeeds in an overcrowded profession, or in a competitive examination; whoever is preferred to another in any contest for an object which both desire, reaps benefit from the loss of others, from their wasted exertion and their disappointment. But it is, by common admission, better for the general interest of mankind, that persons should pursue their objects undeterred by this sort of consequences. In other words, society admits no right, either legal or moral, in the disappointed competitors to immunity from this kind of suffering; and feels called on to interfere, only when means of success have been employed which it is contrary to the general interest to permit—namely, fraud or treachery, and force.

Again, trade is a social act. Whoever undertakes to sell any description of goods to the public, does what affects the interest of other persons, and of society in general; and thus his conduct, in principle, comes within the jurisdiction of society: accordingly, it was once held to be the duty of governments, in all cases which were considered of importance, to fix prices, and regulate the processes of manufacture. But it is now recognised, though not till after a long struggle, that both the cheapness and the good quality of commodities are most effectually provided for by leaving the producers and sellers perfectly free, under the sole check of equal freedom to the buyers for supplying themselves elsewhere. This is the so-called doctrine of Free Trade, which rests on grounds different from, though equally solid with, the principle of individual liberty asserted in this Essay. Restrictions on trade, or on production for purposes of trade, are indeed restraints; and all restraint, *quâ* restraint, is an evil: but the restraints in question affect only that part of conduct which society is competent to restrain, and are wrong solely because they do not really produce the results which it is desired to produce by them. As the principle of individual liberty is not involved in the doctrine of Free Trade, so neither is it in most of the questions which arise respecting the limits of that doctrine; as, for example, what amount of public control is admissible for the prevention of fraud by adulteration; how far sanitary precautions, or arrangements to protect workpeople employed in dangerous occupations, should be enforced on employers. Such questions involve considerations of liberty, only in so far as leaving people to themselves is always better, *cæteris paribus,* than controlling them: but that they may be legitimately controlled for these ends is in principle undeniable. On the other hand, there are questions relating to interference with trade which are essentially questions of liberty; such as the Maine Law, already touched upon; the prohibition of the importation of opium into China; the restriction of the sale of poisons; all cases, in short, where the object of the interference is to make it impossible or difficult to obtain a particular commodity. These interferences are objectionable, not as infringements on the liberty of the producer or seller, but on that of the buyer.

One of these examples, that of the sale of poisons, opens a new question; the proper limits of what may be called the functions of police; how far liberty may legitimately be invaded for the prevention of crime, or of accident. It is one of the undisputed functions of government to take precautions against crime before it has been committed, as well as to detect and punish it afterwards. The preventive function of government, however, is far more liable to be abused, to the prejudice of liberty, than the punitory function; for there is hardly any part of the legitimate freedom of action of a human being which would not admit of being represented, and fairly too, as increasing the facilities for some form or other of delinquency. Nevertheless, if a public authority, or even a private person, sees any one evidently preparing to commit a crime, they are not bound to look on inactive until the crime is committed, but may interfere to prevent it. If poisons were never bought or used for any purpose except the commission of murder it would be right to prohibit their manufacture and sale. They may, however, be wanted not only for innocent but for useful purposes, and restrictions cannot be imposed in the one case without operating in the other. Again, it is a proper office of public authority to guard against accidents. If either a public officer or any one else saw a person attempting to cross a bridge which had been ascertained to be unsafe, and there were no time to warn him of his danger, they might seize him and turn him back, without any real infringement of his liberty; for liberty consists in doing what one desires, and he does not desire to fall into the river. Nevertheless, when there is not a certainty, but only a danger of mischief, no one but the person himself can judge of the sufficiency of the motive which may prompt him to incur the risk: in this case, therefore (unless he is a child, or delirious, or in some state of excitement or absorption incompatible with the full use of the reflecting faculty), he ought, I conceive, to be only warned of the danger; not forcibly prevented from exposing himself to it. Similar considerations, applied to such a question as the sale of poisons, may enable us to decide which among the possible modes of regulation are or are not contrary to principle. Such a precaution, for example, as that of labelling the drug with some word expressive of its dangerous character, may be enforced without violation of liberty: the buyer cannot wish not to know that the thing he possesses has poisonous qualities. But to require in all cases the certificate of a medical practitioner would make it sometimes impossible, always expensive, to obtain the article for legitimate uses. The only mode apparent to me, in which difficulties may be thrown in the way of crime committed through this means, without any infringement worth taking into account upon the liberty of those who desire the poisonous substance for other purposes, consists in providing what, in the apt language of Bentham, is called " preappointed evidence." This provision is familiar to every one in the case of contracts. It is usual and right that the law, when a contract is entered into, should require as the condition of its enforcing performance, that certain formalities should be observed, such as signatures, attestation of witnesses, and the like, in order that in case of subsequent dispute there may be evidence to prove that the contract was really entered into, and that there was nothing in the circumstances to render it legally invalid: the effect being to throw great obstacles in the way of fictitious contracts, or contracts made in circumstances which, if known, would destroy their validity. Precautions of a similar nature might be enforced in the sale of articles adapted to be instruments of crime. The seller, for example, might be required to enter in a register the exact time of the transaction, the name and address of the buyer, the precise quality and quantity sold; to ask the purpose for which it was wanted, and record the answer he received. When there was no medical prescription, the presence of some third person might be required, to bring home the fact to the purchaser, in case there should afterwards be reason to believe that the article had been applied to criminal purposes. Such regulations would in general be no material impediment to obtaining the article, but a very considerable one to making an improper use of it without detection.

The right inherent in society, to ward off crimes against itself by antecedent precautions, suggests the obvious limitations to the maxim, that purely self-regarding misconduct cannot properly be meddled with in the way of prevention or punishment. Drunkenness, for example, in ordinary cases, is not a fit subject for legislative interference; but I should deem it perfectly legitimate that a person, who had once been convicted of any act of violence to others under the influence of drink, should be placed under a special legal restriction, personal to himself; that if he were afterwards found drunk, he should be liable to a penalty, and that if when in that state he committed another offence, the punishment to which he would be liable for that other offence should be increased in severity. The making himself drunk, in a person whom drunkenness excites to do harm to others, is a crime against others. So, again, idleness, except in a person receiving support from the public, or except when it constitutes a breach of contract, cannot without tyranny be made a subject of legal punishment; but if, either from idleness or from any other avoidable cause, a man fails to perform his legal duties to others, as for instance to support his children, it is no tyranny to force him to fulfil that obligation, by compulsory labour, if no other means are available.

Again, there are many acts which, being directly injurious

only to the agents themselves, ought not to be legally interdicted, but which, if done publicly, are a violation of good
manners, and coming thus within the category of offences
against others, may rightly be prohibited. Of this kind are
offences against decency; on which it is unnecessary to
dwell, the rather as they are only connected indirectly with
our subject, the objection to publicity being equally strong
in the case of many actions not in themselves condemnable, nor
supposed to be so.

There is another question to which an answer must be found,
consistent with the principles which have been laid down. In
cases of personal conduct supposed to be blamable, but which
respect for liberty precludes society from preventing or punishing because the evil directly resulting falls wholly on the agent;
what the agent is free to do, ought other persons to be
equally free to counsel or instigate? This question is not free
from difficulty. The case of a person who solicits another
to do an act is not strictly a case of self-regarding conduct.
To give advice or offer inducements to any one is a social
act, and may, therefore, like actions in general which affect
others, be supposed amenable to social control. But a little reflection corrects the first impression, by showing that if the
case is not strictly within the definition of individual liberty,
yet the reasons on which the principle of individual liberty
is grounded are applicable to it. If people must be allowed,
in whatever concerns only themselves, to act as seems best
to themselves, at their own peril, they must equally be free
to consult with one another about what is fit to be so done;
to exchange opinions, and give and receive suggestions. Whatever it is permitted to do, it must be permitted to advise to
do. The question is doubtful only when the instigator derives
a personal benefit from his advice; when he makes it his
occupation, for subsistence or pecuniary gain, to promote what
society and the State consider to be an evil. Then, indeed,
a new element of complication is introduced; namely, the
existence of classes of persons with an interest opposed
to what is considered as the public weal, and whose mode of
living is grounded on the counteraction of it. Ought this
to be interfered with, or not? Fornication, for example, must

be tolerated, and so must gambling; but should a person be free to be a pimp, or to keep a gambling-house? The case is one of those which lie on the exact boundary line between two principles, and it is not at once apparent to which of the two it properly belongs. There are arguments on both sides. On the side of toleration it may be said that the fact of following anything as an occupation, and living or profiting by the practice of it, cannot make that criminal which would otherwise be admissible; that the act should either be consistently permitted or consistently prohibited; that if the principles which we have hitherto defended are true, society has no business, *as* society, to decide anything to be wrong which concerns only the individual; that it cannot go beyond dissuasion, and that one person should be as free to persuade as another to dissuade. In opposition to this it may be contended, that although the public, or the State, are not warranted in authoritatively deciding, for purposes of repression or punishment, that such or such conduct affecting only the interests of the individual is good or bad, they are fully justified in assuming, if they regard it as bad, that its being so or not is at least a disputable question: That, this being supposed, they cannot be acting wrongly in endeavouring to exclude the influence of solicitations which are not disinterested, of instigators who cannot possibly be impartial—who have a direct personal interest on one side, and that side the one which the State believes to be wrong, and who confessedly promote it for personal objects only. There can surely, it may be urged, be nothing lost, no sacrifice of good, by so ordering matters that persons shall make their election, either wisely or foolishly, on their own prompting, as free as possible from the arts of persons who stimulate their inclinations for interested purposes of their own. Thus (it may be said) though the statutes respecting unlawful games are utterly indefensible—though all persons should be free to gamble in their own or each other's houses, or in any place of meeting established by their own subscriptions, and open only to the members and their visitors—yet public gambling-houses should not be permitted. It is true that the prohibition is never effectual, and that, whatever amount of tyrannical power may be given to the police, gambling-houses can always be maintained under other pretences; but they may be compelled to conduct their operations with a certain degree of secrecy and mystery, so that nobody knows anything about them but those who seek them; and more than this society ought not to aim at. There is considerable force in these arguments. I will not venture to decide whether they are sufficient to justify the moral anomaly of punishing the accessary, when the principal is (and must be) allowed to go free; of finding or imprisoning the procurer, but not the fornicator—the gambling-house keeper, but not the gambler. Still less ought the common operations of buying and selling to be interfered with on analogous grounds. Almost every article which is bought and sold may be used in excess, and the sellers have a pecuniary interest in encouraging that excess; but no argument can be founded on this, in favour, for instance, of the Maine Law; because the class of dealers in strong drinks, though interested in their abuse, are indispensably required for the sake of their legitimate use. The interest, however, of these dealers in promoting intemperance is a real evil, and justifies the State in imposing restrictions and requiring guarantees which, but for that justification, would be infringements of legitimate liberty.

A further question is, whether the State, while it permits, should nevertheless indirectly discourage conduct which it deems contrary to the best interests of the agent; whether, for example, it should take measures to render the means of drunkenness more costly, or add to the difficulty of procuring them by limiting the number of the places of sale. On this as on most other practical questions, many distinctions require to be made. To tax stimulants for the sole purpose of making them more difficult to be obtained, is a measure differing only in degree from their entire prohibition; and would be justifiable only if that were justifiable. Every increase of cost is a prohibition, to those whose means do not come up to the augmented price; and to those who do, it is a penalty laid on them for gratifying a particular taste. Their choice of pleasures, and their mode of expending their income, after satisfying their legal and moral obligations to the State and to individuals, are their own concern, and must rest with their own judgment. These considerations may seem at first sight to condemn the selection of stimulants as special subjects of taxation for purposes of revenue. But it must be remembered that taxation for fiscal purposes is absolutely inevitable; that in most countries it is necessary that a considerable part of that taxation should be indirect; that the State, therefore, cannot help imposing penalties, which to some persons may be prohibitory, on the use of some articles of consumption. It is hence the duty of the State to consider, in the imposition of taxes, what commodities the customers can best spare; and *à fortiori,* to select in preference those of which it deems the use, beyond a very moderate quantity, to be positively injurious. Taxation, therefore, of stimulants, up to the point which produces the largest amount of revenue (supposing that the State needs all the revenue which it yields) is not only admissible, but to be approved of.

The question of making the sale of these commodities a more or less exclusive privilege, must be answered differently, according to the purposes to which the restriction is intended to be subservient. All places of public resort require the restraint of a police, and places of this kind peculiarly, because offences against society are especially apt to originate there. It is, therefore, fit to confine the power of selling these commodities (at least for consumption on the spot) to persons of known or vouched-for respectability of conduct; to make such regulations respecting hours of opening and closing as may be requisite for public surveillance, and to withdraw the licence if breaches of the peace repeatedly take place through the connivance or incapacity of the keeper of the house, or if it becomes a rendezvous for concocting and preparing offences against the law. Any further restriction I do not conceive to be, in principle, justifiable. The limitation in number, for instance, of beer and spirit houses, for the express purpose of rendering them more difficult of access, and diminishing the occasions of temptation, not only exposes all to an inconvenience because there are some by whom the facility would be abused, but is suited only to a state of society in which the labouring classes are avowedly treated as children or savages, and placed under an education of restraint, to fit them for future admission to the privileges of freedom. This is not the principle on which the labouring classes are professedly governed in any free country; and no person who sets due value on freedom will give his adhesion to their being so governed, unless after all efforts have been exhausted to educate them for freedom and govern them as freemen, and it has been definitively proved that they can only be governed as children. The bare statement of the alternative shows the absurdity of supposing that such efforts have been made in any case which needs be considered here. It is only because the institutions of this country are a mass of inconsistencies, that things find admittance into our practice which belong to the system of despotic, or what is called paternal, government, while the general freedom of our institutions precludes the exercise of the amount of control necessary to render the restraint of any real efficacy as a moral education.

It was pointed out in an early part of this Essay, that the liberty of the individual, in things wherein the individual is alone concerned, implies a corresponding liberty in any number of individuals to regulate by mutual agreement such things as regard them jointly, and regard no persons but themselves. This question presents no difficulty, so long as the will of all the persons implicated remains unaltered; but since that will may change, it is often necessary, even in things in which they alone are concerned, that they should enter into engagements with one another; and when they do, it is fit, as a general rule, that those engagements should be kept. Yet, in the laws, probably, of every country, this general rule has some exceptions. Not only persons are not held to engagements which violate the rights of third parties, but it is sometimes considered a sufficient reason for releasing them from an engagement, that it is injurious to themselves. In this and most civilised countries, for example, an engagement by which a person should sell himself, or allow himself to be sold, as a slave, would be null and void; neither enforced by law nor by opinion. The ground for thus limiting his power of voluntarily disposing of his own lot in life, is apparent, and is very clearly seen in this extreme case. The reason for not interfering, unless for the sake of others, with a person's voluntary acts, is consideration for his liberty. His voluntary choice is evidence that what he so chooses is desirable, or at least endurable, to him, and his good is on the whole best provided for by allowing him to take his own means of pursuing it. But by selling himself for a slave, he abdicates his liberty; he foregoes any future use of it beyond that single act. He therefore defeats, in his own case, the very purpose which is the justification of allowing him to dispose of himself. He is no longer free; but is thenceforth in a position which has no longer the presumption in its favour, that would be afforded by his voluntarily remaining in it. The principle of freedom cannot require that he should be free not to be free. It is not freedom to be allowed to alienate his freedom. These reasons, the force of which is so conspicuous in this peculiar case, are evidently of far wider application; yet a limit is everywhere set to them by the necessities of life, which continually require, not indeed that we should resign our freedom, but that we should consent to this and the other limitation of it. The principle, however, which demands uncontrolled freedom of action in all that concerns only the agents themselves, requires that those who have become bound to one another, in things which concern no third party, should be able to release one another from the engagement: and even without such voluntary release there are perhaps no contracts or engagements, except those that relate to money or money's worth, of which one can venture to say that there ought to be no liberty whatever of retraction. Baron Wilhelm von Humboldt, in the excellent essay from which I have already quoted, states it as his conviction, that engagements which involve personal relations or services should never be legally binding beyond a limited duration of time; and that the most important of these engagements, marriage, having the peculiarity that its objects are frustrated unless the feelings of both the parties are in harmony with it, should require nothing more than the declared will of either party to dissolve it. This subject is too important, and too complicated, to be discussed in a parenthesis, and I touch on it only so far as is necessary for purposes of illustration. If the conciseness and generality of Baron Humboldt's dissertation had not obliged him in this instance to content himself with enunciating his conclusion without discussing the premises, he would doubtless have recognised that the question cannot be decided on grounds so simple as those to which he confines himself. When a person, either by express promise or by conduct, has encouraged another to rely upon his continuing to act in a certain way— to build expectations and calculations, and stake any part of his plan of life upon that supposition—a new series of moral obligations arises on his part towards that person, which may possibly be overruled, but cannot be ignored. And again, if the relation between two contracting parties has been followed by consequences to others; if it has placed third parties in any peculiar position, or, as in the case of marriage, has even called third parties into existence, obligations arise on the part of both the contracting parties towards those third persons, the fulfilment of which, or at all events the mode of fulfilment, must be greatly affected by the continuance or disruption of the relation between the original parties to the contract. It does not follow, nor can I admit, that these obligations extend to requiring the fulfilment of the contract at all costs to the happiness of the reluctant party; but they are a necessary element in the question; and even if, as von Humboldt maintains, they ought to make no difference in the *legal* freedom of the parties to release themselves from the engagement (and I also hold that they ought not to make *much* difference), they necessarily make a great difference in the *moral* freedom. A person is bound to take all these circumstances into account before resolving on a step which may affect such important interests of others; and if he does not allow proper weight to those interests, he is morally responsible for the wrong. I have made these obvious remarks for the better illustration of the general principle of liberty, and not because they are at all needed on the particular question, which, on the contrary, is usually discussed as if the interest of children was everything, and that of grown persons nothing.

I have already observed that, owing to the absence of any

recognised general principles, liberty is often granted where
it should be withheld, as well as withheld where it should
be granted; and one of the cases in which, in the modern
European world, the sentiment of liberty is the strongest,
is a case where, in my view, it is altogether misplaced.
A person should be free to do as he likes in his own concerns;
but he ought not to be free to do as he likes in acting for
another, under the pretext that the affairs of the other are his
own affairs. The State, while it respects the liberty of each
in what specially regards himself, is bound to maintain a
vigilant control over his exercise of any power which it
allows him to possess over others. This obligation is almost
entirely disregarded in the case of the family relations, a case,
in its direct influence on human happiness, more important
than all others taken together. The almost despotic power
of husbands over wives needs not be enlarged upon here,
because nothing more is needed for the complete removal
of the evil than that wives should have the same rights, and
should receive the protection of law in the same manner, as all
other persons; and because, on this subject, the defenders
of established injustice do not avail themselves of the plea
of liberty, but stand forth openly as the champions of power.
It is in the case of children that misapplied notions of
liberty are a real obstacle to the fulfilment by the State of
its duties. One would almost think that a man's children
were supposed to be literally, and not metaphorically, a
part of himself, so jealous is opinion of the smallest interference of law with his absolute and exclusive control over
them; more jealous than of almost any interference with
his own freedom of action : so much less do the generality of
mankind value liberty than power. Consider, for example,
the case of education. Is it not almost a self-evident axiom,
that the State should require and compel the education, up
to a certain standard, of every human being who is born
its citizen? Yet who is there that is not afraid to recognise
and assert this truth? Hardly any one indeed will deny
that it is one of the most sacred duties of the parents (or,
as law and usage now stand, the father), after summoning
a human being into the world, to give to that being an

education fitting him to perform his part well in life towards others and towards himself. But while this is unanimously declared to be the father's duty, scarcely anybody, in this country, will bear to hear of obliging him to perform it. Instead of his being required to make any exertion or sacrifice for securing education to his child, it is left to his choice to accept it or not when it is provided gratis! It still remains unrecognised, that to bring a child into existence without a fair prospect of being able, not only to provide food for its body, but instruction and training for its mind, is a moral crime, both against the unfortunate offspring and against society; and that if the parent does not fulfil this obligation, the State ought to see it fulfilled, at the charge, as far as possible, of the parent.

Were the duty of enforcing universal education once admitted there would be an end to the difficulties about what the State should teach, and how it should teach, which now convert the subject into a mere battlefield for sects and parties, causing the time and labour which should have been spent in educating to be wasted in quarrelling about education. If the government would make up its mind to require for every child a good education, it might save itself the trouble of providing one. It might leave to parents to obtain the education where and how they pleased, and content itself with helping to pay the school fees of the poorer classes of children, and defraying the entire school expenses of those who have no one else to pay for them. The objections which are urged with reason against State education do not apply to the enforcement of education by the State, but to the State's taking upon itself to direct that education; which is a totally different thing. That the whole or any large part of the education of the people should be in State hands, I go as far as any one in deprecating. All that has been said of the importance of individuality of character, and diversity in opinions and modes of conduct, involves, as of the same unspeakable importance, diversity of education. A general State education is a mere contrivance for moulding people to be exactly like one another: and as the mould in which it casts them is that which pleases the predominant power in the government, whether this be a monarch, a priesthood, an aristocracy, or the majority of the existing generation; in proportion as it is efficient and successful, it establishes a despotism over the mind, leading by natural tendency to one over the body. An education established and controlled by the State should only exist, if it exist at all, as one among many competing experiments, carried on for the purpose of example and stimulus, to keep the others up to a certain standard of excellence. Unless, indeed, when society in general is in so backward a state that it could not or would not provide for itself any proper institutions of education unless the government undertook the task : then, indeed, the government may, as the less of two great evils, take upon itself the business of schools and universities, as it may that of joint stock companies, when private enterprise, in a shape fitted for undertaking great works of industry, does not exist in the country. But in general, if the country contains a sufficient number of persons qualified to provide education under government auspices, the same persons would be able and willing to give an equally good education on the voluntary principle, under the assurance of remuneration afforded by a law rendering education compulsory, combined with State aid to those unable to defray the expense.

The instrument for enforcing the law could be no other than public examinations, extending to all children, and beginning at an early age. An age might be fixed at which every child must be examined, to ascertain if he (or she) is able to read. If a child proves unable, the father, unless he has some sufficient ground of excuse, might be subjected to a moderate fine, to be worked out, if necessary, by his labour, and the child might be put to school at his expense. Once in every year the examination should be renewed, with a gradually extending range of subjects, so as to make the universal acquisition, and what is more, retention, of a certain minimum of general knowledge virtually compulsory. Beyond that minimum there should be voluntary examinations on all subjects, at which all who come up to a certain standard of proficiency might claim a certificate. To prevent the State from exercising, through these arrangements, an improper influence over opinion, the knowledge required for passing an examination (beyond the merely instrumental parts of knowledge, such as languages and their use) should, even in the higher classes of examinations, be confined to facts and positive science exclusively. The examinations on religion, politics, or other disputed topics, should not turn on the truth or falsehood of opinions, but on the matter of fact that such and such an opinion is held, on such grounds, by such authors, or schools, or churches. Under this system, the rising generation would be no worse off in regard to all disputed truths than they are at present; they would be brought up either churchmen or dissenters as they now are, the State merely taking care that they should be instructed churchmen, or instructed dissenters. There would be nothing to hinder them from being taught religion, if their parents chose, at the same schools where they were taught other things. All attempts by the State to bias the conclusions of its citizens on disputed subjects are evil; but it may very properly offer to ascertain and certify that a person possesses the knowledge requisite to make his conclusions, on any given subject, worth attending to. A student of philosophy would be the better for being able to stand an examination both in Locke and in Kant, whichever of the two he takes up with, or even if with neither : and there is no reasonable objection to examining an atheist in the evidences of Christianity, provided he is not required to profess a belief in them. The examinations, however, in the higher branches of knowledge should, I conceive, be entirely voluntary. It would be giving too dangerous a power to governments were they allowed to exclude any one from professions, even from the profession of teacher, for alleged deficiency of qualifications : and I think, with Wilhelm von Humboldt, that degrees, or other public certificates of scientific or professional acquirements, should be given to all who present themselves for examination, and stand the test; but that such certificates should confer no advantage over competitors other than the weight which may be attached to their testimony by public opinion.

It is not in the matter of education only that misplaced

notions of liberty prevent moral obligations on the part of parents from being recognised, and legal obligations from being imposed, where there are the strongest grounds for the former always, and in many cases for the latter also. The fact itself, of causing the existence of a human being, is one of the most responsible actions in the range of human life. To undertake this responsibility—to bestow a life which may be either a curse or a blessing—unless the being on whom it is to be bestowed will have at least the ordinary chances of a desirable existence, is a crime against that being. And in a country either over-peopled, or threatened with being so, to produce children, beyond a very small number, with the effect of reducing the reward of labour by their competition, is a serious offence against all who live by the remuneration of their labour. The laws which, in many countries on the Continent, forbid marriage unless the parties can show that they have the means of supporting a family, do not exceed the legitimate powers of the State : and whether such laws be expedient or not (a question mainly dependent on local circumstances and feelings), they are not objectionable as violations of liberty. Such laws are interferences of the State to prohibit a mischievous act—an act injurious to others which ought to be a subject of reprobation, and social stigma, even when it is not deemed expedient to superadd legal punishment. Yet the current ideas of liberty, which bend so easily to real infringements of the freedom of the individual in things which concern only himself, would repel the attempt to put any restraint upon his inclinations when the consequence of their indulgence is a life or lives of wretchedness and depravity to the offspring, with manifold evils to those sufficiently within reach to be in any way affected by their actions. When we compare the strange respect of mankind for liberty, with their strange want of respect for it, we might imagine that a man had an indispensable right to do harm to others, and no right at all to please himself without giving pain to any one.

I have reserved for the last place a large class of questions respecting the limits of government interference, which, though closely connected with the subject of this Essay, do not, in strictness, belong to it. These are cases in which the reasons against interference do not turn upon the principle of liberty : the question is not about restraining the actions of individuals, but about helping them; it is asked whether the government should do, or cause to be done, something for their benefit, instead of leaving it to be done by themselves, individually or in voluntary combination.

The objections to government interference, when it is not such as to involve infringement of liberty, may be of three kinds.

The first is, when the thing to be done is likely to be better done by individuals than by the government. Speaking generally, there is no one so fit to conduct any business, or to determine how or by whom it shall be conducted, as those who are personally interested in it. This principle condemns the interferences, once so common, of the legislature, or the officers of government, with the ordinary processes of industry. But this part of the subject has been sufficiently enlarged upon by political economists, and is not particularly related to the principles of this Essay.

The second objection is more nearly allied to our subject. In many cases, though individuals may not do the particular thing so well, on the average, as the officers of government, it is nevertheless desirable that it should be done by them, rather than by the government, as a means to their own mental education—a mode of strengthening their active faculties, exercising their judgment, and giving them a familiar knowledge of the subjects with which they are thus left to deal. This is a principal, though not the sole, recommendation of jury trial (in cases not political); of free and popular local and municipal institutions; of the conduct of industrial and philanthropic enterprises by voluntary associations. These are not questions of liberty, and are connected with that subject only by remote tendencies; but they are questions of development. It belongs to a different occasion from the present to dwell on these things as parts of national education; as being, in truth, the peculiar training of a citizen, the practical part of the political education of a free people, taking them out of the narrow circle of personal and family selfishness, and accustoming them to the comprehension of joint interests, the management of joint concerns—habituating them to act from public or semi-public motives, and guide their conduct by aims which unite instead of isolating them from one another. Without these habits and powers, a free constitution can neither be worked nor preserved; as is exemplified by the too-often transitory nature of political freedom in countries where it does not rest upon a sufficient basis of local liberties. The management of purely local business by the localities, and of the great enterprises of industry by the union of those who voluntarily supply the pecuniary means, is further recommended by all the advantages which have been set forth in this Essay as belonging to individuality of development, and diversity of modes of action. Government operations tend to be everywhere alike. With individuals and voluntary associations, on the contrary, there are varied experiments, and endless diversity of experience. What the State can usefully do is to make itself a central depository, and active circulator and diffuser, of the experience resulting from many trials. Its business is to enable each experimentalist to benefit by the experiments of others; instead of tolerating no experiments but its own.

The third and most cogent reason for restricting the interference of government is the great evil of adding unnecessarily to its power. Every function superadded to those already exercised by the government causes its influence over hopes and fears to be more widely diffused, and converts, more and more, the active and ambitious part of the public into hangers-on of the government, or of some party which aims at becoming the government. If the roads, the railways, the banks, the insurance offices, the great joint-stock companies, the universities, and the public charities, were all of them branches of the government; if, in addition, the municipal corporations and local boards, with all that now devolves on them, became departments of the central administration; if the employés of all these different enterprises were appointed and paid by the government, and looked to the government for every rise in life; not all the freedom of the press and popular constitution of the legislature would make this or any other country free otherwise than in name. And the evil would be greater, the more efficiently and scientifically the administrative machinery was constructed—the more skilful the arrangements for obtaining the best qualified hands and heads with which to work it. In England it has of late been proposed that all the members of the civil service of govern- ment should be selected by competitive examination, to obtain for these employments the most intelligent and instructed persons procurable; and much has been said and written for and against this proposal. One of the arguments most insisted on by its opponents is that the occupation of a permanent official servant of the State does not hold out sufficient prospects of emolument and importance to attract the highest talents, which will always be able to find a more inviting career in the professions, or in the service of com- panies and other public bodies. One would not have been surprised if this argument had been used by the friends of the proposition, as an answer to its principal difficulty. Coming from the opponents it is strange enough. What is urged as an objection is the safety-valve of the proposed system. If indeed all the high talent of the country *could* be drawn into the service of the government, a proposal tending to bring about that result might well inspire uneasiness. If every part of the business of society which required organised concert, or large and comprehensive views, were in the hands of the government, and if government offices were universally filled by the ablest men, all the enlarged culture and practised intelligence in the country, except the purely speculative, would be concentrated in a numerous bureaucracy, to whom alone the rest of the community would look for all things : the multitude for direction and dictation in all they had to do; the able and aspiring for personal advancement. To be admitted into the ranks of this bureaucracy, and when admitted, to rise therein, would be the sole objects of ambition. Under this *régime,* not only is the outside public ill-qualified, for want of practical experience, to criticise or check the mode of operation of the bureaucracy, but even if the accidents of despotic or the natural working of popular institutions occasionally raise to the summit a ruler or rulers of reforming inclinations, no reform can be effected which is contrary to the interests of the bureaucracy. Such is the melancholy condition of the Russian empire, as shown in the accounts of those who have had sufficient opportunity of observation. The Czar himself is powerless against the bureaucratic body; he can send any one of them to Siberia, but he cannot govern without them, or against their will. On every decree of his they have a tacit veto, by merely refraining from carrying it into effect. In countries of more advanced civilisation and of a more insurrectionary spirit, the public, accustomed to expect everything to be done for them by the State, or at least to do nothing for themselves without asking from the State not only leave to do it, but even how it is to be done, naturally hold the State responsible for all evil which befalls them, and when the evil exceeds their amount of patience, they rise against the government, and make what is called a revolution; whereupon somebody else, with or without legitimate authority from the nation, vaults into the seat, issues his orders to the bureaucracy, and everything goes on much as it did before; the bureaucracy being unchanged, and nobody else being capable of taking their place.

A very different spectacle is exhibited among a people accustomed to transact their own business. In France, a large part of the people, having been engaged in military service, many of whom have held at least the rank of non-commissioned officers, there are in every popular insurrection several persons competent to take the lead, and improvise some tolerable plan of action. What the French are in military affairs, the Americans are in every kind of civil business; let them be left without a government, every body of Americans is able to improvise one, and to carry on that or any other public business with a sufficient amount of intelligence, order, and decision. This is what every free people ought to be: and a people capable of this is certain to be free; it will never let itself be enslaved by any man or body of men because these are able to seize and pull the reins of the central administration. No bureaucracy can hope to make such a people as this do or undergo anything that they do not like. But where everything is done through the bureaucracy, nothing to which the bureaucracy is really adverse can be done at all. The constitution of such countries is an organisation of the experience and practical ability of the nation into a disciplined body for the purpose of governing the rest; and the more perfect that organisation is in itself, the more successful in drawing to itself and educating for itself the persons of greatest capacity from all ranks of the community, the more complete is the bondage of all, the members of the bureaucracy included. For the governors are as much the slaves of their organisation and discipline as the governed are of the governors. A Chinese mandarin is as much the tool and creature of a despotism as the humblest cultivator. An individual Jesuit is to the utmost degree of abasement the slave of his order, though the order itself exists for the collective power and importance of its members.

It is not, also, to be forgotten, that the absorption of all the principal ability of the country into the governing body is fatal, sooner or later, to the mental activity and progressiveness of the body itself. Banded together as they are—working a system which, like all systems, necessarily proceeds in a great measure by fixed rules—the official body are under the constant temptation of sinking into indolent routine, or, if they now and then desert that mill-horse round, of rushing into some half-examined crudity which has struck the fancy of some leading member of the corps; and the sole check to these closely allied, though seemingly opposite, tendencies, the only stimulus which can keep the ability of the body itself up to a high standard, is liability to the watchful criticism of equal ability outside the body. It is indispensable, therefore, that the means should exist, independently of the government, of forming such ability, and furnishing it with the opportunities and experience necessary for a correct judgment of great practical affairs. If we would possess permanently a skilful and efficient body of functionaries—above all, a body able to originate and willing to adopt improvements; if we would not have our bureaucracy degenerate into a pedantocracy, this body must not engross all the occupations which form and cultivate the faculties for the government of mankind.

To determine the point at which evils, so formidable to
human freedom and advancement, begin, or rather at which
they begin to predominate over the benefits attending the
collective application of the force of society, under its recognised chiefs, for the removal of the obstacles which stand
in the way of its well-being; to secure as much of the advantages of centralised power and intelligence as can be had
without turning into governmental channels too great a
proportion of the general activity— is one of the most difficult
and complicated questions in the art of government. It is, in
a great measure, a question of detail, in which many and various
considerations must be kept in view, and no absolute rule
can be laid down. But I believe that the practical principle
in which safety resides, the ideal to be kept in view, the
standard by which to test all arrangements intended for
overcoming the difficulty, may be conveyed in these words:
the greatest dissemination of power consistent with efficiency;
but the greatest possible centralisation of information, and
diffusion of it from the centre. Thus, in municipal administration, there would be, as in the New England States, a very
minute division among separate officers, chosen by the localities,
of all business which is not better left to the persons directly
interested; but besides this, there would be, in each department of local affairs, a central superintendence, forming a
branch of the general government. The organ of this superintendence would concentrate, as in a focus, the variety
of information and experience derived from the conduct of
that branch of public business in all the localities, from
everything analogous which is done in foreign countries,
and from the general principles of political science. This
central organ should have a right to know all that is done,
and its special duty should be that of making the knowledge
acquired in one place available for others. Emancipated
from the petty prejudices and narrow views of a locality
by its elevated position and comprehensive sphere of observation, its advice would naturally carry much authority; but
its actual power, as a permanent institution, should, I conceive,
be limited to compelling the local officers to obey the laws
laid down for their guidance. In all things not provided for

by general rules, those officers should be left to their own judgment, under responsibility to their constituents. For the violation of rules, they should be responsible to law, and the rules themselves should be laid down by the legislature; the central administrative authority only watching over their execution, and if they were not properly carried into effect, appealing, according to the nature of the case, to the tribunals to enforce the law, or to the constituencies to dismiss the functionaries who had not executed it according to its spirit. Such, in its general conception, is the central superintendence which the Poor Law Board is intended to exercise over the administrators of the Poor Rate throughout the country. Whatever powers the Board exercises beyond this limit were right and necessary in that peculiar case, for the cure of rooted habits of maladministration in matters deeply affecting not the localities merely, but the whole community; since no locality has a moral right to make itself by mismanagement a nest of pauperism, necessarily overflowing into other localities, and impairing the moral and physical condition of the whole labouring community. The powers of administrative coercion and subordinate legislation possessed by the Poor Law Board (but which, owing to the state of opinion on the subject, are very scantily exercised by them), though perfectly justifiable in a case of first rate national interest, would be wholly out of place in the superintendence of interests purely local. But a central organ of information and instruction for all the localities would be equally valuable in all departments of administration. A government cannot have too much of the kind of activity which does not impede, but aids and stimulates, individual exertion and development. The mischief begins when, instead of calling forth the activity and powers of individuals and bodies, it substitutes its own activity for theirs; when, instead of informing, advising, and, upon occasion, denouncing, it makes them work in fetters, or bids them stand aside and does their work instead of them. The worth of a State, in the long run, is the worth of the individuals composing it; and a State which postpones the interests of *their* mental expansion and elevation to a little more of administrative skill, or of that semblance of it which practice gives, in the details of business; a State which dwarfs its men, in order that they may be more docile instruments in its hands even for beneficial purposes—will find that with small men no great thing can really be accomplished; and that the perfection of machinery to which it has sacrificed everything will in the end avail it nothing, for want of the vital power which, in order that the machine might work more smoothly, it has preferred to banish.

UTILITARIANISM

by John Stuart Mill

CHAPTER I

GENERAL REMARKS

There are few circumstances among those which make up the present condition of human knowledge, more unlike what might have been expected, or more significant of the backward state in which speculation on the most important subjects still lingers, than the little progress which has been made in the decision of the controversy respecting the criterion of right and wrong. From the dawn of philosophy, the question concerning the *summum bonum,* or, what is the same thing, concerning the foundation of morality, has been accounted the main problem in speculative thought, has occupied the most gifted intellects, and divided them into sects and schools, carrying on a vigorous warfare against one another. And after more than two thousand years the same discussions continue, philosophers are still ranged under the same contending banners, and neither thinkers nor mankind at large seem nearer to being unanimous on the subject, than when the youth Socrates listened to the old Protagoras, and asserted (if Plato's dialogue be grounded on a real conversation) the theory of utilitarianism against the popular morality of the so-called sophist.

It is true that similar confusion and uncertainty, and in some cases similar discordance, exist respecting the first principles of all the sciences, not excepting that which is deemed the most certain of them, mathematics; without much impairing, generally indeed without impairing at all, the trustworthiness of the conclusions of those sciences. An apparent anomaly, the explanation of which is, that the detailed doctrines of a science are not usually deduced from, nor depend for their

evidence upon, what are called its first principles. Were it not
so, there would be no science more precarious, or whose conclusions were more insufficiently made out, than algebra;
which derives none of its certainty from what are commonly
taught to learners as its elements, since these, as laid down
by some of its most eminent teachers, are as full of fictions
as English law, and of mysteries as theology. The truths
which are ultimately accepted as the first principles of a science,
are really the last results of metaphysical analysis, practised
on the elementary notions with which the science is con-
versant; and their relation to the science is not that of
foundations to an edifice, but of roots to a tree, which may
perform their office equally well though they be never dug
down to and exposed to light. But though in science the
particular truths precede the general theory, the contrary
might be expected to be the case with a practical art, such
as morals or legislation. All action is for the sake of some
end, and rules of action, it seems natural to suppose, must
take their whole character and colour from the end to which
they are subservient. When we engage in a pursuit, a clear
and precise conception of what we are pursuing would
seem to be the first thing we need, instead of the last we are
to look forward to. A test of right and wrong must be the
means, one would think, of ascertaining what is right or wrong,
and not a consequence of having already ascertained it.

The difficulty is not avoided by having recourse to the
popular theory of a natural faculty, a sense or instinct, informing us of right and wrong. For—besides that the existence
of such a moral instinct is itself one of the matters in dispute
—those believers in it who have any pretensions to philosophy,
have been obliged to abandon the idea that it discerns what
is right or wrong in the particular case in hand, as our
other senses discern the sight or sound actually present. Our
moral faculty, according to all those of its interpreters who
are entitled to the name of thinkers, supplies us only with
the general principles of moral judgments; it is a branch of our
reason, not of our sensitive faculty; and must be looked to
for the abstract doctrines of morality, not for perception of
it in the concrete. The intuitive, no less than what may be

termed the inductive, school of ethics, insists on the necessity of general laws. They both agree that the morality of an individual action is not a question of direct perception, but of the application of a law to an individual case. They recognise also, to a great extent, the same moral laws; but differ as to their evidence, and the source from which they derive their authority. According to the one opinion, the principles of morals are evident *à priori,* requiring nothing to command assent, except that the meaning of the terms be understood. According to the other doctrine, right and wrong, as well as truth and falsehood, are questions of observation and experience. But both hold equally that morality must be deduced from principles; and the intuitive school affirm as strongly as the inductive, that there is a science of morals. Yet they seldom attempt to make out a list of the *à priori* principles which are to serve as the premises of the science; still more rarely do they make any effort to reduce those various principles to one first principle, or common ground of obligation. They either assume the ordinary precepts of morals as of *à priori* authority, or they lay down as the common groundwork of those maxims, some generality much less obviously authoritative than the maxims themselves, and which has never succeeded in gaining popular acceptance. Yet to support their pretensions there ought either to be some one fundamental principle or law, at the root of all morality, or if there be several, there should be a determinate order of precedence among them; and the one principle, or the rule for deciding between the various principles when they conflict, ought to be self-evident.

To inquire how far the bad effects of this deficiency have been mitigated in practice, or to what extent the moral beliefs of mankind have been vitiated or made uncertain by the absence of any distinct recognition of an ultimate standard, would imply a complete survey and criticism of past and present ethical doctrine. It would, however, be easy to show that whatever steadiness or consistency these moral beliefs have attained, has been mainly due to the tacit influence of a standard not recognised. Although the non-existence of an acknowledged first principle has made ethics not so much a guide as a consecration of men's actual sentiments, still, as men's sentiments, both of favour and of aversion, are greatly influenced by what they suppose to be the effects of things upon their happiness, the principle of utility, or as Bentham latterly called it, the greatest happiness principle, has had a large share in forming the moral doctrines even of those who most scornfully reject its authority. Nor is there any school of thought which refuses to admit that the influence of actions on happiness is a most material and even predominant consideration in many of the details of morals, however unwilling to acknowledge it as the fundamental principle of morality, and the source of moral obligation. I might go much further, and say that to all those *à priori* moralists who deem it necessary to argue at all, utilitarian arguments are indispensable. It is not my present purpose to criticise these thinkers; but I cannot help referring, for illustration, to a systematic treatise by one of the most illustrious of them, the *Metaphysics of Ethics,* by Kant. This remarkable man, whose system of thought will long remain one of the landmarks in the history of philosophical speculation, does, in the treatise in question, lay down a universal first principle as the origin and ground of moral obligation; it is this :—" So act, that the rule on which thou actest would admit of being adopted as a law by all rational beings." But when he begins to deduce from this precept any of the actual duties of morality, he fails, almost grotesquely, to show that there would be any contradiction, any logical (not to say physical) impossibility, in the adoption by all rational beings of the most outrageously immoral rules of conduct. All he shows is that the *consequences* of their universal adoption would be such as no one would choose to incur.

On the present occasion, I shall, without further discussion of the other theories, attempt to contribute something towards the understanding and appreciation of the Utilitarian or Happiness theory, and towards such proof as it is susceptible of. It is evident that this cannot be proof in the ordinary and popular meaning of the term. Questions of ultimate ends are not amenable to direct proof. Whatever can be proved to be good, must be so by being shown to be a means to something admitted to be good without proof. The medical art is proved to be good by its conducing to health; but how is it possible to prove that health is good? The art of music is good, for the reason, among others, that it produces pleasure; but what proof is it possible to give that pleasure is good? If, then, it is asserted that there is a comprehensive formula, including all things which are in themselves good, and that whatever else is good, is not so as an end, but as a mean, the formula may be accepted or rejected, but is not a subject of what is commonly understood by proof. We are not, however, to infer that its acceptance or rejection must depend on blind impulse, or arbitrary choice. There is a larger meaning of the word proof, in which this question is as amenable to it as any other of the disputed questions of philosophy. The subject is within the cognisance of the rational faculty; and neither does that faculty deal with it solely in the way of intuition. Considerations may be presented capable of determining the intellect either to give or withhold its assent to the doctrine; and this is equivalent to proof.

We shall examine presently of what nature are these considerations; in what manner they apply to the case, and what rational grounds, therefore, can be given for accepting or rejecting the utilitarian formula. But it is a preliminary condition of rational acceptance or rejection, that the formula should be correctly understood. I believe that the very imperfect notion ordinarily formed of its meaning, is the chief obstacle which impedes its reception; and that could it be cleared, even from only the grosser misconceptions, the question would be greatly simplified, and a large proportion of its difficulties removed. Before, therefore, I attempt to enter into the philosophical grounds which can be given for assenting to the utilitarian standard, I shall offer some illustrations of the doctrine itself; with the view of showing more clearly what it is, distinguishing it from what it is not, and disposing of such of the practical objections to it as either originate in, or are closely connected with, mistaken interpretations of its meaning. Having thus prepared the ground, I shall afterwards endeavour to throw such light as I can upon the question, considered as one of philosophical theory.

CHAPTER II

WHAT UTILITARIANISM IS

A passing remark is all that needs be given to the ignorant blunder of supposing that those who stand up for utility as the test of right and wrong, use the term in that restricted and merely colloquial sense in which utility is opposed to pleasure. An apology is due to the philosophical opponents of utilitarianism, for even the momentary appearance of confounding them with any one capable of so absurd a misconception; which is the more extraordinary, inasmuch as the contrary accusation, of referring everything to pleasure, and that too in its grossest form, is another of the common charges against utilitarianism: and, as has been pointedly remarked by an able writer, the same sort of persons, and often the very same persons, denounce the theory "as impracticably dry when the word utility precedes the word pleasure, and as too practicably voluptuous when the word pleasure precedes the word utility." Those who know anything about the matter are aware that every writer, from Epicurus to Bentham, who maintained the theory of utility, meant by it, not something to be contradistinguished from pleasure, but pleasure itself, together with exemption from pain; and instead of opposing the useful to the agreeable or the ornamental, have always declared that the useful means these, among other things. Yet the common herd, including the herd of writers, not only in newspapers and periodicals, but in books of weight and pretension, are perpetually falling into this shallow mistake. Having caught up the word utilitarian, while knowing nothing whatever about it but its sound, they habitually express by it the rejection, or the neglect, of pleasure in some of its forms; of beauty, of ornament, or of amusement. Nor is the term thus ignorantly misapplied solely in disparagement, but occasionally in compliment; as though it implied superiority to frivolity and the mere pleasures of the moment. And this perverted use is the only one in which the word is popularly known, and the one from which the new generation are acquiring their sole notion of its meaning. Those who introduced the word, but who had for many years discontinued it as a distinctive appellation, may well feel themselves called to resume it, if by doing so they can hope to contribute anything towards rescuing it from this utter degradation.[1]

The creed which accepts as the foundation of morals, Utility, or the Greatest Happiness Principle, holds that actions are right in proportion as they tend to promote happiness, wrong as they tend to produce the reverse of happiness. By happiness is intended pleasure, and the absence of pain; by unhappiness, pain, and the privation of pleasure. To give a clear view of the moral standard set up by the theory, much more requires to be said; in particular, what things it includes in the ideas of pain and pleasure; and to what extent this is left an open question. But these supplementary explanations do not affect the theory of life on which this theory of morality is grounded—namely, that pleasure, and freedom from pain, are the only things desirable as ends; and that all desirable things (which are as numerous in the utilitarian as in any other scheme) are desirable either for the pleasure inherent in themselves, or as means to the promotion of pleasure and the prevention of pain.

Now, such a theory of life excites in many minds, and among them in some of the most estimable in feeling and purpose, inveterate dislike. To suppose that life has (as they express it) no higher end than pleasure—no better and nobler object of desire and pursuit—they designate as utterly mean

---

[1] The author of this essay has reason for believing himself to be the first person who brought the word utilitarian into use. He did not invent it, but adopted it from a passing expression in Mr. Galt's *Annals of the Parish.* After using it as a designation for several years, he and others abandoned it from a growing dislike to anything resembling a badge or watchword of sectarian distinction. But as a name for one single opinion, not a set of opinions—to denote the recognition of utility as a standard, not any particular way of applying it—the term supplies a want in the language, and offers, in many cases, a convenient mode of avoiding tiresome circumlocution.

and grovelling; as a doctrine worthy only of swine, to whom
the followers of Epicurus were, at a very early period, contemptuously likened; and modern holders of the doctrine
are occasionally made the subject of equally polite comparisons
by its German, French, and English assailants.

When thus attacked, the Epicureans have always answered,
that it is not they, but their accusers, who represent human
nature in a degrading light; since the accusation supposes
human beings to be capable of no pleasures except those of
which swine are capable. If this supposition were true, the
charge could not be gainsaid, but would then be no longer
an imputation; for if the sources of pleasure were precisely
the same to human beings and to swine, the rule of life
which is good enough for the one would be good enough for
the other. The comparison of the Epicurean life to that of
beasts is felt as degrading, precisely because a beast's pleasures
do not satisfy a human being's conception of happiness.
Human beings have faculties more elevated than the animal
appetites, and when once made conscious of them, do not
regard anything as happiness which does not include their
gratification. I do not, indeed, consider the Epicureans to have
been by any means faultless in drawing out their scheme of
consequences from the utilitarian principle. To do this in
any sufficient manner, many Stoic, as well as Christian elements
require to be included. But there is no known Epicurean
theory of life which does not assign to the pleasures of the
intellect, of the feelings and imagination, and of the moral
sentiments, a much higher value as pleasures than to those
of mere sensation. It must be admitted, however, that utilitarian writers in general have placed the superiority of mental
over bodily pleasures chiefly in the greater permanency, safety,
uncostliness, etc., of the former—that is, in their circumstantial
advantages rather than in their intrinsic nature. And on all
these points utilitarians have fully proved their case; but they
might have taken the other, and, as it may be called, higher
ground, with entire consistency. It is quite compatible with
the principle of utility to recognise the fact, that some
kinds of pleasure are more desirable and more valuable than
others. It would be absurd that while, in estimating all other

things, quality is considered as well as quantity, the estimation of pleasures should be supposed to depend on quantity alone.

If I am asked, what I mean by difference of quality in pleasures, or what makes one pleasure more valuable than another, merely as a pleasure, except its being greater in amount, there is but one possible answer. Of two pleasures, if there be one to which all or almost all who have experience of both give a decided preference, irrespective of any feeling of moral obligation to prefer it, that is the more desirable pleasure. If one of the two is, by those who are competently acquainted with both, placed so far above the other that they prefer it, even though knowing it to be attended with a greater amount of discontent, and would not resign it for any quantity of the other pleasure which their nature is capable of, we are justified in ascribing to the preferred enjoyment a superiority in quality, so far out-weighing quantity as to render it, in comparison, of small account.

Now it is an unquestionable fact that those who are equally acquainted with, and equally capable of appreciating and enjoying, both, do give a most marked preference to the manner of existence which employs their higher faculties. Few human creatures would consent to be changed into any of the lower animals, for a promise of the fullest allowance of a beast's pleasures; no intelligent human being would consent to be a fool, no instructed person would be an ignoramus, no person of feeling and conscience would be selfish and base, even though they should be persuaded that the fool, the dunce, or the rascal is better satisfied with his lot than they are with theirs. They would not resign what they possess more than he for the most complete satisfaction of all the desires which they have in common with him. If they ever fancy they would, it is only in cases of unhappiness so extreme, that to escape from it they would exchange their lot for almost any other, however undesirable in their own eyes. A being of higher faculties requires more to make him happy, is capable probably of more acute suffering, and certainly accessible to it at more points, than one of an inferior type; but in spite of these liabilities, he can never really wish to sink into what he feels to be a lower grade of existence. We may give what explanation we please of this unwillingness; we may attribute it to pride, a name which is given indiscriminately to some of the most and to some of the least estimable feelings of which mankind are capable : we may refer it to the love of liberty and personal independence, an appeal to which was with the Stoics one of the most effective means for the inculcation of it; to the love of power, or to the love of excitement, both of which do really enter into and contribute to it : but its most appropriate appellation is a sense of dignity, which all human beings possess in one form or another, and in some, though by no means in exact, proportion to their higher faculties, and which is so essential a part of the happiness of those in whom it is strong, that nothing which conflicts with it could be, otherwise than momentarily, an object of desire to them. Whoever supposes that this preference takes place at a sacrifice of happiness—that the superior being, in anything like equal circumstances, is not happier than the inferior—confounds the two very different ideas, of happiness, and content. It is indisputable that the being whose capacities of enjoyment are low, has the greatest chance of having them fully satisfied; and a highly endowed being will always feel that any happiness which he can look for, as the world is constituted, is imperfect. But he can learn to bear its imperfections, if they are at all bearable; and they will not make him envy the being who is indeed unconscious of the imperfections, but only because he feels not at all the good which those imperfections qualify. It is better to be a human being dissatisfied than a pig satisfied; better to be Socrates dissatisfied than a fool satisfied. And if the fool, or the pig, are of a different opinion, it is because they only know their own side of the question. The other party to the comparison knows both sides.

It may be objected, that many who are capable of the higher pleasures, occasionally, under the influence of temptation, postpone them to the lower. But this is quite compatible with a full appreciation of the intrinsic superiority of the higher. Men often, from infirmity of character, make their election for the nearer good, though they know it to be the less valuable; and this no less when the choice is beween two bodily pleasures, than when it is between bodily and mental. They pursue sensual indulgences to the injury of health, though perfectly aware that health is the greater good. It may be further objected, that many who begin with youthful enthusiasm for everything noble, as they advance in years sink into indolence and selfishness. But I do not believe that those who undergo this very common change, voluntarily choose the lower description of pleasures in preference to the higher. I believe that before they devote themselves exclusively to the one, they have already become incapable of the other. Capacity for the nobler feelings is in most natures a very tender plant, easily killed, not only by hostile influences, but by mere want of sustenance; and in the majority of young persons it speedily dies away if the occupations to which their position in life has devoted them, and the society into which it has thrown them, are not favourable to keeping that higher capacity in exercise. Men lose their high aspirations as they lose their intellectual tastes, because they have not time or opportunity for indulging them; and they addict themselves to inferior pleasures, not because they deliberately prefer them, but because they are either the only ones to which they have access, or the only ones which they are any longer capable of enjoying. It may be questioned whether any one who has remained equally susceptible to both classes of pleasures, ever knowingly and calmly preferred the lower; though many, in all ages, have broken down in an ineffectual attempt to combine both.

From this verdict of the only competent judges, I apprehend there can be no appeal. On a question which is the best worth having of two pleasures, or which of two modes of existence is the most grateful to the feelings, apart from its moral attributes and from its consequences, the judgment of those who are qualified by knowledge of both, or, if they differ, that of the majority among them, must be admitted as final. And there needs be the less hesitation to accept this judgment respecting the quality of pleasures, since there is no other tribunal to be referred to even on the question of quantity. What means are there of determining which is the acutest of two pains, or the intensest of two pleasurable sensations, except the general suffrage of those who are familiar with both? Neither pains nor pleasures are homogeneous, and pain is always heterogeneous with pleasure. What is there to decide whether a particular pleasure is worth purchasing at the cost of a particular pain, except the feelings and judgment of the experienced? When, therefore, those feelings and judgment declare the pleasures derived from the higher faculties to be preferable *in kind,* apart from the question of intensity, to those of which the animal nature, disjoined from the higher faculties, is susceptible, they are entitled on this subject to the same regard.

I have dwelt on this point, as being a necessary part of a perfectly just conception of Utility or Happiness, considered as the directive rule of human conduct. But it is by no means an indispensable condition to the acceptance of the utilitarian standard; for that standard is not the agent's own greatest happiness, but the greatest amount of happiness altogether; and if it may possibly be doubted whether a noble character is always the happier for its nobleness, there can be no doubt that it makes other people happier, and that the world in general is immensely a gainer by it. Utilitarianism, therefore, could only attain its end by the general cultivation of nobleness of character, even if each individual were only benefited by the nobleness of others, and his own, so far as happiness is concerned, were a sheer deduction from the benefit. But the bare enunciation of such an absurdity as this last, renders refutation superfluous.

According to the Greatest Happiness Principle, as above explained, the ultimate end, with reference to and for the sake of which all other things are desirable (whether we are considering our own good or that of other people), is an existence exempt as far as possible from pain, and as rich as possible in enjoyments, both in point of quantity and quality; the test of quality, and the rule for measuring it against quantity, being the preference felt by those who in their opportunities of experience, to which must be added their

habits of self-consciousness and self-observation, are best furnished with the means of comparison. This, being, according
to the utilitarian opinion, the end of human action, is
necessarily also the standard of morality; which may accordingly be defined, the rules and precepts for human conduct,
by the observance of which an existence such as has been
described might be, to the greatest extent possible, secured
to all mankind; and not to them only, but, so far as the
nature of things admits, to the whole sentient creation.

Against this doctrine, however, arises another class of
objectors, who say that happiness, in any form, cannot be the
rational purpose of human life and action; because, in the
first place, it is unattainable : and they contemptuously ask,
what right hast thou to be happy? a question which Mr.
Carlyle clenches by the addition, What right, a short time ago,
hast thou even *to be?* Next, they say, that men can do
without happiness; that all noble human beings have felt
this, and could not have become noble but by learning the
lesson of Entsagen, or renunciation; which lesson, thoroughly
learnt and submitted to, they affirm to be the beginning and
necessary condition of all virtue.

The first of these objections would go to the root of the
matter were it well founded; for if no happiness is to be
had at all by human beings, the attainment of it cannot
be the end of morality, or of any rational conduct. Though,
even in that case, something might still be said for the
utilitarian theory; since utility includes not solely the pursuit
of happiness, but the prevention or mitigation of unhappiness;
and if the former aim be chimerical, there will be all the
greater scope and more imperative need for the latter,
so long at least as mankind think fit to live, and do not take
refuge in the simultaneous act of suicide recommended under
certain conditions by Novalis. When, however, it is thus
positively asserted to be impossible that human life should
be happy, the assertion, if not something like a verbal
quibble, is at least an exaggeration. If by happiness be
meant a continuity of highly pleasurable excitement, it is
evident enough that this is impossible. A state of exalted
pleasure lasts only moments, or in some cases, and with

some intermissions, hours or days, and is the occasional brilliant flash of enjoyment, not its permanent and steady flame. Of this the philosophers who have taught that happiness is the end of life were as fully aware as those who taunt them. The happiness which they meant was not a life of rapture; but moments of such, in an existence made up of few and transitory pains, many and various pleasures, with a decided predominance of the active over the passive, and having as the foundation of the whole, not to expect more from life than it is capable of bestowing. A life thus composed, to those who have been fortunate enough to obtain it, has always appeared worthy of the name of happiness. And such an existence is even now the lot of many, during some considerable portion of their lives. The present wretched education, and wretched social arrangements, are the only real hindrance to its being attainable by almost all.

The objectors perhaps may doubt whether human beings, if taught to consider happiness as the end of life, would be satisfied with such a moderate share of it. But great numbers of mankind have been satisfied with much less. The main constituents of a satisfied life appear to be two, either of which by itself is often found sufficient for the purpose : tranquillity, and excitement. With much tranquillity, many find that they can be content with very little pleasure : with much excitement, many can reconcile themselves to a considerable quantity of pain. There is assuredly no inherent impossibility in enabling even the mass of mankind to unite both; since the two are so far from being incompatible that they are in natural alliance, the prolongation of either being a preparation for, and exciting a wish for, the other. It is only those in whom indolence amounts to a vice, that do not desire excitement after an interval of repose : it is only those in whom the need of excitement is a disease, that feels the tranquillity which follows excitement dull and insipid, instead of pleasurable in direct proportion to the excitement which preceded it. When people who are tolerably fortunate in their outward lot do not find in life sufficient enjoyment to make it valuable to them, the cause generally is, caring for nobody but themselves. To

those who have neither public nor private affections, the
excitements of life are much curtailed, and in any case
dwindle in value as the time approaches when all selfish
interests must be terminated by death : while those who
leave after them objects of personal affection, and especially
those who have also cultivated a fellow-feeling with the
collective interests of mankind, retain as lively an interest in
life on the eve of death as in the vigour of youth and health.
Next to selfishness, the principal cause which makes life
unsatisfactory is want of mental cultivation. A cultivated mind
—I do not mean that of a philosopher, but any mind to which
the fountains of knowledge have been opened, and which has
been taught, in any tolerable degree, to exercise its faculties
—finds sources of inexhaustible interest in all that surrounds
it; in the objects of nature, the achievements of art, the
imaginations of poetry, the incidents of history, the ways of
mankind, past and present, and their prospects in the future.
It is possible, indeed, to become indifferent to all this, and that
too without having exhausted a thousandth part of it; but
only when one has had from the beginning no moral or
human interest in these things, and has sought in them
only the gratification of curiosity.

Now there is absolutely no reason in the nature of things
why an amount of mental culture sufficient to give an
intelligent interest in these objects of contemplation, should
not be the inheritance of every one born in a civilised country.
As little is there an inherent necessity that any human being
should be a selfish egotist, devoid of every feeling or care
but those which centre in his own miserable individuality.
Something far superior to this is sufficiently common even now,
to give ample earnest of what the human species may be made.
Genuine private affections, and a sincere interest in the
public good, are possible, though in unequal degrees, to
every rightly brought up human being. In a world in which
there is so much to interest, so much to enjoy, and so much
also to correct and improve, every one who has this moderate
amount of moral and intellectual requisites is capable of
an existence which may be called enviable; and unless
such a person, through bad laws, or subjection to the will of

others, is denied the liberty to use the sources of happiness within his reach, he will not fail to find this enviable existence, if he escape the positive evils of life, the great sources of physical and mental suffering—such as indigence, disease, and the unkindness, worthlessness, or premature loss of objects of affection. The main stress of the problem lies, therefore, in the contest with these calamities, from which it is a rare good fortune entirely to escape; which as things now are, cannot be obviated, and often cannot be in any material degree mitigated. Yet no one whose opinion deserves a moment's consideration can doubt that most of the great positive evils of the world are in themselves removable, and will, if human affairs continue to improve, be in the end reduced within narrow limits. Poverty, in any sense implying suffering, may be completely extinguished by the wisdom of society, combined with the good sense and providence of individuals. Even that most intractable of enemies, disease, may be indefinitely reduced in dimensions by good physical and moral education, and proper control of noxious influences; while the progress of science holds out a promise for the future of still more direct conquests over this detestable foe. And every advance in that direction relieves us from some, not only of the chances which cut short our own lives, but, what concerns us still more, which deprive us of those in whom our happiness is wrapt up. As for vicissitudes of fortune, and other disappointments connected with worldly circumstances, these are principally the effect either of gross imprudence, of ill-regulated desires, or of bad or imperfect social institutions. All the grand sources, in short, of human suffering are in a great degree, many of them almost entirely, conquerable by human care and effort; and though their removal is grievously slow—though a long succession of generations will perish in the breach before the conquest is completed, and this world becomes all that, if will and knowledge were not wanting, it might easily be made—yet every mind sufficiently intelligent and generous to bear a part, however small and unconspicuous, in the endeavour, will draw a noble enjoyment from the contest itself, which he would not for any bribe in the form of selfish indulgence consent to be without.

And this leads to the true estimation of what is said by the objectors concerning the possibility, and the obligation, of learning to do without happiness. Unquestionably it is possible to do without happiness; it is done involuntarily by nineteen-twentieths of mankind, even in those parts of our present world which are least deep in barbarism; and it often has to be done voluntarily by the hero or the martyr, for the sake of something which he prizes more than his individual happiness. But this something, what is it, unless the happiness of others, or some of the requisites of happiness? It is noble to be capable of resigning entirely one's own portion of happiness, or chances of it : but, after all, this self-sacrifice must be for some end; it is not its own end; and if we are told that its end is not happiness, but virtue, which is better than happiness, I ask, would the sacrifice be made if the hero or martyr did not believe that it would earn for others immunity from similar sacrifices? Would it be made if he thought that his renunciation of happiness for himself would produce no fruit for any of his fellow creatures, but to make their lot like his, and place them also in the condition of persons who have renounced happiness? All honour to those who can abnegate for themselves the personal enjoyment of life, when by such renunciation they contribute worthily to increase the amount of happiness in the world; but he who does it, or professes to do it, for any other purpose, is no more deserving of admiration than the ascetic mounted on his pillar. He may be an inspiring proof of what men *can* do, but assuredly not an example of what they *should*.

Though it is only in a very imperfect state of the world's arrangements that any one can best serve the happiness of others by the absolute sacrifice of his own, yet so long as the world is in that imperfect state, I fully acknowledge that the readiness to make such a sacrifice is the highest virtue which can be found in man. I will add, that in this condition of the world, paradoxical as the assertion may be, the conscious ability to do without happiness gives the best prospect of realising such happiness as is attainable. For nothing except that consciousness can raise a person above the chances of life, by making him feel that, let fate and fortune do their worst, they have not power to subdue him : which, once felt, frees him from excess of anxiety concerning the evils of life, and enables him, like many a Stoic in the worst times of the Roman Empire, to cultivate in tranquillity the sources of satisfaction accessible to him, without concerning himself about the uncertainty of their duration, any more than about their inevitable end.

Meanwhile, let utilitarians never cease to claim the morality of self devotion as a possession which belongs by as good a right to them, as either to the Stoic or to the Transcendentalist. The utilitarian morality does recognise in human beings the power of sacrificing their own greatest good for the good of others. It only refuses to admit that the sacrifice is itself a good. A sacrifice which does not increase, or tend to increase, the sum total of happiness, it considers as wasted. The only self-renunciation which it applauds, is devotion to the happiness, or to some of the means of happiness, of others; either of mankind collectively, or of individuals within the limits imposed by the collective interests of mankind.

I must again repeat, what the assailants of utilitarianism seldom have the justice to acknowledge, that the happiness which forms the utilitarian standard of what is right in conduct, is not the agent's own happiness, but that of all concerned. As between his own happiness and that of others, utilitarianism requires him to be as strictly impartial as a disinterested and benevolent spectator. In the golden rule of Jesus of Nazareth, we read the complete spirit of the ethics of utility. To do as you would be done by, and to love your neighbour as yourself, constitute the ideal perfection of utilitarian morality. As the means of making the nearest approach to this ideal, utility would enjoin, first, that laws and social arrangements should place the happiness, or (as speaking practically it may be called) the interest, of every individual, as nearly as possible in harmony with the interest of the whole; and secondly, that education and opinion, which have so vast a power over human character, should so use that power as to establish in the mind of every individual an indissoluble association between his own happiness and the good of the whole; especially between his own happiness and the practice of such modes of conduct, negative and positive, as regard for the universal happiness prescribes; so that not only he may be unable to conceive the possibility of happiness to himself, consistently with conduct opposed to the general good, but also that a direct impulse to promote the general good may be in every individual one of the habitual motives of action, and the sentiments connected therewith may fill a large and prominent place in every human being's sentient existence. If the impugners of the utilitarian morality represented it to their own minds in this its true character, I know not what recommendation possessed by any other morality they could possibly affirm to be wanting to it; what more beautiful or more exalted developments of human nature any other ethical system can be supposed to foster, or what springs of action, not accessible to the utilitarian, such systems rely on for giving effect to their mandates.

The objectors to utilitarianism cannot always be charged with representing it in a discreditable light. On the contrary, those among them who entertain anything like a just idea of its disinterested character, sometimes find fault with its standard as being too high for humanity. They say it is exacting too much to require that people shall always act from the inducement of promoting the general interests of society. But this is to mistake the very meaning of a standard of morals, and confound the rule of action with the motive of it. It is the business of ethics to tell us what are our duties, or by what test we may know them; but no system of ethics requires that the sole motive of all we do shall be a feeling of duty; on the contrary, ninety-nine hundredths of all our actions are done from other motives, and rightly so done, if the rule of duty does not condemn them. It is the more unjust to utilitarianism that this particular misapprehension should be made a ground of objection to it, inasmuch as utilitarian moralists have gone beyond almost all others in affirming that the motive has nothing to do with the morality of the action, though much with the worth of the agent. He who saves a fellow-creature from drowning does what is morally right, whether his motive be duty, or the hope of being paid for his trouble; he who betrays the friend that trusts him, is guilty of a crime, even if his object be to serve another friend to whom he is under greater obligation. But to speak only of actions done from the motive of duty, and in direct obedience to principle : it is a mis-apprehension of the utilitarian mode of thought, to conceive it as implying that people should fix their minds upon so wide a generality as the world, or society at large. The great majority of good actions are intended not for the benefit of the world, but for that of individuals, of which the good of the world is made up; and the thoughts of the most virtuous man need not on these occasions travel beyond the particular persons concerned, except so far as is necessary to assure himself that in benefiting them he is not violating the rights, that is, the legitimate and authorised expectations, of any one else. The multiplication of happiness is, according to the utilitarian ethics, the object of virtue : the occasions on which any person (except one in a thousand) has it in his power to do this on an extended scale, in other words to be a public benefactor, are but exceptional; and on these occasions alone is he called on to consider public utility; in every other case, private utility, the interest or happiness of some few persons, is all he has to attend to. Those alone the influence of whose actions extends to society in general, need concern themselves habitually about so large an object. In the case of abstinences indeed—of things which people forbear to do from moral considerations, though the conse-quences in the particular case might be beneficial—it would be unworthy of an intelligent agent not to be consciously aware that the action is of a class which, if practised generally, would be generally injurious, and that this is the ground of the obligation to abstain from it. The amount of regard for the public interest implied in this recognition, is no greater than is demanded by every system of morals, for they all enjoin to abstain from whatever is manifestly pernicious to society.

The same considerations dispose of another reproach against the doctrine of utility, founded on a still grosser misconception of the purpose of a standard of morality, and of the very meaning of the words right and wrong. It is often affirmed that utilitarianism renders men cold and unsympathising; that it chills their moral feelings towards individuals; that it makes them regard only the dry and hard consideration of the consequences of actions, not taking into their moral estimate the qualities from which those actions emanate. If the assertion means that they do not allow their judgment respecting the rightness or wrongness of an action to be influenced by their opinion of the qualities of the person who does it, this is a complaint not against utilitarianism, but against having any standard of morality at all; for certainly no known ethical standard decides an action to be good or bad because it is done by a good or a bad man, still less because done by an amiable, a brave, or a benevolent man, or the contrary. These considerations are relevant, not to the estimation of actions, but of persons; and there is nothing in the utilitarian theory inconsistent with the fact that there are other things which interest us in persons besides the rightness and wrongness of their actions. The Stoics, indeed, with the paradoxical misuse of language which was part of their system, and by which they strove to raise themselves above all concern about anything but virtue, were fond of saying that he who has that has everything; that he, and only he, is rich, is beautiful, is a king. But no claim of this description is made for the virtuous man by the utilitarian doctrine. Utilitarians are quite aware that there are other desirable possessions and qualities besides virtue, and are perfectly willing to allow to all of them their full worth. They are also aware that a right action does not necessarily indicate a virtuous character, and that actions which are blamable, often proceed from qualities entitled to praise. When this is apparent in any particular case, it modifies their estimation, not certainly of the act, but of the agent. I grant that they are, notwithstanding, of opinion, that in the long run the best proof of a good character is good actions; and resolutely refuse to consider any mental disposition as good, of which the predominant tendency is to produce bad conduct. This makes them unpopular with many people; but it is an unpopularity which they must share with every one who regards the distinction between right and wrong in a serious light; and the reproach is not one which a conscientious utilitarian need be anxious to repel.

If no more be meant by the objection than that many utilitarians look on the morality of actions, as measured by the utilitarian standard, with too exclusive a regard, and do not lay sufficient stress upon the other beauties of character which go towards making a human being lovable or admirable, this may be admitted. Utilitarians who have cultivated their moral feelings, but not their sympathies nor their artistic perceptions, do fall into this mistake; and so do all other moralists under the same conditions. What can be said in excuse for other moralists is equally available for them, namely, that, if there is to be any error, it is better that it should be on that side. As a matter of fact, we may affirm that among utilitarians as among adherents of other systems, there is every imaginable degree of rigidity and of laxity in the application of their standard : some are even puritanically rigorous, while others are as indulgent as can possibly be desired by sinner or by sentimentalist. But on the whole, a doctrine which brings prominently forward the interest that mankind have in the repression and prevention of conduct which violates the moral law, is likely to be inferior to no other in turning the sanctions of opinion against such violations. It is true, the question, What does violate the moral law? is one on which those who recognise different standards of morality are likely now and then to differ. But difference of opinion on moral questions was not first introduced into the world by utilitarianism, while that doctrine does supply, if not always an easy, at all events a tangible and intelligible mode of deciding such differences.

It may not be superfluous to notice a few more of the common misapprehensions of utilitarian ethics, even those which are so obvious and gross that it might appear impossible for any person of candour and intelligence to fall into them; since persons, even of considerable mental endowment, often give themselves so little trouble to understand the bearings of any opinion against which they entertain a prejudice, and men are in general so little conscious of this voluntary ignorance as a defect, that the vulgarest misunderstandings of ethical doctrines are continually met with in the deliberate writings of persons of the greatest pretensions both to high principle and to philosophy. We not uncommonly hear the doctrine of utility inveighed against as a *godless* doctrine. If it be necessary to say anything at all against so mere an assumption, we may say that the question depends upon what idea we have formed of the moral character of the Deity. If it be a true belief that God desires, above all things, the happiness of his creatures, and that this was his purpose in their creation, utility is not only not a godless doctrine, but more profoundly religious than any other. If it be meant that utilitarianism does not recognise the revealed will of God as the supreme law of morals, I answer, that a utilitarian who believes in the perfect goodness and wisdom of God, necessarily believes that whatever God has thought fit to reveal on the subject of morals, must fulfil the requirements of utility in a supreme degree. But others besides utilitarians have been of opinion that the Christian revelation was intended, and is fitted, to inform the hearts and minds of mankind with a spirit which should enable them to find for themselves what is right, and incline them to do it when found, rather than to tell them, except in a very general way, what it is; and that we need a doctrine of ethics, carefully followed out, to *interpret* to us the will of God. Whether this opinion is correct or not, it is superfluous here to discuss; since whatever aid religion, either natural or revealed, can afford to ethical investigation, is as open to the utilitarian moralist as to any other. He can use it as the testimony of God to the usefulness or hurtfulness of any given course of action, by as good a right as others can use it for the indication of a transcendental law, having no connection with usefulness or with happiness.

Again, Utility is often summarily stigmatised as an immoral doctrine by giving it the name of Expediency, and taking advantage of the popular use of that term to contrast it with Principle. But the Expedient, in the sense in which it is opposed to the Right, generally means that which is expedient for the particular interest of the agent himself; as when a minister sacrifices the interests of his country to keep himself in place. When it means anything better than this, it means that which is expedient for some immediate object, some temporary purpose, but which violates a rule whose observance is expedient in a much higher degree. The Expedient, in this sense, instead of being the same thing with the useful, is a branch of the hurtful. Thus, it would often be expedient, for the purpose of getting over some momentary embarrass-ment, or attaining some object immediately useful to ourselves or others, to tell a lie. But inasmuch as the cultivation in ourselves of a sensitive feeling on the subject of veracity, is one of the most useful, and the enfeeblement of that feeling one of the most hurtful, things to which our conduct can be instrumental; and inasmuch as any, even unintentional, deviation from truth, does that much towards weakening the trustworthiness of human assertion, which is not only the principal support of all present social well-being, but the insufficiency of which does more than any one thing that can be named to keep back civilisation, virtue, everything on which human happiness on the largest scale depends; we feel that the violation, for a present advantage, of a rule of such transcendant expediency, is not expedient, and that he who, for the sake of a convenience to himself or to some other individual, does what depends on him to deprive man-kind of the good, and inflict upon them the evil, involved in the greater or less reliance which they can place in each other's word, acts the part of one of their worst enemies. Yet that even this rule, sacred as it is, admits of possible exceptions, is acknowledged by all moralists; the chief of which is when the withholding of some fact (as of information from a malefactor, or of bad news from a person dangerously ill) would save an individual (especially an individual other than oneself) from great and unmerited evil, and when the withholding can only be effected by denial. But in order that the exception may not extend itself beyond the need, and may have the least possible effect in weakening reliance on veracity, it ought to be recognised, and, if possible, its limits defined; and if the principle of utility is good for anything, it must be good for weighing these conflicting utilities against one another, and marking out the region within which one or the other preponderates.

Again, defenders of utility often find themselves called upon to reply to such objections as this—that there is not time, previous to action, for calculating and weighing the effects of any line of conduct on the general happiness. This is exactly as if any one were to say that it is impossible to guide our conduct by Christianity, because there is not time, on every occasion on which anything has to be done, to read through the Old and New Testaments. The answer to the objection is, that there has been ample time, namely, the whole past duration of the human species. During all that time, mankind have been learning by experience the tendencies of actions; on which experience all the prudence, as well as all the morality of life, are dependent. People talk as if the commencement of this course of experience had hitherto been put off, and as if, at the moment when some man feels tempted to meddle with the property or life of another, he had to begin considering for the first time whether murder and theft are injurious to human happiness. Even then I do not think that he would find the question very puzzling; but, at all events, the matter is now done to his hand. It is truly a whimsical supposition that, if mankind were agreed in considering utility to be the test of morality, they would remain without any agreement as to what *is* useful, and would take no measures for having their notions on the subject taught to the young, and enforced by law and opinion. There is no difficulty in proving any ethical standard whatever to work ill, if we suppose universal idiocy to be conjoined with it; but on any hypothesis short of that, mankind must by this time have acquired positive beliefs as to the effects of

some actions on their happiness; and the beliefs which
have thus come down are the rules of morality for the multitude, and for the philosopher until he has succeeded in finding
better. That philosophers might easily do this, even now,
on many subjects; that the received code of ethics is by no
means of divine right; and that mankind have still much
to learn as to the effects of actions on the general happiness,
I admit, or rather, earnestly maintain. The corollaries from
the principle of utility, like the precepts of every practical art,
admit of indefinite improvement, and, in a progressive state
of the human mind, their improvement is perpetually going
on. But to consider the rules of morality as improvable, is one
thing; to pass over the intermediate generalisations entirely,
and endeavour to test each individual action directly by the
first principle, is another. It is a strange notion that the
acknowledgement of a first principle is inconsistent with
the admission of secondary ones. To inform a traveller respecting the place of his ultimate destination, is not to forbid the
use of landmarks and direction-posts on the way. The proposition that happiness is the end and aim of morality, does
not mean that no road ought to be laid down to that goal, or
that persons going thither should not be advised to take one
direction rather than another. Men really ought to leave off
talking a kind of nonsense on this subject, which they would
neither talk nor listen to on other matters of practical con-
cernment. Nobody argues that the art of navigation is not
founded on astronomy, because sailors cannot wait to calculate
the National Almanack. Being rational creatures, they go
to sea with it ready calculated; and all rational creatures
go out upon the sea of life with their minds made up on the
common questions of right and wrong, as well as on many of
the far more difficult questions of wise and foolish. And this,
as long as foresight is a human quality, it is to be presumed
they will continue to do. Whatever we adopt as the fundamental principle of morality, we require subordinate principles
to apply it by; the impossibility of doing without them, being
common to all systems, can afford no argument against any
one in particular; but gravely to argue as if no such secondary principles could be had, and as if mankind had remained

till now, and always must remain, without drawing any general conclusions from the experience of human life, is as high a pitch, I think, as absurdity has ever reached in philosophical controversy.

The remainder of the stock arguments against utilitarianism mostly consist in laying to its charge the common infirmities of human nature, and the general difficulties which embarrass conscientious persons in shaping their course through life. We are told that a utilitarian will be apt to make his own particular case an exception to moral rules, and, when under temptation, will see a utility in the breach of a rule, greater than he will see in its observance. But is utility the only creed which is able to furnish us with excuses for evil doing, and means of cheating our own conscience? They are afforded in abundance by all doctrines which recognise as a fact in morals the existence of conflicting considerations; which all doctrines do, that have been believed by sane persons. It is not the fault of any creed, but of the complicated nature of human affairs, that rules of conduct cannot be so framed as to require no exceptions, and that hardly any kind of action can safely be laid down as either always obligatory or always condemnable. There is no ethical creed which does not temper the rigidity of its laws, by giving a certain latitude, under the moral responsibility of the agent, for accommodation to peculiarities of circumstances; and under every creed, at the opening thus made, self-deception and dishonest casuistry get in. There exists no moral system under which there do not arise unequivocal cases of conflicting obligation. These are the real difficulties, the knotty points both in the theory of ethics, and in the conscientious guidance of personal conduct. They are overcome practically, with greater or with less success, according to the intellect and virtue of the individual; but it can hardly be pretended that any one will be the less qualified for dealing with them, from possessing an ultimate standard to which conflicting rights and duties can be referred. If utility is the ultimate source of moral obligations, utility may be invoked to decide between them when their demands are incompatible. Though the application of the standard may be difficult, it is better than none at all: while in other systems, the moral laws all claiming independent authority, there is no common umpire entitled to interfere between them; their claims to precedence one over another rest on little better than sophistry, and unless determined, as they generally are, by the unacknowledged influence of considerations of utility, afford a free scope for the action of personal desires and partialities. We must remember that only in these cases of conflict between secondary principles is it requisite that first principles should be appealed to. There is no case of moral obligation in which some secondary principle is not involved; and if only one, there can seldom be any real doubt which one it is, in the mind of any person by whom the principle itself is recognised.

CHAPTER III

OF THE ULTIMATE SANCTION OF THE PRINCIPLE OF UTILITY

The question is often asked, and properly so, in regard to any supposed moral standard—What is its sanction? what are the motives to obey it? or more specifically, what is the source of its obligation? whence does it derive its binding force? It is a necessary part of moral philosophy to provide the answer to this question; which, though frequently assuming the shape of an objection to the utilitarian morality, as if it had some special applicability to that above others, really arises in regard to all standards. It arises, in fact, whenever a person is called on to *adopt* a standard, or refer morality to any basis on which he has not been accustomed to rest it. For the customary morality, that which education and opinion have consecrated, is the only one which presents itself to the mind with the feeling of being *in itself* obligatory; and when a person is asked to believe that this morality *derives* its obligation from some general principle round which custom has not thrown the same halo, the assertion is to him a paradox; the supposed corollaries seem to have a more binding force than the original theorem; the superstructure seems to stand better without, than with, what is represented as its foundation. He says to himself, I feel that I am bound not to rob or murder, betray or deceive; but why am I bound to promote the general happiness? If my own happiness lies in something else, why may I not give that the preference?

If the view adopted by the utilitarian philosophy of the nature of the moral sense be correct, this difficulty will always present itself, until the influences which form moral character have taken the same hold of the principle which they have taken of some of the consequences—until, by the improvement of education, the feeling of unity with our fellow-creatures shall be (what it cannot be denied that Christ intended it to be) as deeply rooted in our character, and to our own consciousness as completely a part of our nature, as the horror of crime is in an ordinary well brought up young person. In the meantime, however, the difficulty has no peculiar application to the doctrine of utility, but is inherent in every attempt to analyse morality and reduce it to principles; which, unless the principle is already in men's minds invested with as much sacredness as any of its applications, always seem to divest them of a part of their sanctity.

The principle of utility either has, or there is no reason why it might not have, all the sanctions which belong to any other system of morals. Those sanctions are either external or internal. Of the external sanctions it is not necessary to speak at any length. They are, the hope of favour and the fear of displeasure, from our fellow-creatures or from the Ruler of the Universe, along with whatever we have of sympathy or affection for them, or of love and awe of Him, inclining us to do his will independently of selfish consequences. There is evidently no reason why all these motives for observance should not attach themselves to the utilitarian morality, as completely and as powerfully as to any other. Indeed, those of them which refer to our fellow-creatures are sure to do so, in proportion to the amount of general intelligence; for whether there be any other ground of moral obligation than the general happiness or not, men do desire happiness; and however imperfect may be their own practice, they desire and commend all conduct in others towards themselves, by which they think their happiness is promoted. With regard to the religious motive, if men believe, as most profess to do, in the goodness of God, those who think that conduciveness to the general happiness is the essence, or even only the criterion of good, must necessarily believe that it is also that which God approves. The whole force therefore of external reward and punishment, whether physical or moral, and whether proceeding from God or from our fellow men, together with all that the capacities of human nature admit of disinterested devotion to either, become available to enforce the utilitarian morality, in proportion as that morality is recognised; and the more powerfully, the more the appliances of education and general cultivation are bent to the purpose.

So far as to external sanctions. The internal sanction of duty, whatever our standard of duty may be, is one and the same—a feeling in our own mind; a pain, more or less intense, attendant on violation of duty, which in properly cultivated moral natures rises, in the more serious cases, into shrinking from it as an impossibility. This feeling, when disinterested, and connecting itself with the pure idea of duty, and not with some particular form of it, or with any of the merely accessory circumstances, is the essence of Conscience; though in that complex phenomenon as it actually exists, the simple fact is in general all encrusted over with collateral associations, derived from sympathy, from love, and still more from fear; from all the forms of religious feeling; from the recollections of childhood and of all our past life; from self-esteem, desire of the esteem of others, and occasionally even self-abasement. This extreme complication is, I apprehend, the origin of the sort of mystical character which, by a tendency of the human mind of which there are many other examples, is apt to be attributed to the idea of moral obligation, and which leads people to believe that the idea cannot possibly attach itself to any other objects than those which, by a supposed mysterious law, are found in our present experience to excite it. Its binding force, however, consists in the existence of a mass of feeling which must be broken through in order to do what violates our standard of right, and which, if we do nevertheless violate that standard, will probably have to be encountered afterwards in the form of remorse. Whatever theory we have of the nature or origin of conscience, this is what essentially constitutes it.

The ultimate sanction, therefore, of all morality (external motives apart) being a subjective feeling in our own minds, I see nothing embarrassing to those whose standard is utility, in the question, what is the sanction of that particular standard? We may answer, the same as of all other moral standards—the conscientious feelings of mankind. Undoubtedly this sanction has no binding efficacy on those who do not

possess the feelings it appeals to; but neither will these
persons be more obedient to any other moral principle than
to the utilitarian one. On them morality of any kind has no
hold but through the external sanctions. Meanwhile the
feelings exist, a fact in human nature, the reality of which,
and the great power with which they are capable of acting
on those in whom they have been duly cultivated, are proved
by experience. No reason has ever been shown why they may
not be cultivated to as great intensity in connection with the
utilitarian, as with any other rule of morals.

There is, I am aware, a disposition to believe that a person
who sees in moral obligation a transcendental fact, an objective
reality belonging to the province of " Things in themselves,"
is likely to be more obedient to it than one who believes
it to be entirely subjective, having its seat in human consciousness only. But whatever a person's opinion may be on
this point of Ontology, the force he is really urged by is his
own subjective feeling, and is exactly measured by its strength.
No one's belief that duty is an objective reality is stronger than
the belief that God is so; yet the belief in God, apart from
the expectation of actual reward and punishment, only operates
on conduct through, and in proportion to, the subjective
religious feeling. The sanction, so far as it is disinterested,
is always in the mind itself; and the notion therefore of
the transcendental moralists must be, that this sanction will
not exist *in* the mind unless it is believed to have its root out
of the mind; and that if a person is able to say to himself,
This which is restraining me, and which is called my conscience,
is only a feeling in my own mind, he may possibly draw
the conclusion that when the feeling ceases the obligation
ceases, and that if he find the feeling inconvenient, he may
disregard it, and endeavour to get rid of it. But is this
danger confined to the utilitarian morality? Does the belief
that moral obligation has its seat outside the mind make the
feeling of it too strong to get rid of? The fact is so far
otherwise, that all moralists admit and lament the ease
with which, in the generality of minds, conscience can be
silenced or stifled. The question, Need I obey my conscience?
is quite as often put to themselves by persons who never

heard of the principle of utility, as by its adherents. Those whose conscientious feelings are so weak as to allow of their asking this question, if they answer it affirmatively, will not do so because they believe in the transcendental theory, but because of the external sanctions.

It is not necessary, for the present purpose, to decide whether the feeling of duty is innate or implanted. Assuming it to be innate, it is an open question to what objects it naturally attaches itself; for the philosophic supporters of that theory are now agreed that the intuitive perception is of principles of morality and not of the details. If there be anything innate in the matter, I see no reason why the feeling which is innate should not be that of regard to the pleasures and pains of others. If there is any principle of morals which is intuitively obligatory, I should say it must be that. If so, the intuitive ethics would coincide with the utilitarian, and there would be no further quarrel between them. Even as it is, the intuitive moralists, though they believe that there are other intuitive moral obligations, do already believe this to be one; for they unanimously hold that a large *portion* of morality turns upon the consideration due to the interests of our fellow-creatures. Therefore, if the belief in the transcendental origin of moral obligation gives any additional efficacy to the internal sanction, it appears to me that the utilitarian principle has already the benefit of it.

On the other hand, if, as is my own belief, the moral feelings are not innate, but acquired, they are not for that reason the less natural. It is natural to man to speak, to reason, to build cities, to cultivate the ground, though these are acquired faculties. The moral feelings are not indeed a part of our nature, in the sense of being in any perceptible degree present in all of us; but this, unhappily, is a fact admitted by those who believe the most strenuously in their transcendental origin. Like the other acquired capacities above referred to, the moral faculty, if not a part of our nature, is a natural outgrowth from it; capable, like them, in a certain small degree of springing up spontaneously; and susceptible of being brought up by cultivation to a high degree of development. Unhappily it is also susceptible, by a sufficient use of the external sanctions and of the force of early impressions, of being cultivated in almost any direction: so that there is hardly anything so absurd or so mischievous that it may not, by means of these influences, be made to act on the human mind with all the authority of conscience. To doubt that the same potency might be given by the same means to the principle of utility, even if it had no foundation in human nature, would be flying in the face of all experience.

But moral associations which are wholly of artificial creation, when intellectual culture goes on, yield by degrees to the dissolving force of analysis: and if the feeling of duty, when associated with utility, would appear equally arbitrary; if there were no leading department of our nature, no powerful class of sentiments, with which that association would harmonise, which would make us feel it congenial, and incline us not only to foster it in others (for which we have abundant interested motives), but also to cherish it in ourselves; if there were not, in short, a natural basis of sentiment for utilitarian morality, it might well happen that this association also, even after it had been implanted by education, might be analysed away.

But there *is* this basis of powerful natural sentiment; and this it is which, when once the general happiness is recognised as the ethical standard, will constitute the strength of the utilitarian morality. This firm foundation is that of the social feelings of mankind; the desire to be in unity with our fellow-creatures, which is already a powerful principle in human nature, and happily one of those which tend to become stronger, even without express inculcation, from the influences of advancing civilisation. The social state is at once so natural, so necessary, and so habitual to man, that, except in some unusual circumstances or by an effort of voluntary abstraction, he never conceives himself otherwise than as a member of a body; and this association is riveted more and more, as mankind are further removed from the state of savage independence. Any condition, therefore, which is essential to a state of society, becomes more and more an inseparable part of every person's conception of the state of things which he is born into, and which is the destiny of

a human being. Now, society between human beings, except
in the relation of master and slave, is manifestly impossible on
any other footing than that the interests of all are to be consulted. Society between equals can only exist on the understanding that the interests of all are to be regarded equally.
And since in all states of civilisation, every person, except
an absolute monarch, has equals, every one is obliged to live
on these terms with somebody; and in every age some
advance is made towards a state in which it will be impossible
to live permanently on other terms with anybody. In this way
people grow up unable to conceive as possible to them a
state of total disregard of other people's interests. They are
under a necessity of conceiving themselves as at least abstain-
ing from all the grosser injuries, and (if only for their own
protection) living in a state of constant protest against them.
They are also familiar with the fact of co-operating with
others, and proposing to themselves a collective, not an
individual interest as the aim (at least for the time being)
of their actions. So long as they are co-operating, their ends
are identified with those of others; there is at least a temporary
feeling that the interests of others are their own interests.
Not only does all strengthening of social ties, and all healthy
growth of society, give to each individual a stronger personal
interest in practically consulting the welfare of others; it also
leads him to identify his *feelings* more and more with
their good, or at least with an even greater degree of
practical consideration for it. He comes, as though in-
stinctively, to be conscious of himself as a being who
of course pays regard to others. The good of others becomes
to him a thing naturally and necessarily to be attended to,
like any of the physical conditions of our existence. Now,
whatever amount of this feeling a person has, he is urged
by the strongest motives both of interest and of sympathy
to demonstrate it, and to the utmost of his power encourage
it in others; and even if he has none of it himself, he is
as greatly interested as any one else that others should have
it. Consequently the smallest germs of the feeling are laid
hold of and nourished by the contagion of sympathy and
the influences of education; and a complete web of cor-

roborative association is woven round it, by the powerful agency of the external sanctions. This mode of conceiving ourselves and human life, as civilisation goes on, is felt to be more and more natural. Every step in political improvement renders it more so, by removing the sources of opposition of interest, and levelling those inequalities of legal privilege between individuals or classes, owing to which there are large portions of mankind whose happiness it is still practicable to disregard. In an improving state of the human mind, the influences are constantly on the increase, which tend to generate in each individual a feeling of unity with all the rest; which, if perfect, would make him never think of, or desire, any beneficial condition for himself, in the benefits of which they are not included. If we now suppose this feeling of unity to be taught as a religion, and the whole force of education, of institutions, and of opinion, directed, as it once was in the case of religion, to make every person grow up from infancy surrounded on all sides both by the profession and the practice of it, I think that no one, who can realise this conception, will feel any misgiving about the sufficiency of the ultimate sanction for the Happiness morality. To any ethical student who finds the realisation difficult, I recommend, as a means of facilitating it, the second of M. Comte's two principal works, the *Traité de Politique Positive*. I entertain the strongest objections to the system of politics and morals set forth in that treatise; but I think it has super-abundantly shown the possibility of giving to the service of humanity, even without the aid of belief in a Providence, both the psychological power and the social efficacy of a religion; making it take hold of human life, and colour all thought, feeling, and action, in a manner of which the greatest ascendancy ever exercised by any religion may be but a type and foretaste; and of which the danger is, not that it should be insufficient, but that it should be so excessive as to interfere unduly with human freedom and individuality.

Neither is it necessary to the feeling which constitutes the binding force of the utilitarian morality on those who recognise it, to wait for those social influences which would make its obligation felt by mankind at large. In the comparatively

early state of human advancement in which we now live, a
person cannot indeed feel that entireness of sympathy with
all others, which would make any real discordance in the
general direction of their conduct in life impossible; but
already a person in whom the social feeling is at all developed,
cannot bring himself to think of the rest of his fellow-
creatures as struggling rivals with him for the means of
happiness, whom he must desire to see defeated in their
object in order that he may succeed in his. The deeply
rooted conception which every individual even now has of
himself as a social being, tends to make him feel it one of
his natural wants that there should be harmony between
his feelings and aims and those of his fellow-creatures. If
differences of opinion and of mental culture make it impossible for him to share many of their actual feelings—
perhaps make him denounce and defy those feelings—he still
needs to be conscious that his real aim and theirs do not
conflict; that he is not opposing himself to what they really
wish for, namely their own good, but is, on the contrary,
promoting it. This feeling in most individuals is much inferior
in strength to their selfish feelings, and is often wanting
altogether. But to those who have it, it possesses all the
characters of a natural feeling. It does not present itself
to their minds as a superstition of education, or a law
despotically imposed by the power of society, but as an
attribute which it would not be well for them to be without.
This conviction is the ultimate sanction of the greatest happiness morality. This it is which makes any mind, of well-
developed feelings, work with, and not against, the outward
motives to care for others, afforded by what I have called
the external sanctions; and when those sanctions are wanting,
or act in an opposite direction, constitutes in itself a powerful
internal binding force, in proportion to the sensitiveness
and thoughtfulness of the character; since few but those
whose mind is a moral blank, could bear to lay out their
course of life on the plan of paying no regard to others
except so far as their own private interest compels.

CHAPTER IV

OF WHAT SORT OF PROOF THE PRINCIPLE OF UTILITY IS SUSCEPTIBLE

It has already been remarked, that questions of ultimate ends do not admit of proof, in the ordinary acceptation of the term. To be incapable of proof by reasoning is common to all first principles; to the first premises of our knowledge, as well as to those of our conduct. But the former, being matters of fact, may be the subject of a direct appeal to the faculties which judge of fact—namely, our senses, and our internal consciousness. Can an appeal be made to the same faculties on questions of practical ends? Or by what other faculty is cognisance taken of them?

Questions about ends are, in other words, questions what things are desirable. The utilitarian doctrine is, that happiness is desirable, and the only thing desirable, as an end; all other things being only desirable as means to that end. What ought to be required of this doctrine—what conditions is it requisite that the doctrine should fulfil—to make good its claim to be believed?

The only proof capable of being given that an object is visible, is that people actually see it. The only proof that a sound is audible, is that people hear it: and so of the other sources of our experience. In like manner, I apprehend, the sole evidence it is possible to produce that anything is desirable, is that people do actually desire it. If the end which the utilitarian doctrine proposes to itself were not, in theory and in practice, acknowledged to be an end, nothing could ever convince any person that it was so. No reason can be given why the general happiness is desirable, except that each person, so far as he believes it to be attainable, desires his own happiness. This, however, being a fact, we have not only all the proof which the case admits of, but all which it is possible to require, that happiness is a good: that each person's happiness is a good to that person, and the general happiness, therefore, a good to the aggregate of all persons. Happiness has made out its title as *one* of the ends of conduct, and consequently one of the criteria of morality.

But it has not, by this alone, proved itself to be the sole criterion. To do that, it would seem, by the same rule, necessary to show, not only that people desire happiness, but that they never desire anything else. Now it is palpable that they do desire things which, in common language, are decidedly distinguished from happiness. They desire, for example, virtue, and the absence of vice, no less really than pleasure and the absence of pain. The desire of virtue is not as universal, but it is as authentic a fact, as the desire of happiness. And hence the opponents of the utilitarian standard deem that they have a right to infer that there are other ends of human action besides happiness, and that happiness is not the standard of approbation and disapprobation.

But does the utilitarian doctrine deny that people desire virtue, or maintain that virtue is not a thing to be desired? The very reverse. It maintains not only that virtue is to be desired, but that it is to be desired disinterestedly, for itself. Whatever may be the opinion of utilitarian moralists as to the original conditions by which virtue is made virtue; however they may believe (as they do) that actions and dispositions are only virtuous because they promote another end than virtue; yet this being granted, and it having been decided, from considerations of this description, what *is* virtuous, they not only place virtue at the very head of the things which are good as means to the ultimate end, but they also recognise as a psychological fact the possibility of its being, to the individual, a good in itself, without looking to any end beyond it; and hold, that the mind is not in a right state, not in a state conformable to Utility, not in the state most conducive to the general happiness, unless it does love virtue in this manner—as a thing desirable in itself, even although, in the individual instance, it should not produce those other desirable consequences which it tends to produce, and on account of which it is held to be virtue. This opinion is not, in the smallest degree, a departure from the Happiness principle The ingredients of happiness are very various, and each of them is desirable in itself, and not merely when considered as swelling an aggregate. The principle of utility does not mean that any given pleasure, as music, for instance, or any given exemption from pain, as for example health, is to be looked upon as means to a collective something termed happiness, and to be desired on that account. They are desired and desirable in and for themselves; besides being means, they are a part of the end. Virtue, according to the utilitarian doctrine, is not naturally and originally part of the end, but it is capable of becoming so; and in those who love it disinterestedly it has become so, and is desired and cherished, not as a means to happiness, but as a part of their happiness.

To illustrate this farther, we may remember that virtue is not the only thing, originally a means, and which if it were not a means to anything else, would be and remain indifferent, but which by association with what it is a means to, comes to be desired for itself, and that too with the utmost intensity. What, for example, shall we say of the love of money? There is nothing originally more desirable about money than about any heap of glittering pebbles. Its worth is solely that of the things which it will buy; the desires for other things than itself, which it is a means of gratifying. Yet the love of money is not only one of the strongest moving forces of human life, but money is, in many cases, desired in and for itself; the desire to possess it is often stronger than the desire to use it, and goes on increasing when all the desires which point to ends beyond it, to be compassed by it, are falling off. It may, then, be said truly, that money is desired not for the sake of an end, but as part of the end. From being a means to happiness, it has come to be itself a principal ingredient of the individual's conception of happiness. The same may be said of the majority of the great objects of human life—power, for example, or fame; except that to each of these there is a certain amount of immediate pleasure annexed, which has at least the semblance of being naturally inherent of fame, is the immense aid they give to the attainment of in them; a thing which cannot be said of money. Still, however, the strongest natural attraction, both of power and

our other wishes; and it is the strong association thus generated between them and all our objects of desire, which gives to the direct desire of them the intensity it often assumes, so as in some characters to surpass in strength all other desires. In these cases the means have become a part of the end, and a more important part of it than any of the things which they are means to. What was once desired as an instrument for the attainment of happiness, has come to be desired for its own sake. In being desired for its own sake it is, however, desired as *part* of happiness. The person is made, or thinks he would be made, happy by its mere possession; and is made unhappy by failure to obtain it. The desire of it is not a different thing from the desire of happiness, any more than the love of music, or the desire of health. They are included in happiness. They are some of the elements of which the desire of happiness is made up. Happiness is not an abstract idea, but a concrete whole; and these are some of its parts. And the utilitarian standard sanctions and approves their being so. Life would be a poor thing, very ill provided with sources of happiness, if there were not this provision of nature, by which things originally indifferent, but conducive to, or otherwise associated with, the satisfaction of our primitive desires, become in themselves sources of pleasure more valuable than the primitive pleasures, both in permanency, in the space of human existence that they are capable of covering, and even in intensity.

Virtue, according to the utilitarian conception, is a good of this description. There was no original desire of it, or motive to it, save its conduciveness to pleasure, and especially to protection from pain. But through the association thus formed, it may be felt a good in itself, and desired as such with as great intensity as any other good; and with this difference between it and the love of money, of power, or of fame, that all of these may, and often do, render the individual noxious to the other members of the society to which he belongs, whereas there is nothing which makes him so much a blessing to them as the cultivation of the disinterested love of virtue. And consequently, the utilitarian standard, while it tolerates and approves those other acquired desires, up to the point beyond which they would be more injurious to the general happiness than promotive of it, enjoins and requires the cultivation of the love of virtue up to the greatest strength possible, as being above all things important to the general happiness.

It results from the preceding considerations, that there is in reality nothing desired except happiness. Whatever is desired otherwise than as a means to some end beyond itself, and ultimately to happiness, is desired as itself a part of happiness, and is not desired for itself until it has become so. Those who desire virtue for its own sake, desire it either because the consciousness of it is a pleasure, or because the consciousness of being without it is a pain, or for both reasons united; as in truth the pleasure and pain seldom exist separately, but almost always together, the same person feeling pleasure in the degree of virtue attained, and pain in not having attained more. If one of these gave him no pleasure, and the other no pain, he would not love or desire virtue, or would desire it only for the other benefits which it might produce to himself or to persons whom he cared for.

We have now, then, an answer to the question, of what sort of proof the principle of utility is susceptible. If the opinion which I have now stated is psychologically true—if human nature is so constituted as to desire nothing which is not either a part of happiness or a means of happiness, we can have no other proof, and we require no other, that these are the only things desirable. If so, happiness is the sole end of human action, and the promotion of it the test by which to judge of all human conduct; from whence it necessarily follows that it must be the criterion of morality, since a part is included in the whole.

And now to decide whether this is really so; whether mankind do desire nothing for itself but that which is a pleasure to them, or of which the absence is a pain; we have evidently arrived at a question of fact and experience, dependent, like all similar questions, upon evidence. It can only be determined by practised self-consciousness and self-observation, assisted by observation of others. I believe that these sources of evidence, impartially consulted, will declare that desiring a thing and finding it pleasant, aversion to it and thinking of it as painful, are phenomena entirely inseparable, or rather two parts of the same phenomenon; in strictness of language, two different modes of naming the same psychological fact : that to think of an object as desirable. (unless for the sake of its consequences), and to think of it as pleasant, are one and the same thing; and that to desire anything, except in proportion as the idea of it is pleasant, is a physical and metaphysical impossibility.

So obvious does this appear to me, that I expect it will hardly be disputed : and the objection made will be, not that desire can possibly be directed to anything ultimately except pleasure and exemption from pain, but that the will is a different thing from desire; that a person of confirmed virtue, or any other person whose purposes are fixed, carries out his purposes without any thought of the pleasure he has in contemplating them, or expects to derive from their fulfilment; and persists in acting on them, even though these pleasures are much diminished, by changes in his character or decay of his passive sensibilities, or are out-weighed by the pains which the pursuit of the purposes may bring upon him. All this I fully admit, and have stated it elsewhere, as positively and emphatically as any one. Will, the active phenomenon, is a different thing from desire, the state of passive sensibility, and though originally an offshoot from it, may in time take root and detach itself from the parent stock; so much so, that in the case of an habitual purpose, instead of willing the thing because we desire it, we often desire it only because we will it. This, however, is but an instance of that familiar fact, the power of habit, and is nowise confined to the case of virtuous actions. Many indifferent things, which men originally did from a motive of some sort, they continue to do from habit. Sometimes this is done unconsciously, the consciousness coming only after the action : at other times with conscious volition, but volition which has become habitual, and is put in operation by the force of habit, in opposition perhaps to the deliberate preference, as often happens with those who have contracted habits of

vicious or hurtful indulgence. Third and last comes the case
in which the habitual act of will in the individual instance
is not in contradiction to the general intention prevailing
at other times, but in fulfilment of it; as in the case of
the person of confirmed virtue, and of all who pursue
deliberately and consistently any determinate end. The distinction between will and desire thus understood is an authentic and highly important psychological fact; but the fact
consists solely in this—that will, like all other parts of our constitution, is amenable to habit, and that we may will from
habit what we no longer desire for itself, or desire only because
we will it. It is not the less true that will, in the beginning,
is entirely produced by desire; including in that term the
repelling influence of pain as well as the attractive one of
pleasure. Let us take into consideration, no longer the person
who has a confirmed will to do right, but him in whom
that virtuous will is still feeble, conquerable by temptation,
and not to be fully relied on; by what means can it be
strengthened? How can the will to be virtuous, where it does
not exist in sufficient force, be implanted or awakened? Only
by making the person *desire* virtue—by making him think
of it in a pleasurable light, or of its absence in a painful one.
It is by associating the doing right with pleasure, or the
doing wrong with pain, or by eliciting and impressing and
bringing home to the person's experience the pleasure naturally
involved in the one or the pain in the other, that it is
possible to call forth that will to be virtuous, which, when
confirmed, acts without any thought of either pleasure or
pain. Will is the child of desire, and passes out of the
dominion of its parent only to come under that of habit.
That which is the result of habit affords no presumption of
being intrinsically good; and there would be no reason for
wishing that the purpose of virtue should become independent
of pleasure and pain, were it not that the influence of the
pleasurable and painful associations which prompt to virtue
is not sufficiently to be depended on for unerring constancy
of action until it has acquired the support of habit. Both
in feeling and in conduct, habit is the only thing which
imparts certainty; and it is because of the importance to others

of being able to rely absolutely on one's feelings and conduct, and to oneself of being able to rely on one's own, that the will to do right ought to be cultivated into this habitual independence. In other words, this state of the will is a means to good, not intrinsically a good; and does not contradict the doctrine that nothing is a good to human beings but in so far as it is either itself pleasurable, or a means of attaining pleasure or averting pain.

But if this doctrine be true, the principle of utility is proved. Whether it is or not must now be left to the consideration of the thoughtful reader.

CHAPTER V

ON THE CONNECTION BETWEEN JUSTICE AND UTILITY

In all ages of speculation, one of the strongest obstacles to the reception of the doctrine that Utility or Happiness is the criterion of right and wrong, has been drawn from the idea of Justice. The powerful sentiment, and apparently clear perception, which that word recalls with a rapidity and certainty resembling an instinct, have seemed to the majority of thinkers to point to an inherent quality in things; to show that the Just must have an existence in Nature as something absolute, generically distinct from every variety of the Expedient, and, in idea, opposed to it, though (as is commonly acknowledged) never, in the long run, disjoined from it in fact.

In the case of this, as of our other moral sentiments, there is no necessary connection between the question of its origin, and that of its binding force. That a feeling is bestowed on us by Nature, does not necessarily legitimate all its promptings. The feeling of justice might be a peculiar instinct, and might yet require, like our other instincts, to be controlled and enlightened by a higher reason. If we have intellectual instincts, leading us to judge in a particular way, as well as animal instincts that prompt us to act in a particular way, there is no necessity that the former should be more infallible in their sphere than the latter in theirs: it may as well happen that wrong judgments are occasionally suggested by those, as wrong actions by these. But though it is one thing to believe that we have natural feelings of justice, and another to acknowledge them as an ultimate criterion of conduct, these two opinions are very closely connected in point of fact. Mankind are always predisposed to believe that any subjective feeling, not otherwise accounted for, is a revelation of some objective reality. Our present object is to determine whether the reality, to which the feeling of justice corresponds, is one which needs any such special revelation; whether the justice or injustice of an action is a thing intrinsically peculiar, and distinct from all its other qualities, or only a combination of certain of those qualities, presented under a peculiar aspect. For the purpose of this inquiry it is practically important to consider whether the feeling itself, of justice and injustice, is *sui generis* like our sensations of colour and taste, or a derivative feeling, formed by a combination of others. And this it is the more essential to examine, as people are in general willing enough to allow, that objectively the dictates of Justice coincide with a part of the field of General Expediency; but inasmuch as the subjective mental feeling of Justice is different from that which commonly attaches to simple expediency, and, except in the extreme cases of the latter, is far more imperative in its demands, people find it difficult to see, in Justice, only a particular kind or branch of general utility, and think that its superior binding force requires a totally different origin.

To throw light upon this question, it is necessary to attempt to ascertain what is the distinguishing character of justice, or of injustice : what is the quality, or whether there is any quality, attributed in common to all modes of conduct designated as unjust (for justice, like many other moral attributes, is best defined by its opposite), and distinguishing them from such modes of conduct as are disapproved, but without having that particular epithet of disapprobation applied to them. If in everything which men are accustomed to characterise as just or unjust, some one common attribute or collection of attributes is always present, we may judge whether this particular attribute or combination of attributes would be capable of gathering round it a sentiment of that peculiar character and intensity by virtue of the general laws of our emotional constitution, or whether the sentiment is inexplicable, and requires to be regarded as a special provision of Nature. If we find the former to be the case, we shall, in resolving this question, have resolved also the main problem : if the latter, we shall have to seek for some other mode of investigating it.

To find the common attributes of a variety of objects, it is necessary to begin by surveying the objects themselves in the concrete. Let us therefore advert successively to the various modes of action, and arrangements of human affairs, which are classed, by universal or widely spread opinion, as Just or as Unjust. The things well known to excite the sentiments associated with those names are of a very multifarious character. I shall pass them rapidly in review, without studying any particular arrangement.

In the first place, it is mostly considered unjust to deprive any one of his personal liberty, his property, or any other thing which belongs to him by law. Here, therefore, is one instance of the application of the terms just and unjust in a perfectly definite sense, namely, that it is just to respect, unjust to violate, the *legal rights* of any one. But this judgment admits of several exceptions, arising from the other forms in which the notions of justice and injustice present themselves. For example, the person who suffers the deprivation may (as the phrase is) have *forfeited* the rights which he is so deprived of : a case to which we shall return presently. But also,

Secondly; the legal rights of which he is deprived, may be rights which *ought* not to have belonged to him; in other words, the law which confers on him these rights, may be a bad law. When it is so, or when (which is the same thing for our purpose) it is supposed to be so, opinions will differ as to the justice or injustice of infringing it. Some maintain that no law, however bad, ought to be disobeyed by an individual citizen; that his opposition to it, if shown at all, should only be shown in endeavouring to get it altered by competent authority. This opinion (which condemns many of the most illustrious benefactors of mankind, and would often protect pernicious institutions against the only weapons which, in the state of things existing at the time, have any chance of succeeding against them) is defended, by those who hold it, on grounds of expediency; principally on that of the importance, to the common interest of mankind, of maintaining inviolate the sentiment of submission to law. Other persons, again, hold the directly contrary opinion, that any law, judged to be bad, may blamelessly be disobeyed, even though it be not judged to be unjust, but only inexpedient; while others would confine the licence of disobedience to the case of unjust laws : but again, some say, that all laws which are inexpedient are unjust; since every law imposes some restriction on the natural liberty of mankind, which restriction is an injustice, unless legitimated by tending to their good. Among these diversities of opinion, it seems to be universally admitted that there may be unjust laws, and that law, consequently, is not the ultimate criterion of justice, but may give to one person a benefit, or impose on another an evil, which justice condemns. When, however, a law is thought to be unjust, it seems always to be regarded as being so in the same way in which a breach of law is unjust, namely, by infringing somebody's right; which, as it cannot in this case be a legal right, receives a different appellation, and is called a moral right. We may say, therefore, that a second case of injustice consists in taking or withholding from any person that to which he has a *moral right*.

Thirdly, it is universally considered just that each person should obtain that (whether good or evil) which he *deserves*; and unjust that he should obtain a good, or be made to undergo an evil, which he does not deserve. This is, perhaps, the clearest and most emphatic form in which the idea of justice is conceived by the general mind. As it involves the notion of desert, the question arises, what constitutes desert? Speaking in a general way, a person is understood to deserve good if he does right, evil if he does wrong; and in a more particular sense, to deserve good from those to whom he does or has done good, and evil from those to whom he does or has done evil. The precept of returning good for evil has never been regarded as a case of the fulfilment of justice, but as one in which the claims of justice are waived, in obedience to other considerations.

Fourthly, it is confessedly unjust to *break faith* with any one : to violate an engagement, either express or implied, or disappoint expectations raised by our own conduct, at least if we have raised those expectations knowingly and voluntarily. Like the other obligations of justice already spoken of, this one is not regarded as absolute, but as capable of being overruled by a stronger obligation of justice on the other side; or by such conduct on the part of the person concerned as is deemed to absolve us from our obligation to him, and to constitute a *forfeiture* of the benefit which he has been led to expect.

Fifthly, it is, by universal admission, inconsistent with justice to be *partial*; to show favour or preference to one person over another, in matters to which favour and preference do not properly apply. Impartiality, however, does not seem to be regarded as a duty in itself, but rather as instrumental to some other duty; for it is admitted that favour and preference are not always censurable, and indeed the cases in which they are condemned are rather the exception than the rule. A person would be more likely to be blamed than applauded for giving his family or friends no superiority in good offices over strangers, when he could do so without violating any other duty; and no one thinks it unjust to seek one person in preference to another as a friend, connection, or companion. Impartiality where rights are concerned is of course obligatory, but this is involved in the more general obligation of giving to every one his right. A tribunal, for example, must be impartial, because it is bound to award, without regard to any other consideration, a disputed object to the one of two parties who has the right to it. There are other cases in which impartiality means, being solely influenced by desert; as with those who, in the capacity of judges, preceptors, or parents, administer reward and punishment as such. There are cases, again, in which it means, being solely influenced by consideration for the public interest; as in making a selection among candidates for a government employment. Impartiality, in short, as an obligation of justice, may be said to mean, being exclusively influenced by the considerations which it is supposed ought to influence the particular case in hand; and resisting the solicitation of any motives which prompt to conduct different from what those considerations would dictate.

Nearly allied to the idea of impartiality is that of *equality*; which often enters as a component part both into the conception of justice and into the practice of it, and, in the eyes of many persons, constitutes its essence. But in this, still more than in any other case, the notion of justice varies in different persons, and always conforms in its variations to their notion of utility. Each person maintains that equality is the dictate of justice, except where he thinks that expediency requires inequality. The justice of giving equal protection to the rights of all, is maintained by those who support the most outrageous inequality in the rights themselves. Even in slave countries it is theoretically admitted that the rights of the slave, such as they are, ought to be as sacred as those of the master; and that a tribunal which fails to enforce them with equal strictness is wanting in justice; while, at the same time, institutions which leave to the slave scarcely any rights to enforce, are not deemed unjust, because they are not deemed inexpedient. Those who think that utility requires distinctions of rank, do not consider it unjust that riches and social privileges should be unequally dispensed; but those who think this inequality inexpedient, think it unjust also. Whoever thinks that government is necessary, sees no injustice in as much inequality as is constituted by giving to the magistrate powers not granted to other people. Even among those who hold levelling doctrines, there are as many questions of justice as there are differences of opinion about expediency. Some Communists consider it unjust that the produce of the labour of the community should be shared on any other principle than that of exact equality; others think it just that those should receive most whose wants are greatest; while others hold that those who work harder, or who produce more, or whose services are more valuable to the community, may justly claim a larger quota in the division of the produce. And the sense of natural justice may be plausibly appealed to in behalf of every one of these opinions.

Among so many diverse applications of the term Justice,

which yet is not regarded as ambiguous, it is a matter of some difficulty to seize the mental link which holds them together, and on which the moral sentiment adhering to the term essentially depends. Perhaps, in this embarrassment, some help may be derived from the history of the word, as indicated by its etymology.

In most, if not in all, languages, the etymology of the word which corresponds to Just, points distinctly to an origin connected with the ordinances of law. *Justum* is a form of *jussum*, that which has been ordered. Δίκαιον comes directly from δίκη, a suit at law. *Recht*, from which came *right* and *righteous*, is synonymous with law. The courts of justice, the administration of justice, are the courts and the administration of law. *La justice*, in French, is the established term for judicature. I am not committing the fallacy imputed with some show of truth to Horne Tooke, of assuming that a word must still continue to mean what it originally meant. Etymology is slight evidence of what the idea now signified is, but the very best evidence of how it sprang up. There can, I think, be no doubt that the *idée mère*, the primitive element, in the formation of the notion of justice, was conformity to law. It constituted the entire idea among the Hebrews, up to the birth of Christianity; as might be expected in the case of a people whose laws attempted to embrace all subjects on which precepts were required, and who believed those laws to be a direct emanation from the Supreme Being. But other nations, and in particular the Greeks and Romans, who knew that their laws had been made originally, and still continued to be made, by men, were not afraid to admit that those men might make bad laws; might do, by law, the same things, and from the same motives, which if done by individuals without sanction of law, would be called unjust. And hence the sentiment of injustice came to be attached, not to all violations of law, but only to violations of such laws as *ought* to exist, including such as ought to exist, but do not; and to laws themselves, if supposed to be contrary to what ought to be law. In this manner the idea of law and of its injunctions was still predominant in the notion of justice, even when the laws actually in force ceased to be accepted as the standard of it.

It is true that mankind consider the idea of justice and its obligations as applicable to many things which neither are, nor is it desired that they should be, regulated by law. Nobody desires that laws should interfere with the whole detail of private life; yet every one allows that in all daily conduct a person may and does show himself to be either just or unjust. But even here, the idea of the breach of what ought to be law, still lingers in a modified shape. It would always give us pleasure, and chime in with our feelings of fitness, that acts which we deem unjust should be punished, though we do not always think it expedient that this should be done by the tribunals. We forego that gratification on account of incidental inconveniences. We should be glad to see just conduct enforced and injustice repressed, even in the minutest details, if we were not, with reason, afraid of trusting the magistrate with so unlimited an amount of power over individuals. When we think that a person is bound in justice to do a thing, it is an ordinary form of language to say, that he ought to be compelled to do it. We should be gratified to see the obligation enforced by anybody who had the power. If we see that its enforcement by law would be inexpedient, we lament the impossibility, we consider the impunity given to injustice as an evil, and strive to make amends for it by bringing a strong expression of our own and the public disapprobation to bear upon the offender. Thus the idea of legal constraint is still the generating idea of the notion of justice, though undergoing several transformations before that notion, as it exists in an advanced state of society, becomes complete.

The above is, I think, a true account, as far as it goes, of the origin and progressive growth of the idea of injustice. But we must observe, that it contains, as yet, nothing to distinguish that obligation from moral obligation in general. For the truth is, that the idea of penal sanction, which is the essence of law, enters not only into the conception of injustice, but into that of any kind of wrong. We do not call anything wrong, unless we mean to imply that a person ought to be punished in some way or other for doing it; if not by law, by the opinion of his fellow-creatures; if not by opinion, by the reproaches of his own conscience. This seems the real turning point of the distinction between morality and simple expediency. It is a part of the notion of Duty in every one of its forms, that a person may rightfully be compelled to fulfil it. Duty is a thing which may be *exacted* from a person, as one exacts a debt. Unless we think that it may be exacted from him, we do not call it his duty. Reasons of prudence, or the interest of other people, may militate against actually exacting it; but the person himself, it is clearly understood, would not be entitled to complain. There are other things, on the contrary, which we wish that people should do, which we like or admire them for doing, perhaps dislike or despise them for not doing, but yet admit that they are not bound to do; it is not a case of moral obligation; we do not blame them, that is, we do not think that they are proper objects of punishment. How we come by these ideas of deserving and not deserving punishment, will appear, perhaps, in the sequel; but I think there is no doubt that this distinction lies at the bottom of the notions of right and wrong; that we call any conduct wrong, or employ, instead, some other term of dislike or disparagement, according as we think that the person ought, or ought not, to be punished for it; and we say, it would be right to do so and so, or merely that it would be desirable or laudable, according as we would wish to see the person whom it concerns, compelled, or only persuaded and exhorted, to act in that manner.[1]

This, therefore, being the characteristic difference which marks off, not justice, but morality in general, from the remaining provinces of Expediency and Worthiness; the character is still to be sought which distinguishes justice from other branches of morality. Now it is known that ethical

---

[1] See this point enforced and illustrated by Professor Bain, in an admirable chapter (entitled " The Ethical Emotions, or the Moral Sense "), of the second of the two treatises composing his elaborate and profound work on the Mind.

writers divide moral duties into two classes, denoted by
the ill-chosen expressions, duties of perfect and of imperfect
obligation; the latter being those in which, though the
act is obligatory, the particular occasions of performing it
are left to our choice; as in the case of charity or beneficence, which we are indeed bound to practise, but not towards
any definite person, nor at any prescribed time. In the more
precise language of philosophic purists, duties of perfect obligation are those duties in virtue of which a correlative *right*
resides in some person or persons; duties of imperfect
obligation are those moral obligations which do not give
birth to any right. I think it will be found that this distinction exactly coincides with that which exists between
justice and the other obligations of morality. In our survey
of the various popular acceptations of justice, the term
appeared generally to involve the idea of a personal right
—a claim on the part of one or more individuals, like that
which the law gives when it confers a proprietary or other
legal right. Whether the injustice consists in depriving a
person of a possession, or in breaking faith with him, or in
treating him worse than he deserves, or worse than other
people who have no greater claims, in each case the supposition implies two things—a wrong done, and some assignable person who is wronged. Injustice may also be done by
treating a person better than others; but the wrong in
this case is to his competitors, who are also assignable persons.
It seems to me that this feature in the case—a right in some
person, correlative to the moral obligation—constitutes the
specific difference between justice, and generosity or beneficence. Justice implies something which is not only
right to do, and wrong not to do, but which some individual
person can claim from us as his moral right. No one has a
moral right to our generosity or beneficence, because we are
not morally bound to practise those virtues towards any given
individual. And it will be found with respect to this as to
every correct definition, that the instances which seem to
conflict with it are those which most confirm it. For if a
moralist attempts, as some have done, to make out that
mankind generally, though not any given individual, have a

right to all the good we can do them, he at once, by that thesis, includes generosity and beneficence within the category of justice. He is obliged to say, that our utmost exertions are *due* to our fellow-creatures, thus assimilating them to a debt; or that nothing less can be a sufficient *return* for what society does for us, thus classing the case as one of gratitude; both of which are acknowledged cases of justice. Wherever there is a right, the case is one of justice, and not of the virtue of beneficence : and whoever does not place the distinction between justice and morality in general, where we have now placed it, will be found to make no distinction between them at all, but to merge all morality in justice.

Having thus endeavoured to determine the distinctive elements which enter into the composition of the idea of justice, we are ready to enter on the inquiry, whether the feeling, which accompanies the idea, is attached to it by a special dispensation of nature, or whether it could have grown up, by any known laws, out of the idea itself; and in particular, whether it can have originated in considerations of general expediency.

I conceive that the sentiment itself does not arise from anything which would commonly, or correctly, be termed an idea of expediency; but that though the sentiment does not, whatever is moral in it does.

We have seen that the two essential ingredients in the sentiment of justice are, the desire to punish a person who has done harm, and the knowledge or belief that there is some definite individual or individuals to whom harm has been done.

Now it appears to me, that the desire to punish a person who has done harm to some individual is a spontaneous outgrowth from two sentiments, both in the highest degree natural, and which either are or resemble instincts; the impulse of self-defence, and the feeling of sympathy.

It is natural to resent, and to repel or retaliate, any harm done or attempted against ourselves, or against those with whom we sympathise. The origin of this sentiment it is not necessary here to discuss. Whether it be an instinct or a result of intelligence, it is, we know, common to all animal nature; for every animal tries to hurt those who have hurt, or who it thinks are about to hurt, itself or its young. Human beings, on this point, only differ from other animals in two particulars. First, in being capable of sympathising, not solely with their offspring, or, like some of the more noble animals, with some superior animal who is kind to them, but with all human, and even with all sentient, beings. Secondly, in having a more developed intelligence, which gives a wider range to the whole of their sentiments, whether self-regarding or sympathetic. By virtue of his superior intelligence, even apart from his superior range of sympathy, a human being is capable of apprehending a community of interest between himself and the human society of which he forms a part, such that any conduct which threatens the security of the society generally, is threatening to his own, and calls forth his instinct (if instinct it be) of self-defence. The same superiority of intelligence, joined to the power of sympathising with human beings generally, enables him to attach himself to the collective idea of his tribe, his country, or mankind, in such a manner that any act hurtful to them, raises his instinct of sympathy, and urges him to resistance.

The sentiment of justice, in that one of its elements which consists of the desire to punish, is thus, I conceive, the natural feeling of retaliation or vengeance, rendered by intellect and sympathy applicable to those injuries, that is, to those hurts, which wound us through, or in common with, society at large. This sentiment, in itself, has nothing moral in it; what is moral is, the exclusive subordination of it to the social sympathies, so as to wait on and obey their call. For the natural feeling would make us resent indiscriminately whatever any one does that is disagreeable to us; but when moralised by the social feeling, it only acts in the directions conformable to the general good : just persons resenting a hurt to society, though not otherwise a hurt to themselves, and not resenting a hurt to themselves, however painful, unless it be of the kind which society has a common interest with them in the repression of.

It is no objection against this doctrine to say, that when we feel our sentiment of justice outraged, we are not thinking of society at large or of any collective interest, but only of the indi-

vidual case. It is common enough certainly, though the reverse
of commendable, to feel resentment merely because we have
suffered pain; but a person whose resentment is really a
moral feeling, that is, who considers whether an act is blamable before he allows himself to resent it—such a person,
though he may not say expressly to himself that he is standing
up for the interest of society, certainly does feel that he is
asserting a rule which is for the benefit of others as well
as for his own. If he is not feeling this—if he is regarding
the act solely as it affects him individually—he is not consciously just; he is not concerning himself about the justice
of his actions. This is admitted even by anti-utilitarian
moralists. When Kant (as before remarked) propounds as the
fundamental principle of morals, " So act, that thy rule of
conduct might be adopted as a law by all rational beings,"
he virtually acknowledges that the interest of mankind collectively, or at least of mankind indiscriminately, must be in the
mind of the agent when conscientiously deciding on the morality of the act. Otherwise he uses words without a meaning:
for, that a rule even of utter selfishness could not *possibly* be
adopted by all rational beings—that there is any insuperable
obstacle in the nature of things to its adoption—cannot be
even plausibly maintained. To give any meaning to Kant's
principle, the sense put upon it must be, that we ought to shape
our conduct by a rule which all rational beings might adopt
with benefit to their collective interest.

To recapitulate : the idea of justice supposes two things; a
rule of conduct, and a sentiment which sanctions the rule. The
first must be supposed common to all mankind, and intended
for their good. The other (the sentiment) is a desire that punishment may be suffered by those who infringe the rule. There
is involved, in addition, the conception of some definite person
who suffers by the infringement; whose rights (to use the
expression appropriated to the case) are violated by it. And
the sentiment of justice appears to me to be, the animal desire
to repel or retaliate a hurt or damage to oneself, or to those
with whom one sympathises, widened so as to include all
persons, by the human capacity of enlarged sympathy, and the
human conception of intelligent self-interest. From the latter

elements, the feeling derives its morality; from the former, its peculiar impressiveness, and energy of self-assertion.

I have, throughout, treated the idea of a *right* residing in the injured person, and violated by the injury, not as a separate element in the composition of the idea and sentiment, but as one of the forms in which the other two elements clothe themselves. These elements are, a hurt to some assignable person or persons on the one hand, and a demand for punishment on the others. An examination of our own minds, I think, will show, that these two things include all that we mean when we speak of violation of a right. When we call anything a person's right, we mean that he has a valid claim on society to protect him in the possession of it, either by the force of law, or by that of education and opinion. If he has what we consider a sufficient claim, on whatever account, to have something guaranteed to him by society, we say that he has a right to it. If we desire to prove that anything does not belong to him by right, we think this done as soon as it is admitted that society ought not to take measures for securing it to him, but should leave him to chance, or to his own exertions. Thus, a person is said to have a right to what he can earn in fair professional competition; because society ought not to allow any other person to hinder him from endeavouring to earn in that manner as much as he can. But he has not a right to three hundred a-year, though he may happen to be earning it; because society is not called on to provide that he shall earn that sum. On the contrary, if he owns ten thousand pounds three per cent. stock, he *has* a right to three hundred a-year; because society has come under an obligation to provide him with an income of that amount.

To have a right, then, is, I conceive, to have something which society ought to defend me in the possession of. If the objector goes on to ask, why it ought? I can give him no other reason than general utility. If that expression does not seem to convey a sufficient feeling of the strength of the obligation, nor to account for the peculiar energy of the feeling, it is because there goes to the composition of the sentiment, not a rational only, but also an animal element, the thirst

for retaliation; and this thirst derives its intensity, as well as
its moral justification, from the extraordinarily important and
impressive kind of utility which is concerned. The interest
involved is that of security, to every one's feelings the
most vital of all interests. All other earthly benefits are needed
by one person, not needed by another; and many of them can,
if necessary, be cheerfully foregone, or replaced by something
else; but security no human being can possibly do without;
on it we depend for all our immunity from evil, and for
the whole value of all and every good, beyond the passing
moment; since nothing but the gratification of the instant
could be of any worth to us, if we could be deprived of
anything the next instant by whoever was momentarily stronger
than ourselves. Now this most indispensable of all necessaries,
after physical nutriment, cannot be had, unless the machinery
for providing it is kept unintermittedly in active play. Our
notion, therefore, of the claim we have on our fellow-
creatures to join in making safe for us the very groundwork
of our existence, gathers feelings around it so much more
intense than those concerned in any of the more common
cases of utility, that the difference in degree (as is often the
case in psychology) becomes a real difference in kind. The
claim assumes that character of absoluteness, that apparent
infinity, and incommensurability with all other considerations,
which constitute the distinction between the feeling of right
and wrong and that of ordinary expediency and inexpediency.
The feelings concerned are so powerful, and we count so
positively on finding a responsive feeling in others (all being
alike interested), that *ought* and *should* grow into *must,*
and recognised indispensability becomes a moral necessity,
analogous to physical, and often not inferior to it in binding
force.

If the preceding analysis, or something resembling it, be not
the correct account of the notion of justice; if justice be
totally independent of utility, and be a standard *per se,* which
the mind can recognise by simple introspection of itself; it
is hard to understand why that internal oracle is so ambiguous,

and why so many things appear either just or unjust, according to the light in which they are regarded.

We are continually informed that Utility is an uncertain standard, which every different person interprets differently, and that there is no safety but in the immutable, ineffaceable, and unmistakable dictates of Justice, which carry their evidence in themselves, and are independent of the fluctuations of opinion. One would suppose from this that on questions of justice there could be no controversy; that if we take that for our rule, its application to any given case could leave us in as little doubt as a mathematical demonstration. So far is this from being the fact, that there is as much difference of opinion, and as much discussion, about what is just, as about what is useful to society. Not only have different nations and individuals different notions of justice, but in the mind of one and the same individual, justice is not some one rule, principle, or maxim, but many, which do not always coincide in their dictates, and in choosing between which, he is guided either by some extraneous standard, or by his own personal predilections.

For instance, there are some who say, that it is unjust to punish any one for the sake of example to others; that punishment is just, only when intended for the good of the sufferer himself. Others maintain the extreme reverse, contending that to punish persons who have attained years of discretion, for their own benefit, is despotism and injustice, since if the matter at issue is solely their own good, no one has a right to control their own judgment of it; but that they may justly be punished to prevent evil to others, this being the exercise of the legitimate right of self-defence. Mr. Owen, again, affirms that it is unjust to punish at all; for the criminal did not make his own character; his education, and the circumstances which surrounded him, have made him a criminal, and for these he is not responsible. All these opinions are extremely plausible; and so long as the question is argued as one of justice simply, without going down to the principles which lie under justice and are the source of its authority, I am unable to see how any of these reasoners can be refuted. For in truth every one of the three builds upon rules of justice confessedly true. The first appeals to the acknowledged injustice of singling out an individual, and making him a sacrifice, without his consent, for other people's benefit. The second relies on the acknowledged justice of self-defence, and the admitted injustice of forcing one person to conform to another's notions of what constitutes his good. The Owenite invokes the admitted principle, that it is unjust to punish any one for what he cannot help. Each is triumphant so long as he is not compelled to take into consideration any other maxims of justice than the one he has selected; but as soon as their several maxims are brought face to face, each disputant seems to have exactly as much to say for himself as the others. No one of them can carry out his own notion of justice without trampling upon another equally binding. These are difficulties; they have always been felt to be such; and many devices have been invented to turn rather than to overcome them. As a refuge from the last of the three, men imagined what they called the freedom of the will; fancying that they could not justify punishing a man whose will is in a thoroughly hateful state, unless it be supposed to have come into that state through no influence of anterior circumstances. To escape from the other difficulties, a favourite contrivance has been the fiction of a contract, whereby at some unknown period all the members of society engaged to obey the laws, and consented to be punished for any disobedience to them; thereby giving to their legislators the right, which it is assumed they would not otherwise have had, of punishing them, either for their own good or for that of society. This happy thought was considered to get rid of the whole difficulty, and to legitimate the infliction of punishment, in virtue of another received maxim of justice, *Volenti non fit injuria;* that is not unjust which is done with the consent of the person who is supposed to be hurt by it. I need hardly remark, that even if the consent were not a mere fiction, this maxim is not superior in authority to the others which it is brought in to supersede. It is, on the contrary, an instructive specimen of the loose and irregular manner in which supposed principles of justice grow up.

This particular one evidently came into use as a help to the coarse exigencies of courts of law, which are sometimes obliged to be content with very uncertain presumptions, on account of the greater evils which would often arise from any attempt on their part to cut finer. But even courts of law are not able to adhere consistently to the maxim, for they allow voluntary engagements to be set aside on the ground of fraud, and sometimes on that of mere mistake or misinformation.

Again, when the legitimacy of inflicting punishment is admitted, how many conflicting conceptions of injustice come to light in discussing the proper apportionment of punishments to offences. No rule on the subject recommends itself so strongly to the primitive and spontaneous sentiment of justice, as the *lex talionis,* an eye for an eye and a tooth for a tooth. Though this principle of the Jewish and of the Mahomedan law has been generally abandoned in Europe as a practical maxim, there is, I suspect, in most minds, a secret hankering after it; and when retribution accidentally falls on an offender in that precise shape, the general feeling of satisfaction evinced bears witness how natural is the sentiment to which this repayment in kind is acceptable. With many, the test of justice in penal infliction is that the punishment should be proportioned to the offence; meaning that it should be exactly measured by the moral guilt of the culprit (whatever be their standard for measuring moral guilt): the consideration, what amount of punishment is necessary to deter from the offence, having nothing to do with the question of justice, in their estimation: while there are others to whom that consideration is all in all; who maintain that it is not just, at least for man, to inflict on a fellow-creature, whatever may be his offences, any amount of suffering beyond the least that will suffice to prevent him from repeating, and others from imitating, his misconduct.

To take another example from a subject already once referred to. In a co-operative industrial association, is it just or not that talent or skill should give a title to superior remuneration? On the negative side of the question it is argued, that whoever does the best he can, deserves equally

well, and ought not in justice to be put in a position of
inferiority for no fault of his own; that superior abilities
have already advantages more than enough, in the admiration they excite, the personal influence they command, and
the internal sources of satisfaction attending them, without
adding to these a superior share of the world's goods; and
that society is bound in justice rather to make compensation to
the less favoured, for this unmerited inequality of advantages,
than to aggravate it. On the contrary side it is contended, that
society receives more from the more efficient labourer; that his
services being more useful, society owes him a larger return
for them; that a greater share of the joint result is actually
his work, and not to allow his claim to it is a kind of robbery;
that if he is only to receive as much as others, he can only
be justly required to produce as much, and to give a smaller
amount of time and exertion, proportioned to his superior
efficiency. Who shall decide between these appeals to conflicting principles of justice? Justice has in this case two
sides to it, which it is impossible to bring into harmony,
and the two disputants have chosen opposite sides; the
one looks to what it is just that the individual should receive,
the other to what it is just that the community should give.
Each, from his own point of view, is unanswerable; and
any choice between them, on grounds of justice, must be
perfectly arbitrary. Social utility alone can decide the preference.

How many, again, and how irreconcilable, are the standards
of justice to which reference is made in discussing the repar-
tition of taxation. One opinion is, that payment to the State
should be in numerical proportion to pecuniary means. Others
think that justice dictates what they term graduated taxation;
taking a higher percentage from those who have more to
spare. In point of natural justice a strong case might be made
for disregarding means altogether, and taking the same
absolute sum (whenever it could be got) from every one:
as the subscribers to a mess, or to a club, all pay the same
sum for the same privileges, whether they can all equally
afford it or not. Since the protection (it might be said)
of law and government is afforded to, and is equally required

by all, there is no injustice in making all buy it at the same price. It is reckoned justice, not injustice, that a dealer should charge to all customers the same price for the same article, not a price varying according to their means of payment. This doctrine, as applied to taxation, finds no advocates, because it conflicts so strongly with man's feelings of humanity and of social expediency; but the principle of justice which it invokes is as true and as binding as those which can be appealed to against it. Accordingly it exerts a tacit influence on the line of defence employed for other modes of assessing taxation. People feel obliged to argue that the State does more for the rich man than for the poor, as a justification for its taking more from them: though this is in reality not true, for the rich would be far better able to protect themselves, in the absence of law and government, than the poor, and indeed would probably be successful in converting the poor into their slaves. Others, again, so far defer to the same conception of justice, as to maintain that all should pay an equal capitation tax for the protection of their persons (these being of equal value to all), and an unequal tax for the protection of their property, which is unequal. To this others reply, that the all of one man is as valuable to him as the all of another. From these confusions there is no other mode of extrication than the utilitarian.

Is, then, the difference between the Just and the Expedient a merely imaginary distinction? Have mankind been under a delusion in thinking that justice is a more sacred thing than policy, and that the latter ought not to be listened to after the former has been satisfied? By no means. The exposition we have given of the nature and origin of the sentiment, recognises a real distinction; and no one of those who profess the most sublime contempt for the consequences of actions as an element in their morality, attaches more importance to the distinction than I do. While I dispute the pretensions of any theory which sets up an imaginary standard of justice not grounded on utility, I account the justice which is grounded on utility to be the chief part, and incomparably the most sacred and binding part, of all morality. Justice is a name for certain classes of moral rules, which concern the essentials of human well-being more nearly, and are therefore of more absolute obligation, than any other rules for the guidance of life; and the notion which we have found to be the essence of the idea of justice, that of a right residing in an individual, implies and testifies to this more binding obligation.

The moral rules which forbid mankind to hurt one another (in which we must never forget to include wrongful interference with each other's freedom) are more vital to human well-being than any maxims, however important, which only point out the best mode of managing some department of human affairs. They have also the peculiarity, that they are the main element in determining the whole of the social feelings of mankind. It is their observance which alone preserves peace among human beings: if obedience to them were not the rule, and disobedience the exception, every one would see in every one else an enemy, against whom he must be perpetually guarding himself. What is hardly less important, these are the precepts which mankind have the strongest and the most direct inducements for impressing upon one another. By merely giving to each other prudential instruction or exhortation, they may gain, or think they gain, nothing: in inculcating on each other the duty of positive beneficence they have an unmistakable interest, but far less in degree: a person may possibly not need the benefits of others; but he always needs that they should not do him hurt. Thus the moralities which protect every individual from being harmed by others, either directly or by being hindered in his freedom of pursuing his own good, are at once those which he himself has most at heart, and those which he has the strongest interest in publishing and enforcing by word and deed. It is by a person's observance of these that his fitness to exist as one of the fellowship of human beings is tested and decided; for on that depends his being a nuisance or not to those with whom he is in contact. Now it is these moralities primarily which compose the obligation of justice. The most marked cases of injustice, and those which give the tone to the feeling of repugnance which characterises the sentiment, are acts of wrongful aggression, or wrongful exercise of power over some one; the next are those which consist in wrongfully withholding from him something which is his due; in both cases, inflicting on him a positive hurt, either in the form of direct suffering, or of the privation of some good which he had reasonable ground, either of a physical or of a social kind, for counting upon.

The same powerful motives which command the observance of these primary moralities, enjoin the punishment of those who violate them; and as the impulses of self-defence, of defence of others, and of vengeance, are all called forth against such persons, retribution, or evil for evil, becomes closely connected with the sentiment of justice, and is universally included in the idea. Good for good is also one of the dictates of justice; and this, though its social utility is evident, and though it carries with it a natural human feeling, has not at first sight that obvious connection with hurt or injury, which, existing in the most elementary cases of just and unjust, is the source of the characteristic intensity of the sentiment. But the connection, though less obvious, is not less real. He who accepts benefits, and denies a return of them when needed, inflicts a real hurt, by disappointing one of the most natural and reasonable of expectations, and one which he must at least tacitly have encouraged, otherwise the benefits would seldom have been conferred. The important rank, among human evils and wrongs, of the disappointment of expectation, is shown in the fact that it constitutes the principal criminality of two such highly immoral acts as a breach of friendship and a breach of promise. Few hurts which human beings can sustain are greater, and none wound more, than when that on which they habitually and with full assurance relied, fails them in the hour of need; and few wrongs are greater than this mere withholding of good; none excite more resentment, either in the person suffering, or in a sympathising spectator. The principle, therefore, of giving to each what they deserve, that is, good for good as well as evil for evil, is not only included within the idea of Justice as we have defined it, but is a proper object of that intensity of sentiment, which places the Just, in human estimation, above the simply Expedient.

Most of the maxims of justice current in the world, and commonly appealed to in its transactions, are simply instrumental to carrying into effect the principles of justice which we have now spoken of. That a person is only responsible for what he has done voluntarily, or could voluntarily have avoided; that it is unjust to condemn any person unheard; that the punishment ought to be proportioned to the offence, and the like, are maxims intended to prevent the just principle of evil for evil from being perverted to the infliction of evil without justification. The greater part of these common maxims have come into use from the practice of courts of justice, which have been naturally led to a more complete recognition and elaboration than was likely to suggest itself to others, of the rules necessary to enable them to fulfil their double function, of inflicting punishment when due, and of awarding to each person his right.

That first of judicial virtues, impartiality, is an obligation of justice, partly for the reason last mentioned; as being a necessary condition of the fulfilment of the other obligations of justice. But this is not the only source of the exalted rank, among human obligations, of those maxims of equality and impartiality, which, both in popular estimation and in that of the most enlightened, are included among the precepts of justice. In one point of view, they may be considered as corollaries from the principles already laid down. If it is a duty to do to each according to his deserts, returning good for good as well as repressing evil by evil, it necessarily follows that we should treat all equally well (when no higher duty forbids) who have deserved equally well of *us*, and that society should treat all equally well who have deserved equally well of *it*, that is, who have deserved equally well absolutely. This is the highest abstract standard of social and distributive justice; towards which all institutions, and the efforts of all virtuous citizens, should be made in the utmost possible degree to converge. But this great moral duty rests upon a still deeper foundation, being a direct emanation from the first principle of morals, and not a mere logical corollary from secondary or derivative doctrines. It is involved in the very meaning of Utility, or the Greatest Happiness Principle. That principle is a mere form of words without rational signification, unless one person's happiness, supposed equal in degree (with the proper allowance made for kind), is counted for exactly as much as another's. Those conditions being supplied, Bentham's dictum, "everybody to count for one, nobody for more than one," might be written under the principle of utility as an explanatory commentary.[2] The equal

[2] This implication, in the first principle of the utilitarian scheme, of perfect impartiality between persons, is regarded by Mr. Herbert Spencer (in his *Social Statics*) as a disproof of the pretensions of utility to be a sufficient guide to right; since (he says) the principle of utility presupposes the anterior principle, that everybody has an equal right to happiness. It may be more correctly described as supposing that equal amounts of happiness are equally desirable, whether felt by the same or by different persons. This, however, is not a *pre*-supposition; not a premise needful to support the principle of utility, but the very principle itself; for what is the principle of utility, if it be not that "happiness" and "desirable" are synonymous terms? If there is any anterior principle implied, it can be no other than this, that the truths of arithmetic are applicable to the valuation of happiness, as of all other measurable quantities.

[Mr. Herbert Spencer, in a private communication on the subject of the preceding Note, objects to being considered an opponent of utilitarianism, and states that he regards happiness as the ultimate end of morality; but deems that end only partially attainable by empirical generalisations from the observed results of conduct, and completely attainable only by deducing, from the laws of life and the conditions of existence, what kinds of action necessarily tend to produce happiness, and what kinds to produce unhappiness. With the exception of the word "necessarily," I have no dissent to express from this doctrine; and (omitting that word) I am not aware that any modern advocate of utilitarianism is of a different opinion. Bentham, certainly, to whom in the *Social Statics* Mr. Spencer particularly referred, is, least of all writers, chargeable with unwillingness to deduce the effect of actions on happiness from the laws of human nature and the universal conditions of human life. The common charge against him is of relying too exclusively upon such deductions, and declining altogether to be bound by the generalisations from specific experience which Mr. Spencer thinks that utilitarians generally confine themselves to. My own opinion (and, as I collect, Mr. Spencer's) is, that in ethics, as in all other

claim of everybody to happiness in the estimation of the
moralist and of the legislator, involves an equal claim to all
the means of happiness, except in so far as the inevitable
conditions of human life, and the general interest, in which
that of every individual is included, set limits to the maxim;
and those limits ought to be strictly construed. As every
other maxim of justice, so this is by no means applied or
held applicable universally; on the contrary, as I have
already remarked, it bends to every person's ideas of social
expediency. But in whatever case it is deemed applicable
at all, it is held to be the dictate of justice. All persons
are deemed to have a *right* to equality of treatment, except
when some recognised social expediency requires the reverse.
And hence all social inequalities which have ceased to be
considered expedient, assume the character not of simple
inexpediency, but of injustice, and appear so tyrannical, that
people are apt to wonder how they ever could have been
tolerated; forgetful that they themselves perhaps tolerate
other inequalities under an equally mistaken notion of expediency, the correction of which would make that which
they approve seem quite as monstrous as what they have
at last learnt to condemn. The entire history of social improvement has been a series of transitions, by which one
custom or institution after another, from being a supposed
primary necessity of social existence, has passed into the rank
of a universally stigmatised injustice and tyranny. So it has
been with the distinctions of slaves and freemen, nobles and
serfs, patricians and plebeians; and so it will be, and in part
already is, with the aristocracies of colour, race, and sex.

It appears from what has been said, that justice is a name
for certain moral requirements, which, regarded collectively,
stand higher in the scale of social utility, and are therefore of
more paramount obligation, than any others; though particular cases may occur in which some other social duty is

---

branches of scientific study, the consilience of the results of both
these processes, each corroborating and verifying the other, is requisite to give to any general proposition the kind and degree of
evidence which constitutes scientific proof.]

so important, as to overrule any one of the general maxims of justice. Thus, to save a life, it may not only be allowable, but a duty, to steal, or take by force, the necessary food or medicine, or to kidnap, and compel to officiate, the only qualified medical practitioner. In such cases, as we do not call anything justice which is not a virtue, we usually say, not that justice must give way to some other moral principle, but that what is just in ordinary cases is, by reason of that other principle, not just in the particular case. By this useful accommodation of language, the character of indefeasibility attributed to justice is kept up, and we are saved from the necessity of maintaining that there can be laudable injustice.

The considerations which have now been adduced resolve, I conceive, the only real difficulty in the utilitarian theory of morals. It has always been evident that all cases of justice are also cases of expediency: the difference is in the peculiar sentiment which attaches to the former, as contradistinguished from the latter. If this characteristic sentiment has been sufficiently accounted for; if there is no necessity to assume for it any peculiarity of origin; if it is simply the natural feeling of resentment, moralised by being made coextensive with the demands of social good; and if this feeling not only does but ought to exist in all classes of cases to which the idea of justice corresponds; that idea no longer presents itself as a stumbling-block to the utilitarian ethics. Justice remains the appropriate name for certain social utilities which are vastly more important, and therefore more absolute and imperative, than any others are as a class (though not more so than others may be in particular cases); and which, therefore, ought to be, as well as naturally are, guarded by a sentiment not only different in degree, but also in kind; distinguished from the milder feeling which attaches to the mere idea of promoting human pleasure or convenience, at once by the more definite nature of its commands, and by the sterner character of its sanctions.

THE PROVINCE OF JURISPRUDENCE DETERMINED

by John Austin

LECTURE II

(Editor's note: the text here printed has been slightly abridged)

The Divine laws, or the laws of God, are laws set by God to his human creatures. As I have intimated already, and shall show more fully hereafter, they are laws or rules *properly* so called.

Of the Divine laws, or the laws of God, some are *revealed* or promulged, and others are *unrevealed*. Such of the laws of God as are unrevealed are not unfrequently denoted by the following names or phrases: 'the law of nature;' 'natural law;' 'the law manifest to man by the light of nature or reason;' 'the laws, precepts, or dictates of natural religion.'

Such of the Divine laws as are *unrevealed* are laws set by God to his human creatures, but not through the medium of human language, or not expressly.

These are the only laws which he has set to that portion of mankind who are excluded from the light of Revelation.

But if God has given us laws which he has not revealed or promulged, how shall we know them? What are those signs of his pleasure, which we style the *light of nature;* and oppose, by that figurative phrase, to express declarations of his will?

The hypotheses or theories which attempt to resolve this question, may be reduced, I think, to two.

According to one of them, there are human actions

322

which all mankind approve, human actions which all men disapprove; and these universal sentiments arise at the thought of those actions, spontaneously, instantly, and inevitably. Being common to all mankind, and inseparable from the thoughts of those actions, these sentiments are marks or signs of the Divine pleasure. They are proofs that the actions which excite them are enjoined or forbidden by the Deity.

The rectitude or pravity of human conduct, or its agreement or disagreement with the laws of God, is instantly inferred from these sentiments, without the possibility of mistake. He has resolved that our happiness shall depend on our keeping his commandments : and it manifestly consists with his manifest wisdom and goodness, that we should know them promptly and certainly. Accordingly, he has not committed us to the guidance of our slow and fallible *reason*. He has wisely endowed us with *feelings,* which warn us at every step; and pursue us, with their importunate reproaches, when we wander from the path of our duties.

These simple or inscrutable feelings have been compared to those which we derive from the outward senses, and have been referred to a peculiar faculty called the *moral sense* : though, admitting that the feelings exist, and are proofs of the Divine pleasure, I am unable to discover the analogy which suggested the comparison and the name. The objects or appearances which properly are perceived through the senses, are perceived immediately, or without an inference of the understanding. According to the hypothesis which I have briefly stated or suggested, there is always an inference of the understanding, though the inference is short and inevitable. From feelings which arise within us when we think of certain actions, we infer that those actions are enjoined or forbidden by the Deity.

The hypothesis, however, of a *moral sense*, is expressed in other ways.

The laws of God, to which these feelings are the index, are not unfrequently named *innate practical principles,* or *postulates of practical reason* : or they are said to be written on our hearts, by the finger of their great Author, in broad and indelible characters.

Common sense (the most yielding and accommodating of phrases) has been moulded and fitted to the purpose of expressing the hypothesis in question. In all their decisions on the rectitude or pravity of conduct (its agreement or disagreement with the unrevealed law), mankind are said to be determined by *common sense* : this same *common sense* meaning, in this instance, the simple or inscrutable sentiments which I have endeavoured to describe.

Considered as affecting the soul, when the man thinks especially of *his own* conduct, these sentiments, feelings, or emotions, are frequently styled his *conscience.*

According to the other of the adverse theories or hypotheses, the laws of God, which are not revealed or promulged, must be gathered by man from the goodness of God, and from the tendencies of human actions. In other words, the benevolence of God, with the principle of general utility, is our only index or guide to his unrevealed law.

God designs the happiness of all his sentient creatures. Some human actions forward that benevolent purpose, or their tendencies are beneficent or useful. Other human actions are adverse to that purpose, or their tendencies are mischievous or pernicious. The former, as promoting his purpose, God has enjoined. The latter, as opposed to his purpose, God has forbidden. He has given us the faculty of observing; of remembering; of reasoning : and, by duly applying those faculties, we may collect the tendencies of our actions. Knowing the tendencies of our actions, and knowing his benevolent purpose, we know his tacit commands.

Such is a brief summary of this celebrated theory. I should wander to a measureless distance from the main purpose of my lectures, if I stated all the explanations with which that summary must be received. But, to obviate the principal misconceptions to which the theory is obnoxious, I will subjoin as many of those explanations as my purpose and limits will admit.

The theory is this :—Inasmuch as the goodness of God is boundless and impartial, he designs the greatest happiness of all his sentient creatures : he wills that the aggregate of their enjoyments shall find no nearer limit than that which is inevitably set to it by their finite and imperfect nature. From the probable effects of our actions on the greatest happiness of all, or from the tendencies of human actions to increase or diminish that aggregate, we may infer the laws which he has given, but has not expressed or revealed.

Now the *tendency* of a human action (as its tendency is thus understood) is the whole of its tendency: the sum of its probable consequences, in so far as they are important or material: the sum of its remote and collateral, as well as of its direct consequences, in so far as any of its consequences may influence the general happiness.

Trying to collect its tendency (as its tendency is thus understood), we must not consider the action as if it were *single* and *insulated,* but must look at the *class* of actions to which it belongs. The probable *specific* consequences of doing that single act, or forbearing from that single act, or of omitting that single act, are not the objects of the inquiry. The question to be solved is this:—If acts of the *class* were *generally* done, or *generally* forborne or omitted, what would be the probable effect on the general happiness or good?

Considered by itself, a mischievous act may seem to be useful or harmless. Considered by itself, a useful act may seem to be pernicious.

For example, if a poor man steals a handful from the heap of his rich neighbour, the act, considered by itself, is harmless or positively good. One man's poverty is assuaged with the superfluous wealth of another.

But suppose that thefts were general (or that the useful right of property were open to frequent invasions), and mark the result.

Without security for property, there were no inducement to save. Without habitual saving on the part of proprietors, there were no accumulation of capital. Without accumulation of capital, there were no fund for the payment of wages, no division of labour, no elaborate and costly machines: there were none of those helps to labour which augment its productive power, and, therefore, multiply the enjoyments of every individual in the community. Frequent invasions of property would bring the rich to poverty; and, what were a greater evil, would aggravate the poverty of the poor.

If a single and insulated theft seem to be harmless or good, the fallacious appearance merely arises from this: that the vast majority of those who are tempted to steal abstain from invasions of property; and the detriment to security, which is the end produced by a single theft, is overbalanced and concealed by the mass of wealth, the accumulation of which is produced by general security.

Again: If I evade the payment of a tax imposed by a good government, the *specific* effects of the mischievous forbearance are indisputably useful. For the money which I unduly withhold is convenient to myself; and, compared with the bulk of the public revenue, is a quantity too small to be missed. But the regular payment of taxes is necessary to the existence of the government. And I, and the rest of the community, enjoy the security which it gives, because the payment of taxes is rarely evaded.

In the cases now supposed, the act or omission is good, considered as single or insulated; but, considered with the rest of its class, is evil. In other cases, an act or omission is evil, considered as single or insulated; but, considered with the rest of its class, is good.

For example, A punishment, as a solitary fact, is an evil: the pain inflicted on the criminal being added to the mischief of the crime. But, considered as part of a system, a punishment is useful or beneficent. By a dozen or score of punishments, thousands of crimes are prevented. With the sufferings of the guilty few, the security of the many is purchased. By the lopping of a peccant member, the body is saved from decay.

It, therefore, is true generally (for the proposition admits of exceptions), that; to determine the true tendency of an act, forbearance, or omission, we must resolve the following question:—What would be the probable effect on the general happiness or good, if *similar* acts, forbearances, or omissions were general or frequent?

Such is the *test* to which we must usually resort, if we would try the true *tendency* of an act, forbearance, or omission: Meaning, by the true *tendency* of an act, forbearance, or omission, the sum of its probable effects on the general happiness or good, or its agreement or disagreement with the principle of general utility.

But, if this be the ordinary test for trying the tendencies of actions, and if the tendencies of actions be the index to the will of God, it follows that most of his commands are general or universal. The useful acts which he enjoins, and the pernicious acts which he prohibits, he enjoins or prohibits, for the most part, not singly, but by classes : not by commands which are particular, or directed to insulated cases; but by laws or rules which are general, and commonly inflexible.

For example, Certain acts are pernicious, considered as a class : or (in other words) the frequent repetition of the act were adverse to the general happiness, though, in this or that instance, the act might be useful or harmless. Further : Such are the motives or inducements to the commission of acts of the class, that, unless we were determined to forbearance by the fear of punishment, they *would* be frequently committed. Now, if we combine these *data* with the wisdom and goodness of God, we must infer that he forbids such acts, and forbids them *without exception*. In the tenth or the hundredth case, the act might be useful : in the nine, or the ninety and nine, the act would be pernicious. If the act were permitted or tolerated in the rare and anomalous case, the motives to forbear in the others would be weakened or destroyed. In the hurry and tumult of action, it is hard to distinguish justly. To grasp at present enjoyment, and to turn from present uneasiness, is the habitual inclination of us all. And thus, through the weakness of our judgments, and the more dangerous infirmity of our wills, we should frequently *stretch* the exception to cases embraced by the rule.

Consequently, where acts, considered as a class, are useful or pernicious, we must conclude that he enjoins or forbids them, and by a *rule* which probably is inflexible.

Such, I say, is the conclusion at which we must arrive, supposing that the fear of punishment be necessary to incite or restrain.

For the tendency of an act is one thing; the utility of

enjoining or forbidding it is another thing. There are classes of useful acts, which it were useless to enjoin; classes of mischievous acts, which it were useless to prohibit. Sanctions were superfluous. We are sufficiently prone to the useful, and sufficiently averse from the mischievous acts, without the motives which are presented to the will by a lawgiver. Motives *natural* or spontaneous (or motives *other* than those which are created by injunctions and prohibitions) impel us to action in the one case, and hold us to forbearance in the other. In the language of Mr. Locke, 'The mischievous omission or action would bring down evils upon us, which are its *natural* products or consequences; and which, as *natural* inconveniences, operate *without a law.*'

Now, if the measure or test which I have endeavoured to explain be the ordinary measure or test for trying the tendencies of our actions, the most current and specious of the objections, which are made to the theory of utility, is founded in gross mistake, and is open to triumphant refutation.

The theory, be it always remembered, is this:

Our motives to obey the laws which God has given us, are paramount to all others. For the transient pleasures which we may snatch, or the transient pains which we may shun, by violating the duties which they impose, are nothing in comparison with the pains by which those duties are sanctioned.

The greatest possible happiness of all his sentient creatures, is the purpose and effect of those laws. For the benevolence by which they were prompted, and the wisdom with which they were planned, equal the might which enforces them.

But, seeing that such is their purpose, they embrace the *whole* of our conduct; so far, that is, as our conduct may promote or obstruct that purpose; and so far as injunctions and prohibitions are necessary to correct our desires.

In so far as the laws of God are clearly and indisputably revealed, we are bound to guide our conduct by the plain meaning of their terms. In so far as they are not revealed, we must resort to another guide: namely, the probable effect of our conduct on that *general happiness or good* which is the object of the Divine Lawgiver in all his laws and commandments.

In each of these cases the *source* of our duties is the same; though the *proofs* by which we know them are different. The principle of general utility is the *index* to many of these duties; but the principle of general utility is not their *fountain* or *source*. For duties or obligations arise from commands and sanctions. And commands, it is manifest, proceed not from abstractions, but from living and rational beings.

Admit these premises, and the following conclusion is inevitable:—The *whole* of our conduct should be guided by the principle of utility, in so far as the conduct to be pursued has not been determined by Revelation. For, to conform to the principle of maxim with which a law coincides, is equivalent to obeying that law.

Such is the theory: which I have repeated in various forms, and, I fear, at tedious length, in order that my younger hearers might conceive it with due distinctness.

The current and specious objection to which I have adverted, may be stated thus:

'Pleasure and pain (or good and evil) are inseparably connected. Every positive act, and every forbearance or omission, is followed by *both*: immediately or remotely, directly or collaterally, to ourselves or to our fellow-creatures.

'Consequently, if we shape our conduct justly to the principle of general utility, every election which we make between doing or forbearing from an act will be preceded by the following process. *First*: We shall conjecture the consequences of the act, and also the consequences of the forbearance. For these are the competing elements of that *calculation,* which, according to our guiding principle, we are bound to make. *Secondly*: We shall compare the consequences of the act with the consequences of the forbearance, and determine the set of consequences which gives the *balance* of advantage: which yields the larger residue of probable good, or (adopting a different, though exactly equivalent expression) which leaves the smaller residue of probable evil.

'Now let us suppose that we actually tried this process,

before we arrived at our resolves. And then let us mark the absurd and mischievous effects which would inevitably follow our attempts.

Generally speaking, the period allowed for deliberation is brief: and to lengthen deliberation beyond that limited period, is equivalent to forbearance or omission. Consequently, if we performed this elaborate process completely and correctly, we should often defeat its purpose. We should abstain from action altogether, though utility required us to act; or the occasion for acting *usefully* would slip through our fingers, whilst we weighed with anxious scrupulosity, the merits of the act and the forbearance.

'But feeling the necessity of resolving promptly, we should *not* perform the process completely and correctly. We should guess or conjecture hastily the effects of the act and the forbearance, and compare their respective effects with equal precipitancy. Our premises would be false or imperfect; our conclusions, badly deduced. Labouring to adjust our conduct to the principle of general utility, we should work inevitable mischief.

And such were the consequences of following the principle of utility, though we sought the true and the useful with simplicity and in earnest. But, as we commonly prefer our own to the interests of our fellow-creatures, and our own immediate to our own remote interests, it is clear that we should warp the principle to selfish and sinister ends.

'The final cause or purpose of the Divine laws is the general happiness or good. But to trace the effect of our conduct on the general happiness or good is not the way to know them. By consulting and obeying the laws of God we promote our own happiness and the happiness of our fellow-creatures. But we should *not* consult his laws, we should *not* obey his laws, and, so far as in us lay, we should thwart their benevolent design, if we made the general happiness our object or end. In a breath, we should widely deviate *in effect* from the principle of general utility by taking it as the *guide* of our conduct.'

Such, I believe, is the meaning of those—if they have

a meaning—who object to the meaning of utility that it
were a *dangerous* principle of conduct.'

As the objectors are generally persons little accustomed
to clear and determinate thinking, I am not quite certain
that I have conceived the objection exactly. But I have
endeavoured with perfectly good faith to understand their
meaning, and as forcibly as I can to state it, or to state the
most rational meaning which their words can be supposed
to import.

It has been said, in answer to this objection, that it
involves a contradiction in terms. *Danger* is another name
for *probable mischief*: And, surely, we best avert the probable mischiefs of our conduct, by conjecturing and estimating
its probable consequences. To say 'that the principle of
utility were a *dangerous* principle of conduct,' is to say 'that it
were contrary to utility to consult utility.'

Now, though this is so brief and pithy that I heartily wish
it were conclusive, I must needs admit that it scarcely touches
the objection, and falls far short of a crushing reduction to
absurdity. For the objection obviously assumes that we
cannot foresee and estimate the probable effects of our
conduct; that if we attempted to calculate its good and its
evil consequences, our presumptuous attempt at calculation
would lead us to error and sin. What is contended is, that by
the attempt to act according to utility, an attempt which
would not be successful, we should deviate from utility. A
proposition involving when fairly stated nothing like a contradiction.

But, though this is not the refutation, there *is* a refutation.

And first, if utility be our only index to the tacit commands
of the Deity, it is idle to object its imperfections. We must
even make the most of it.

If we were endowed with a *moral sense,* or with a *common
sense,* or with a *practical reason,* we scarcely should construe
his commands by the principle of general utility. If our souls
were furnished out with *innate practical principles* we scarcely
should read his commands in the tendencies of human actions.
For, by the supposition, man would be gifted with a peculiar

organ for acquiring a knowledge of his duties. The duties imposed by the Deity would be subjects of immediate consciousness, and completely exempted from the jurisdiction of observation and induction. An attempt to displace that invincible consciousness, and to thrust the principle of utility into the vacant seat, would be simply impossible and manifestly absurd. An attempt to taste or smell by force of syllogism, were not less hopeful or judicious.

But, if we are not gifted with that peculiar organ, we must take to the principle of utility, let it be never so defective. We must gather our duties, as we can, from the tendencies of human actions; or remain, at our own peril, in ignorance of our duties. We must pick our scabrous way with the help of a glimmering light, or wander in profound darkness.

Whether there be any ground for the hypothesis of a *moral sense,* is a question which I shall duly examine in a future lecture, but which I shall not pursue in the present place. For the present is a convenient place for the introduction of another topic: namely, that they who advance the objection in question misunderstand the theory which they presume to impugn.

Their objection, is founded on the following assumption: —That, if we adjusted our conduct to the principle of general utility, every election which we made between doing and forbearing from an act would be preceded by a *calculation*: by an attempt to conjecture and compare the respective probable consequences of action and forbearance.

Or (changing the expression) their assumption is this:— That, if we adjusted our conduct to the principle of general utility, our conduct would always be determined by an immediate or direct resort to it.

And, granting their assumption, I grant their inference. I grant that the principle of utility were a halting and purblind guide.

But their assumption is groundless. They are battering (and most effectually) a misconception of their own, whilst they fancy they are hard at work demolishing the theory which they hate.

For, according to that theory, our conduct would conform to *rules* inferred from the tendencies of actions, but would not be determined by a direct resort to the principle of general utility. Utility would be the test of our conduct, ultimately, but not immediately : the immediate test of the rules to which our conduct would conform, but not the immediate test of specific or individual actions. Our rules would be fashioned on utility; our conduct, on our rules.

Recall the true test for trying the tendency of an action, and, by a short and easy deduction, you will see that their assumption is groundless.

If we would try the tendency of a specific or individual act, we must not contemplate the act as if it were single and insulated, but must look at the class of acts to which it belongs. We must suppose that acts of the class were generally done or omitted, and consider the probable effect upon the general happiness or good.

We must guess the consequences which would follow, if acts of the class were general; and also the consequences which would follow, if they were generally omitted. We must then compare the consequences on the positive and negative sides, and determine on which of the two the balance of advantage lies.

If it lie on the positive side, the tendency of the act is good : or (adopting a wider, yet exactly equivalent expression) the general happiness requires that *acts* of the *class* shall be done. If it lie on the negative side, the tendency of the act is bad : or (again adopting a wider, yet exactly equivalent expression) the general happiness requires that *acts* of the *class* shall be forborne.

In a breath, if we truly try the tendency of a specific or individual act, we try the tendency of the class to which that act belongs. The *particular* conclusion which we draw, with regard to the single act, implies a *general* conclusion embracing all similar acts.

But, concluding that acts of the class are useful or pernicious, we are forced upon a further inference. Adverting to the known wisdom and the known benevolence of the

Deity, we infer that he enjoins or forbids them by a general and inflexible *rule*.

Such is the inference at which we inevitably arrive, supposing that the acts be *such* as to call for the intervention of a lawgiver.

To *rules* thus inferred, and lodged in the memory, our conduct would conform *immediately* if it were truly adjusted to utility. To consider the specific consequences of single or individual acts, would seldom consist with that ultimate principle. And our conduct would, therefore, be guided by *general* conclusions, or (to speak more accurately) by *rules* inferred from these conclusions.

But, this being admitted, the necessity of pausing and calculating, which the objection in question supposes, is an imaginary necessity. To preface each act or forbearance by a conjecture and comparison of consequences, were clearly superfluous and mischievous. It were clearly superfluous, inasmuch as the result of that process would be embodied in a known *rule*. It were clearly mischievous, inasmuch as the *true* result would be expressed by that rule, whilst the process would probably be faulty, if it were done on the spur of the occasion.

Speaking generally, human conduct, including the human conduct which is subject to the Divine commands, is inevitably guided by *rules*, or by *principles* or *maxims*.

If our experience and observation of particulars were not *generalised*, our experience and observation of particulars would seldom avail us in *practice*. To review on the spur of the occasion a host of particulars, and to obtain from those particulars a conclusion applicable to the case, were a process too slow and uncertain to meet the exigencies of our lives. The inferences suggested to our minds by repeated experience and observation are, therefore, drawn into *principles*, or compressed into *maxims*. These we carry about us ready for use, and apply to individual cases promptly or without hesitation : without reverting to the process by which they were obtained; or without recalling, and arraying before our minds, the numerous and intricate considerations of which they are handy abridgments.

This is the main, though not the only use of *theory*: which ignorant and weak people are in a habit of *opposing* to practice, but which is essential to practice guided by experience and observation.

' 'Tis true in *theory*; but, then, 'tis false in *practice*.' Such is a common talk. This says Noodle; propounding it with a look of the most ludicrous profundity.

But, with due and discreet deference to this worshipful and weighty personage, *that* which is true in *theory* is *also* true in *practice*.

Seeing that a true theory is a *compendium* of particular truths, it is necessarily true as applied to particular cases. The terms of the theory are general and abstract, or the particular truths which the theory implies would not be abbreviated or condensed. But, unless it be true of particulars, and, therefore, true in practice, it has no *truth* at all. *Truth* is always particular, though *language* is commonly general. Unless the terms of a theory can be resolved into particular truths, the theory is mere jargon: a coil of those senseless abstractions which often ensnare the *instructed*; and in which the wits of the ignorant are certainly caught and entangled, when they stir from the track of authority, and venture to think for themselves.

They who talk of theory as if it were the antagonist of practice, or of a thing being true in *theory* but not true in *practice,* mean (if they have a meaning) that the theory in question is false: that the particular truths which it concerns are treated imperfectly or incorrectly; and that, if it were applied in practice, it might, therefore, mislead. They *say* that truth in theory is not truth in practice. They *mean* that a false theory is not a true one, and might lead us to practical errors.

Speaking, then, generally, human conduct is inevitably guided by *rules,* or by *principles* or *maxims*.

The human conduct which is subject to the Divine commands, is not only guided by *rules,* but also by *moral sentiments* associated with those rules.

If I believe (no matter why) that acts of a class or description are enjoined or forbidden by the Deity, a moral sentiment or feeling (or a sentiment or feeling of approbation or disapprobation) is inseparably connected in my mind with the thought or conception of such acts. And by this I am urged to do, or restrained from doing such acts, although I advert not to the reason in which my belief originated, nor recall the Divine rule which I have inferred from that reason.

Now, if the reason in which my belief originated be the useful or pernicious tendency of acts of the class, my conduct is truly adjusted to the principle of general utility, but my conduct is not determined by a direct resort to it. It is directly determined by a *sentiment* associated with acts of the class, and with the rule which I have inferred from their tendency.

If my conduct be truly adjusted to the principle of general utility, my conduct is guided remotely by *calculation*. But immediately, or at the moment of action, my conduct is determined by *sentiment*. I am swayed by *sentiment* as imperiously as I *should* be swayed by it, supposing I were utterly unable to produce a reason for my conduct, and were ruled by the capricious feelings which are styled the moral sense.

For example, Reasons which are quite satisfactory, but somewhat numerous and intricate, convince me that the institution of property is necessary to the general good. Convinced of this, I am convinced that thefts are pernicious. Convinced that thefts are pernicious, I infer that the Deity forbids them by a general and inflexible rule.

Now the train of induction and reasoning by which I arrive at this rule, is somewhat long and elaborate. But I am not compelled to repeat the process, before I can know with certainty that I should forbear from taking your purse. Through my previous habits of thought and by my education, *a sentiment of aversion* has become associated in my mind with the thought or conception of *a theft* : And, without adverting to the reasons which have convinced me that thefts are pernicious, or without adverting to the rule which I have inferred from their pernicious tendency, I am determined by that ready emotion to keep my fingers from your purse.

To think that the theory of utility would *substitute* calculation for sentiment, is a gross and flagrant error : the error of a shallow, precipitate understanding. He who *opposes* calculation and sentiment, opposes the rudder to the sail, or to the breeze which swells the sail. Calculation is the guide, and not the antagonist of sentiment. Sentiment without calculation were blind and capricious; but calculation without sentiment were inert.

To crush the moral sentiments, is not the scope or purpose of the true theory of utility. It seeks to impress those sentiments with a just or beneficent direction: to free us of *groundless* likings, and from the tyranny of senseless antipathies; to fix our love upon the useful, our hate upon the pernicious.

If, then, the principle of utility were the presiding principle of our conduct, our conduct would be determined immediately by Divine *rules,* or rather by moral *sentiments* associated with those rules. And, consequently, the application of the principle of utility to particular or individual cases, would neither be attended by the errors, nor followed by the mischiefs, which the current objection in question supposes.

But these conclusions (like most conclusions) must be taken with limitations.

There certainly are cases (of comparatively rare occurrence) wherein the specific considerations balance or outweigh the general: cases which (in the language of Bacon) are ' immersed in matter ': cases perplexed with peculiarities from which it were dangerous to abstract them; and to which our attention would be directed, if we were true to our presiding principle. It were mischievous to depart from a rule which regarded any of these cases; since every departure from a rule tends to weaken its authority. But so important were the *specific* consequences which would follow our resolves, that the evil of observing the rule might surpass the evil of breaking it. Looking at the reasons from which we had inferred the rule, it were absurd to think it inflexible. We should, therefore, dismiss the *rule;* resort directly to the *principle* upon which our rules were fashioned; and calculate *specific* consequences to the best of our knowledge and ability.

For example, If we take the principle of utility as our

index to the Divine commands, we must infer that obedience
to established government is enjoined generally by the Deity.
For, without obedience to ' the powers which be,' there were
little security and little enjoyment. The ground, however,
of the inference, is the *utility* of government : And if the
protection which it yields be *too costly,* or if it vex us with
needless restraints and load us with *needless* exactions, the
principle which points at submission as our general duty
may counsel and justify resistance. Disobedience to an established government, let it be never so bad, is an evil : For
the mischiefs inflicted by a bad government are less than
the mischiefs of anarchy. So momentous, however, is the
difference between a bad and a good government, that *if it
would lead to a good one,* resistance to a bad one would be
useful. The anarchy attending the transition were an extensive, but a passing evil : The good which would follow
the transition were extensive and lasting. The peculiar good
would outweigh the generic evil : The good which would
crown the change in the insulated and eccentric case, would
more than compensate the evil which is inseparable from
rebellion.

Whether resistance to government be useful or pernicious,
be consistent or inconsistent with the Divine pleasure, is,
therefore, an *anomalous* question. We must try it by a
direct resort to the ultimate or presiding *principle,* and not
by the Divine *rule* which the principle clearly indicates. To
consult the rule, were absurd. For, the rule being general
and applicable to ordinary cases, it ordains obedience to
governments, and excludes the question.

The members of a political society who revolve this
momentous question must, therefore, dismiss the rule, and
calculate specific consequences. They must measure the mischief wrought by the actual government; the chance of
getting better, by resorting to resistance; the evil which
must attend resistance, whether it prosper or fail; and the
good which may follow resistance, in case it be crowned
with success. And, then, by comparing these, the elements of
their moral calculation, they must solve the question before
them to the best of their knowledge and ability.

And in this eccentric or anomalous case, the application of the principle of utility would probably be beset with the difficulties which the current objection in question imputes to it generally. To measure and compare the evils of sub-mission and disobedience, and to determine which of the two would give the balance of advantage, would probably be a difficult and uncertain process. The numerous and competing considerations by which the question must be solved, might well perplex and divide the wise, and the good, and the brave. A Milton or a Hampden might animate their country-men to resistance, but a Hobbes or a Falkland would counsel obedience and peace.

But, though the principle of utility would afford no certain solution, the community would be fortunate, if their opinions and sentiments were formed upon it. The pre-tensions of the opposite parties being tried by an intelligible test, a peaceable compromise of their difference would, at least, be possible. The adherents of the established govern-ment, might think it the most *expedient* : but, as their tensions of the opposite parties being tried by an intelligible liking would depend upon reasons, and not upon names and phrases, they might possibly prefer innovations, of which they would otherwise disapprove, to the mischiefs of a violent contest. They might chance to see the absurdity of upholding the existing order, with a stiffness which must end in anarchy. The party affecting reform, being also intent upon *utility,* would probably accept concessions short of their notions and wishes, rather than persist in the chase of a greater possible good through the evils and the hazards of a war. In short, if the object of each party were measured by the standard of utility, each might compare the worth of its object with the cost of a violent pursuit.

But, if the parties were led by their ears, and not by the principle of utility : if they appealed to unmeaning abstractions, or to senseless fictions; if they mouthed of ' the rights of man,' or ' the sacred rights of sovereigns,' of ' unalienable liberties,' or ' eternal and immutable justice,' of an ' original contract or covenant,' or ' the principles of an inviolable constitution;' neither could compare its object with the cost of a violent pursuit, nor would the difference between them admit of a peaceable compromise. A sacred or unalienable right is truly and indeed *invaluable* : For, seeing that it means nothing, there is nothing with which it can be measured. Parties who rest their pretensions on the jargon to which I have adverted, must inevitably push to their objects through thick and thin, though their objects be straws or feathers as weighed in the balance of utility. Having bandied their fustian phrases, and ' bawled till their lungs be spent,' they must even take to their weapons, and fight their difference out.

It really *is* important (though I feel the audacity of the paradox), that men should think distinctly, and speak with a meaning.

In most of the domestic broils which have agitated civilised communities, the result has been determined or seriously affected, by the nature of the prevalent *talk* : by the nature of the topics or phrases which have figured in the war of words. These topics or phrases have been more than pretexts : more than varnish : more than distinguishing cockades mounted by the opposite parties.

For example, If the bulk of the people of England had thought and reasoned with Mr. Burke, had been imbued with the spirit and had seized the scope of his arguments, her needless and disastrous war with her American colonies would have been stifled at the birth. The stupid and infuriate majority who rushed into that odious war, could perceive and discourse of nothing but the *sovereignty* of the mother country, and her so called *right* to tax her colonial subjects.

But, granting that the mother country was properly the sovereign of the colonies, granting that the fact of her sovereignty was proved by invariable practice, and granting her so called *right* to tax her colonial subjects, this was hardly a topic to move an enlightened people.

Is it the interest of England to insist upon her sovereignty? Is it her interest to exercise her right without the approbation of the colonists? For the chance of a slight revenue to be wrung from her American subjects, and of a trifling relief from the taxation which now oppresses herself, shall she drive those reluctant subjects to assert their alleged independence, visit her own children with the evil of war, squander her treasures and soldiers in trying to keep them down, and desolate the very region from which the revenue must be drawn?—These and the like considerations would have determined the people of England, if their dominant opinions and sentiments had been fashioned on the principle of utility.

And, if these and the like considerations had determined the public mind, the public would have damned the project of taxing and coercing the colonies, and the government would have abandoned the project. For, it is only in the ignorance of the people, and in their consequent mental imbecility, that governments or demagogues can find the means of mischief.

If these and the like considerations had determined the public mind, the expenses and miseries of the war would have been avoided; the connection of England with America would not have been torn asunder; and, in case their common interests had led them to dissolve it quietly, the relation of sovereign and subject, or of parent and child, would have been followed by an equal, but intimate and lasting alliance. For the interests of the two nations perfectly coincide; and the open, and the covert hostilities, with which they plague one another, are the offspring of a bestial antipathy begotten by their original quarrel.

But arguments drawn from utility were not to the dull taste of the stupid and infuriate majority. The rabble, great and small, would hear of nothing but their *right*. ' They'd a *right* to tax the colonists, and tax 'em they would: Ay, *that* they would.' Just as if a *right* were worth a rush of itself, or a something to be cherished and asserted independently of the good that it may bring.

Mr. Burke would have taught them better : would have purged their muddled brains, and ' laid the fever in their souls,' with the healing principle of utility. He asked them what they would get, if the project of coercion should succeed; and implored them to compare the advantage with the hazard and the cost. But the sound practical men still insisted on the *right*; and sagaciously shook their heads at him, as a refiner and a theorist.

If a serious difference shall arise between themselves and Canada, or if a serious difference shall arise between ourselves and Ireland, an attempt will probably be made to cram us with the same stuff. But, such are the mighty strides which reason has taken in the interval, that I hope we shall not swallow it with the relish of our good ancestors. It will probably occur to us to ask, whether she be worth keeping, and whether she be worth keeping at the cost of a war?—I think there is nothing romantic in the hope which I now express; since an admirable speech of Mr. Baring, advising the relinquishment of Canada, was seemingly received, a few years ago, with general assent and approbation.

There are, then, cases, which are anomalous or eccentric; and to which the man, whose conduct was fashioned on utility, would apply that ultimate principle immediately or directly. And, in these anomalous or eccentric cases, the application of the principle would probably be beset with the difficulties which the current objection in question imputes to it generally.

But, even in these cases, the principle would afford an intelligible test, and a likelihood of a just solution : a probability of discovering the conduct required by the general good, and, therefore, required by the commands of a wise and benevolent Deity.

And the anomalies, after all, are comparatively few. In the great majority of cases, the general happiness requires that *rules* shall be observed, and that *sentiments* associated with rules shall be promptly obeyed. If our conduct were truly adjusted to the principle of general utility, our conduct would seldom be determined by an immediate or direct resort to it.

BIBLIOGRAPHY

(I) BENTHAM

Bentham's writings are scattered and the full collection and publication of them is only now being undertaken. The earliest collection of his work is *The Works of Jeremy Bentham* Ed. J. Bowring, London, 1838.

This book also contains a biography. Bowring was a would-be Boswell, and this part of the book has been described by Leslie Stephen as the worst biography ever written.

A Fragment on Government and *An Introduction to the Principle of Morals and Legislation* have been frequently reprinted, for instance with introduction by Wilfrid Harrison, Oxford, 1948.

Discussions of Bentham are to be found, among other places, in Leslie Stephen's *The English Utilitarians,* 3 vols. London, 1900, and John Plamenatz's *The English Utilitarians.* Oxford, 1949.

(II) MILL

a. Major Works of J. S. Mill.

A System of Logic; 2 vols. London, 1843; eighth edition 1872.

Principles of Political Economy; 2 vols. London, 1848; seventh edition 1871. Edited with introduction, notes and commentary by W. J. Ashley, London, 1909.

On Liberty; London, 1859.

Dissertations and Discussions; Mill's own collection of his occasional writings. 2 vols. London, 1859, 4 vols. 1875.

Considerations on Representative Government; London, 1861.

Utilitarianism; London, 1863.

An Examination of Sir William Hamilton's Philosophy; London, 1865.

The Subjection of Women; London, 1869.

Autobiography; published posthumously by Helen Taylor,
     London, 1873. Edited by John Jacob Coss, New York,
     1924. Reissued 1944.
Mill's major writings on moral and political philosophy are
     available in an Everyman's library volume, published
     in 1910 and frequently reprinted.

b. Critical and Biographical works on Mill.
W. L. Courtney's *Life of John Stuart Mill*; London, 1889.
     The earliest full-scale biography.
Michael St. John Packe's *John Stuart Mill*; London, 1954.
     Scholarly biography with most ample bibliography.
Karl Britton's *John Stuart Mill*; Pelican Books, 1953. The
     most useful short account of Mill's life with a clear dis-
     cussion of all the branches of his philosophy.
R. P. Anschutz's *The Philosophy of John Stuart Mill;* London,
     1953. Another, longer, account of his philosophical
     doctrines with a full discussion of them.

CHRONOLOGICAL TABLE

1748   Birth of Bentham.

1776   *Fragment on Government.*

1785   Bentham's journey to Russia.

1789   *Introduction to the Principles of Morals and Legislation.*

1790   *Draught of a code for the Organisation of the Judicial Establishment in France.*

1802   Dumont's *Traité de Legislation Civile et Pénale.*

1806   Birth of J. S. Mill.

1808   Bentham and James Mill meet.

1809   Bentham's *Catechism of Parliamentary Reform.*

1820   J. S. Mill's journey to France.

1823   J. S. Mill entered India House.

1824   Bentham financed the foundation of the Westminster Review.

1828   James Mill's *Analysis of the Human Mind.*

1830   J. S. Mill met Harriet Taylor.

1832   Death of Bentham.
        Reform Bill passed.

1836   Death of James Mill.

1843   Mill's *System of Logic.*

1848   *The Principles of Political Economy.*

1849   Death of John Taylor.

1851   Mill's marriage to Harriet Taylor.

1856 Mill made head of the Examiner's Department in India House.

1858 Mill retired from India House.
Death of Harriet Taylor.

1859 *On Liberty.*

1861 *Utilitarianism.*

1865 Mill elected to Parliament.

1868 Mill defeated by Tory Candidate.
Retired to Avignon with Helen Taylor.

1872 Birth of Bertrand Russell, to whom Mill was " Godfather."

1873 Death of Mill.

INDEX

absolutism, 143

action, Bentham on. 34; Mill on, 252; liberty of, 184-5; love of, 101

acts, classes of, 22-3; estimation of, 271, 322-3

Albigeois, the, 154

Alcibiades, 192

" Alliance, The," 220-2

America, United States of, 105, 116, 195, 219, 220, 246, 340-1

amity, pleasures of, 68, 70

analysis, 284

antipathy (see also sympathy), 52n., 57 and n.

Appropriation Clause, the, 80

a priori moralists, 254

aristocracy, 114-5, 196

Aristotle, 150

Arnold of Brescia, 154

artisan class, 219

arts, the, 122, 265

asceticism, 40-5, 40n., 56n., 177

association, pleasures and pains of, 68, 69, 72, 76, 77n.

atheism, 153

atheists, 156, 198n.

Austin, John, 8, 10, 22-3; his Province of Jurisprudence Determined, 12, 23 (text), 322-42

authority, 113

awkwardness, pain of, 68, 74

backward societies, 135-6

Bacon, Francis, 85, 92, 119, 337

Bain, Professor, 304n.

Baring, Mr., 342

Barnwell, George, 212

Beattie, 90

beauty, 121, 256; love of, 101

Beccaria, 7

benevolence, 206; pleasures and pains of, 68, 71, 75, 76

Bentham, Jeremy: birth and education, 7, 83; career, 8, 11; his disciples, 102

His works: Book of Fallacies, 83; Constitutional Code, 9; Defence of Usury, 83; Deontology, 94, 104; Fragment on Government, 7, 12, 13, 14, 17, 18, 37n., 83; Introduction to the Principles of Morals and Legislation, 7, 16-7, 18, 19; (text) 33-77; quoted by Mill, 87-89; On the Influence of Time and Place in

Matters of Legislation, 112; Table of the Springs of Action, 99, 101; religious writings, 104

His thoughts, 22-3, 27-8, 29, 30, 78-82, 85, 93, 99-106, 254, 256, 319 and n.; its sources, 90; his empiricism, 96-7

His defects as a philosopher, 93-6; his positive achievement, 106-13; his alleged coldness, 120-3; his style, 123-4

Mill's remarks on, 20, 78ff., 97-99, 119-25, 229; Lord Brougham's views of, 125n.

Bible, the, 56, 157n.

Bigendians and Littleendians, 55n.

Blackstone, 15, 16, 18, 110; his Commentaries, 7, 12

Brougham, Lord, 125n.

Brown's " Essays on the Characteristics," 90

Bulwer, E. Lytton, 10

bureaucracy, 245-6, 247

Burke, Edmund, 340-1

business, 200, 203, 243

Byron, Lord, 97

Calvin and Calvinism, 169, 190, 191, 218

Camden, Lord, 83

Carlyle, Thomas, 123, 263

celibacy, 44

censorship, 215; of public opinion, 190

chancery law, 83

character, 189, 192, 262, 269; formation of, 103; national, 105

Châteaubriand, 97

children, 28-9, 135, 211, 230, 238

China, 116, 143, 202, 224, 228, 247

Christ (see also Jesus), divinity of, 152, 157n.

Christianity, 15, 156, 168, 176, 178, 191, 202, 241, 258, 273, 275, 302

Christians, 157n., 179, 198n., 216; persecution of, 151-4, 158-9

Church, the Christian, 81, 83, 133, 144, 147, 159, 178, 195, 241

Cicero, 90, 163

citizenship, training in, 243

civil code (of law), 111

" civilisade," proposed, 224

civilisation, 174, 185, 224-5, 265, 274

class interest, 118, 132

" club " theory of society, 314-5